Sociological Traditions
from Generation to Generation

CONTRIBUTORS

Robert K. Merton
Matilda White Riley
Talcott Parsons
Leonard S. Cottrell, Jr.
Helen MacGill Hughes
Robert Bierstedt
Robin M. Williams, Jr.
G. Franklin Edwards
Jackson Toby
James S. Coleman

SOCIOLOGICAL TRADITIONS FROM GENERATION TO GENERATION

Glimpses of the American Experience

edited by
ROBERT K. MERTON
Columbia University

and

MATILDA WHITE RILEY
National Institute on Aging

ABLEX Publishing Corporation
Norwood, New Jersey 07648

In accord with the request of the editors and contributors, all royalties from the sale of this book go to the Eastern Sociological Society.

Library of Congress Cataloging in Publication Data

Main entry under title:
Sociological traditions from generation to generation.

(Modern sociology)
Includes bibliographies and indexes.
1. Sociology—United States—History—Congresses.
2. Sociologists—United States—History—Congresses.
I. Merton, Robert King, 1910- II. Riley, Matilda White, 1911- III. Series.
HM13.S57   301'.0973   79-26693
ISBN 0-89391-034-1
ISBN 0-89391-061-9 pbk.

ABLEX Publishing Corporation
355 Chestnut Street
Norwood, New Jersey 07648

To the Memory of
Talcott Parsons
Student and Teacher
1902-1979

MODERN SOCIOLOGY:
A Series of Monographs, Treatises, and Texts

Edited by
GERALD M. PLATT

BELLMAN AND JULES-ROSETTE ● *A Paradigm for Looking, 1977*

HAMMOND ● *The Politics of Benevolence: Revival Religion and American Voting Behavior, 1979*

JULES-ROSETTE (Ed.) ● *The New Religions of Africa, 1979*

LOUIS AND SIEBER ● *Bureaucracy and the Dispersed Organization: The Educational Extension Agent Experiment, 1979*

MCCANN ● *Chemistry Transformed: The Paradigmatic Shift from Phlogiston to Oxygen, 1978*

MCHUGH AND BLUM (Eds.) ● *Friends, Enemies and Strangers: Theorizing in Art, Science, and Everyday Life, 1979*

MERTON AND RILEY (Eds.) ● *Sociological Traditions from Generation to Generation: Glimpses of the American Experience, 1980*

ROSENFELD ● *The Legacy of Aging: Inheritance and Disinheritance in Social Perspective, 1979*

SANGIOVANNI ● *Ex-Nuns: A Study of Emergent Role Passage, 1978*

WILKEN ● *Entrepreneurship: A Comparative and Historical Study, 1979*

Contents

Preface

The short biography of this book is soon told. In its most remote origins, it can be said to have begun in the 1930s, when the assumption of an unremitting unilinear accumulation of scientific knowledge was being emphatically questioned by Pitirim Sorokin and others. This helped some of us to develop an interest in the social processes that make for continuities and discontinuities in science. Reflecting upon those processes, we had cause to observe that the persistence of cognitive traditions need not be for the cognitive best, that uninterrupted development in the thought-models of a discipline carries its own hazards of conceptual rigidity, undetected dedicated error and, above all, resistance to new and possibly fundamental ideas. Still, continuity, and not merely over the very short run, is far more characteristic than marked discontinuity in the development of science. The greater part of scientific knowledge in any field of inquiry is selectively transmitted from the immediate past to become, in diverse ways, the cognitive basis required for new departures of thought, including the most radical among them. The fact that the reward system of science, which itself changes as society changes, puts a premium on new knowledge need not divert attention from questions about the ways in which past knowledge is selectively transmitted.

While talking about a range of possible subjects for plenary sessions at the 1978 Annual Meetings of the Eastern Sociological Society (of which one of us, Matilda Riley, was then president), we were led by our longstanding interest in such matters to plan a session devoted to a particular mode of transmission of sociological knowledge. The central idea was to arrange for a quartet of outstanding sociologists of this day to reflect upon their experience as students of masters of sociology in an earlier day. They would describe and interpret the intellectual and other socializing influences exerted upon them by their teachers and the local academic ambience while they were students-in-residence, an influence which, in some cases, continued as they went on to become students-at-a-distance. In this way, they would be telling us something, in reasonably fine-grained detail, about the ways in which sociological orientations are directly transmitted from one generation to the next. A focus on the direct interaction between sociologists of the first rank and their subsequently consequential students, we believed, would provide insight into the distinctive modes of intellectual influence exercised by grand masters of the art and science of sociology upon their immediate students, or apprentices, as distinguished from the modes of their influence upon the many other sociologists who knew them only through their published writings.

Such a session was in fact organized under the title "Sociological Traditions from Generation to Generation," the last part of the title being borrowed from S. N. Eisenstadt's well-known book, *From Generation to Generation* and, more remotely, from a passage in George Cornewall Lewis's *Essay on the Influence of Authority in Matters of Opinion,* published a century before. And then, of course, there is Exodus 17. That session met with so much interest that we were asked, by the next president of the Eastern Sociological Society, Milton M. Gordon, to put together a parallel session for the meetings in 1979. The eight papers presented at those sessions are now brought together in this volume.

The chief difficulty in planning the symposium was, of course, the selecting of a few pairs of masters and students from what seemed to be a wide array of possibilities. These two sessions could plainly provide only a beginning. Constraints of time and locale were severely limiting. Sociological giants of the not-so-distant past such as Durkheim, Simmel, and Pareto at once came to mind as prime possibilities only for us to realize, on second thought, that their students, too, belonged to a generation now past. This led us to tamper a bit with our self-set criteria, conveniently murmuring as we did so that we would not allow them to become fetishes endowed with extravagant power. We knew, of course, that Talcott Parsons was Max Weber's student only in a figurative sense; Parsons had never studied directly under Weber. Yet the asymmetrical relationship between them had proved so consequential for the development of contemporary sociology that it was unthinkable to have it excluded. We knew, too, that Leonard Cottrell had been George Herbert Mead's student for only a short time and that some sociologists who happened to be far removed from the Eastern region of the country had worked more closely with him. But the significance of that direct relationship and our having access to it led us to the same sort of conclusion. And so it went, with great variation in the character of the teacher–student relationships described in these essays. Helen MacGill Hughes was Robert Park's 'student' for over twenty years; Robin Williams studied with Pitirim Sorokin for only twelve months. Franklin Edwards was one of Franklin Frazier's very few graduate students; Jackson Toby was one among a good many of Samuel Stouffer's. Robert Bierstedt became the son-in-law of his teacher, Robert MacIver, and it has been suggested that James Coleman's student relationship to Paul Lazarsfeld was close enough to symbolize a sense of kinship.

These participants were asked to provide distinctly personal accounts that would focus on a central and now historical figure in the intellectual milieux in which they were educated and trained during their time at graduate school. It was suggested to them that their accounts might take up questions such as these:

- What was ---'s sociological orientation when you studied and worked with him?

- What do you find to be the continuing relevance of that orientation for sociology today?

- What sorts of things did you learn during your time as his student that you might not have learned from his writings alone?

- How did he relate to students? Did his work practices make for closeness to students or remoteness from them?

- What do you consider to be his major influence on your own work?

- What was the intellectual ambience at the time? For example, how did members of the department of sociology interact with members of departments regarded as neighboring?

- What were the informal norms and practices in graduate teaching at that time and what are their implications for us today?

These specimen questions were at best only suggestive for we had no intention of having the various accounts cut to the same pattern. But however much the accounts might differ in other respects, we urged upon the authors, perhaps too strongly, that they not be given over to excursions in sentiment. At the same time, we suggested that a plenitude of anecdotes designed to illustrate general observations would give the papers a much-wanted personal flavor.

In the event, the authors escaped the temptation of having their accounts decline into a series of sentimental journeys into nostalgic reminiscence. Nor did the accounts turn out to be a series of testimonials to great scholars set forth in the spirit of amply deserved filial piety. (And having stumbled into this cliché, we pause, as we inspect the sex composition of our panel of authors, to thank those ancient Romans for having provided us with such a wonderfully genderless adjective as 'filial.') Rather than being testimonials, the accounts are typically what the historians describe as testimonies; they are attempts to describe those cognitive and social micro-environments in which eight sociologists found themselves while coming of sociological age during the period ranging from the latter 1920s to the early 1950s.

It is also plain that the papers are both procedurally and substantively well within the thematic context of the 1978 meeting of the Eastern Sociological Society that dealt with Social Change and the Life Course. With regard to procedure, the papers follow a mode early identified by John Aubrey, that seventeenth-century creator of the crisp biographical memoir who, as a child, hit upon the idea of what would become elucidated by Allan Nevins in the twentieth century as "oral history." As Aubrey tells of himself in the incredulous third person: "When a Boy, he did ever love to converse with old men, as Living Histories." (One of his 'living histories,' incidentally, was the even then famed Thomas Hobbes; another, the founder of political arithmetic, William Petty.) Aubrey was of course discovering for himself what is commonplace in nonliterate societies: the utility of elders for the transmission of oral tradition. Applied to our immediate topic, this suggests that one of the few advantages of moving into — shall we say? — advanced middle age is the having acquired a stock of experience and observations that is more than the stuff of oral history. In time, one becomes equipped to transmit, with all the acknowledged and sometimes instructive biases of special cohort perspectives, otherwise eroded portions of the oral tradition of our sociological tribe that can complement its rapidly accumulating abundance of written traditions.

So much for the procedure. With regard to substance, we should note, as the biologist Evelyn Hutchinson liked to point out, that the process of individuals learning from each other gains from the fact that human society has "a fairly well-spread age structure so that all ages are present at once, unlike [say] the situation in wild field mice and more or less annual mammals. . . . " Happily, we sociologists seem to have our share of hardy perennials who remain intellectually fresh over a long succession of years. So it is that we benefit from that biological and social circumstance. Through their own contributions to the discipline, our distinguished panel of oral historicans of sociology give new meaning (for various cohorts in our tribe) to the phrase "contemporaneous ancestors."

Only an inkling need be given of some highlights in the following pages:

- Talcott Parsons's account of how it was that he did not hear of Max Weber until his arrival in Heidelberg, this being followed by a too brief allusion to the ways in which the Weberian tradition was maintained and developed in the United States.

● Leonard Cottrell's response as a student to the social behaviorism of George Herbert Mead and of how it was that, even as part of the glittering array of social science professors and students at Chicago in the late 1930s, Mead seemed to have less influence than might be supposed on the "Chicago school" of sociology.

● Helen MacGill Hughes's reflections on the meanings of her having invariably referred to her mentor, during a relationship of some twenty-five years, as "Doctor Park." And the account of how Park went about translating his everyday, earthy observations into significant theory.

● Robert Bierstedt's account of how Robert MacIver, with the aid of an accomplice named John Dewey, successfully resisted an attempt by the Columbia Faculty of Political Science back in the late 1920s to abolish the Department of Sociology — largely because it could not match the Chicago department at the time.

● Robin Williams's account of Pitirim Sorokin's thunderous rejection of simplistic theories of progress and his equally blunt criticism of totalitarian 'solutions' to social problems; this, together with his appraisal of Sorokin's sociological legacy.

● Franklin Edwards's social portrait of Franklin Frazier's early years and how his family heritage came to be translated into the sociological studies which brought Frazier his fame.

● Jackson Toby's account of the various forms taken by Sam Stouffer's dedication to work and his students and how they, in turn, conspired with Ruth Stouffer to put some order into his life.

● James Coleman's portrait of Paul Lazarsfeld's world and style of work: his obsessive search for the solution to cognitive problems and his distinctive mode of collaboration which served to convert students first into apprentices, then into journeymen, and finally into master craftsmen.

The eight papers provide insight into the lives and contributions of an array of sociologists whose work has entered into major sociological traditions, traditions involving discontinuities as well as continuities of thought as successive generations of scholars have added, subtracted, changed, clarified, and codified. Karl Mannheim spoke to an aspect of this process in his early essay on "The Problem of Generations:" "In contrast to the imaginary society with no generations, our own — in which generation follows generation — is principally characterized by the fact that cultural creation and cultural accumulation are. . . developed by individuals who come into contact with the accumulated heritage."

Some of the varied modes of "coming into contact" can be identified in these fine-grained accounts of direct rather than only mediated contact with major contributors to that heritage. It is evident that styles of scientific work are not transmitted without fail. At least for these scholars who have themselves contributed to one or another sociological tradition, early exposure to this or that master does not result in the masters being 'imprinted' on students for the rest of their days. The process of direct cognitive influence is evidently more complex with young sociologists than with Lorenz's ducklings. Selective response means rejection as well as unfailing acceptance of what the master-and-teacher teaches. The later sociologists, presumably like their masters in *their* comparative youth, took an active role in their interaction with their teachers such that the cognitive outcome of that interaction could not be anticipated merely by knowing what was ostensibly being taught to them. Among other things, the structure of social relations between these mentors and their students evidently induced a degree of ambivalence. In any case, it is not difficult to read between the lines of several of these accounts to find evidence of the notion, which we have advanced elsewhere, that conflict as well as cooperation between age strata of scientists can run deep.

The testimonies provide case materials that can also be usefully examined from the perspective of processes of age stratification. To be sure, the accounts are only suggestive and can be read diversely. Still, they direct our attention to questions such as these:

● Do different but coexisting cohorts of sociologists (and other scientists) tend to adopt criteria of scientific ideas and findings that differ in stringency?

● Correlatively, under what conditions does a shared set of criteria for assessing the scientific worth of ideas and findings transcend differences of age?

● How does the stuff of oral histories contribute to an understanding of ways in which cohort succession affects the cognitive development of a discipline?

However much our reading of the available evidence may be affected by our own place in the system of age stratification in science, we note that these papers do more than raise questions about the idiosyncrasies of a particular array of master sociologists and their outstanding students. For us, at least they underscore the idea that the transmission of knowledge cannot be understood apart from an understanding of the processes of social change. In composite, these testimonies begin to provide a sense of the complexities involved in the selective transmission of sociological traditions from generation to generation.

*　　　*　　　*

We have expressed our thanks to the authors of this book in person and are happy to do so again in print. With scarcely any nudging from us, they have seen to it that both the original and the revised versions of their papers remain directed to the announced purposes of the symposium. To John W. Riley, Jr. we are grateful for having been nothing short of indispensable to this collaborative effort from its beginning. We were greatly helped in initiating and developing the idea central to the essays in this volume by the chapter on masters and apprentices in science in Harriet Zuckerman's *Scientific Elite*. And, finally, we are indebted to Jean Lee, Joan Warmbrun, and most especially to Mary Wilson Miles for aid in monitoring the manuscripts and the reading of proofs.

*   *   *

It may come as a surprise to some readers that the author of the first essay in this volume was a deeply religous man. He would have thought it altogether appropriate to have us turn to Ecclesiastes for our text:

> One generation passeth away, and another generation cometh; but the earth abideth for ever.

Since he appears here as a student known to few of us rather than as the teacher known to many of us, it is with a sense of his fulfillment that we dedicate this book to Talcott Parsons.

Columbia University   R.K.M.

Center for Advanced Study   M.W.R.
    in the Behavioral Sciences

Sociological Traditions
from Generation to Generation

1

On the Oral Transmission
of Knowledge*

Robert K. Merton

THE CONCEPT OF ORAL PUBLICATION[1]

At first glance, the phrase "oral publication" may seem to be a contradiction in terms. But on second thought, the seeming contradiction will be found only to express an unexamined presupposition commonly held in a print culture. A less culture-bound and more etymologically oriented perspective reminds us that for millennia "to publish" has meant "to make public," that is, to make something known to members of a collectivity. Nothing in this general meaning of the word, either in the original Latin *publicare* or in the derivative English *to publish,* restricts the modes of making matters public. After all, the first-century Tacitus could scarcely have had Gutenberg's fifteenth-century movable type in mind when he spoke of 'publishing' the long works which we know as his *Histories* and his *Annals.* Since only minor changes in the technologies of communication occurred for more than a millennium after Tacitus, his use of the word 'publish' meant much the same as it did for, say, Boccaccio, just a century before Gutenberg's printing press, when he wrote of a work which "lay idle on his hands" that he would eventually "send forth to the public (*emittas in*

*I gladly acknowledge support by the National Science Foundation - Grant No. NSF SES 7927238.

[1]Along with unrecorded oral publication of this seemingly contradictory concept, glancing allusions to it can be found in Merton 1976: 118n16; 1979: 98.

1

publicum)'' (Root 1913: 418-19). For Tacitus and Boccaccio were living in scribal cultures rather than in a print culture.

Publication is as the technologies of publication allow. So it happens that in the culture of our time, publication can be taken to refer to any of a variety of modes of making things public: lectures, circulated manuscripts, print, film, radio and television (to say nothing of the newest kinds of photocopying, facsimile transmission and nationwide computer information networks.) In short, ours can be described as a multi-media culture. Each of the various modes of public communication presumably provides distinctive, and sometimes complementary, functions or manages to compete with others in serving similar or identical functions. Of them all, however, pristine (i.e. unrecorded) oral publication is unique. It alone provides no archive that can be consulted at will by contemporary and later generations.

As the earliest and most pervasive means of transmitting information, knowledge, and other traditions from one generation to the next, oral publication of course antedates not only the invention of printing but the invention of writing as well. Only in wholly unlettered or nonliterate cultures—or, in the whiggish stage-theory term preferred by some, only in isolated *pre*literate cultures—are traditions handed down to successive generations solely through word of mouth by storytellers, bards or poet-singers, by grand old men and grand old women, with all the patterns of accumulating deletions, amnesias, elaborations, and other transformations of content in the course of transmission that have been identified by cultural and social anthropologists (as these are set forth, for example, in Vansina's still standard work, *Oral Tradition* [1961] 1973).

The advent of writing and the shift from an oral culture to a scribal culture did not at once lead to the abandoning or loss of the earlier art of transmitting cognitive and other traditions. As noted in the masterly study by Elizabeth Eisenstein[2] centered on the still later historical shift from ''a scribal culture to a print culture,''

> For one thing, the advent of printing did encourage the spread of literacy even while changing the way written texts were handled by already literate elites. For another thing, *even literate groups had to rely much more upon oral transmis-*

---

[2]Composed over a period of some fifteen years, this comprehensive, detailed, and lively two-volume contribution to the historical sociology of knowledge examines the effects of the advent of printing upon ''ways of learning, thinking, and perceiving among the literary elites.'' (This should be stated less restrictively, perhaps, inasmuch as Professor Eisenstein deals with scholarly, technical, and scientific elites in the periods immediately preceding and following Gutenberg.) I resist the temptation to set out the main lines of these analyses in order to get on with the immediate subject of this collective volume.

sion in the age of scribes than they did later on. Many features which are characteristic of oral culture, such as the cultivation of memory arts and the role of a hearing public, were also of great significance among scribal scholars. *Problems associated with oral transmission thus can not be avoided even when dealing with literate* groups (Eisenstein 1979: I,xiii-xiv; italics supplied).

Writing of the period just before and just after the introduction of printing, Eisenstein provides further context for a theme underlying this volume on the transmission of sociological knowledge: social and cognitive differences in the structure of relationships and interaction between teachers and students link up with differences between oral and printed communication:

> Reliance on apprenticeship training, oral communication and special mnemonic devices had gone together with mastering letters in the age of scribes. After the advent of printing, however, the transmission of written information becomes much more efficient. It was not only the craftsman outside universities who profited from the new opportunities to teach himself. Of equal importance was the chance extended to bright undergraduates to reach beyond their teachers' grasp. Gifted students no longer needed to sit at the feet of a given master in order to learn a language or academic skill. Instead they could swiftly achieve mastery on their own, even by sneaking books past their tutors—as did the young would-be astronomer, Tycho Brahe. "Why should old men be preferred to their juniors now that it is possible for the young by diligent study to acquire the same knowledge?" asked the author of a fifteenth-century outline of history (Eisenstein 1979: I, 65-66).

Following out the implications of that fifteenth-century historian's complaint-cum-sociological-insight, we are led to expect that, at least in the domain of science and scholarship, printed publication should have replaced oral publication in the course of the five centuries since Gutenberg. Just as we are further led to expect either a radical change in the age composition of the faculties of universities and other institutions for the transmission of learning or the replacement of such institutions by research institutes on the one hand, designed to produce new knowledge and, on the other, by a variety of archives storing new and past knowledge in forms made possible by print and post-print technologies.

It is something of a sociological puzzle, therefore, that, for all of the abundance of books and journals presumably providing for self-learning, universities still persist as educational institutions and, moreover, that oral publication in the form of lectures, seminars, teaching laboratories, workshops and kindred arrangements remains central to them. What accounts for this obstinate persistence of universities with their heavy accent on oral communication? Is this a case of cultural lag, maintained by powerful vested interests engaged for centuries in perpetuating functionally obsolete or perhaps dysfunctional arrangements for the transmission of learning from generation to generation? Is it a costly survival? Aldous Huxley is somewhat reminiscent of that fifteenth-century historian as he inclines to this opinion:

> Lecturing as a method of instruction dates from classical and mediaeval times, before the invention of printing. When books were worth their weight in gold, professors had to lecture. Cheap printing has radically changed the situation which produced the lecturer of antiquity. And yet—preposterous anomaly!—the lecturer survives and even flourishes. In all the universities of Europe [and, inverted chauvinism aside, one must add: the other continents] his voice still drones and brays just as it droned and brayed in the days of Duns Scotus and Thomas Aquinas. Lecturers are as much an anachronism as bad drains or tallow candles; it is high time they were gotten rid of. (Huxley 1949: 133-134).

Yet, lecturers show no sign of being gotten rid of. We can only skirt the edges of the sociological puzzle posed by their persistence and by intensification of the oral transmission of knowledge and skills first in a print culture and now in a multi-media culture. The systematic research on this question has still largely to be done, but some preliminary observations may provide context.

Although the various modes of transmitting knowledge and skills have appeared *seriatim* in world history, this does not at all mean that each mode wholly replaced the one before it. In speaking of historical shifts from an "oral culture" to a "scribal culture" to a "print culture," one may inadvertently convey a contrary assumption: that the old is simply replaced by the new. But as we have seen from Eisenstein and others, that has not at all been the case. A descriptive term such as "multi-media culture" calls attention to the coexistence of modes of public communication.

The persistence of old modes along with the new suggests that, surface appearances notwithstanding, no two or more of these modes are functionally equivalent, that they do not simply serve the same array of functions with varying degrees of effectiveness. Were it the case that some of these were full functional equivalents, we would be led to suppose a process of evolutionary social selection that would result, over the long run, in the replacement of the less by the more effective. One need be no more enchanted than Aldous Huxley by droning and braying lecturers to advance the hypothesis—the word "guess" will do just as well—that various forms of the oral transmission of knowledge and skills serve functions which the printed book and article do not. Oral publication and printed publication are imbedded in distinct sociocognitive matrices. Spontaneous spoken language differs from written language in cognitive and social attributes and functions, just as spoken language intended for conversion into written language (as with dictation to scribes or secretaries) may differ from both.

Even before we are able to express the difference with pertinent precision, it is scarcely far-fetched to propose that the structures of social and cognitive relations between teachers and students on the one hand and between authors, particularly dead authors, and readers on the other, differ significantly. However, this transparently self-evident claim need not be granted without further thought. As has been suggested elsewhere, the repeated study of classical *writings* particularly in sociology (and in other disciplines occupying the twilight zone between the humanities and the physical and biological sciences) involves an interaction between the printed publications "of the dead author and the live reader." As noted then:

> . . . just as new knowledge has a *retroactive effect* in helping us to recognize anticipations and adumbrations in earlier [printed] work, so changes in current sociological knowledge, problems, and foci of attention enable us to find *new* ideas in a work we had read before. The new context of recent developments in our own intellectual life or in the discipline itself bring into prominence ideas or hints of ideas that escaped notice in an earlier reading. . . What is a familiar experience in the intellectual life of the individual sociologist can become prevalent for entire generations of sociologists. For as each new generation accumulates its own repertoire of knowledge and thus becomes sensitized to new theoretical problems, it comes to see much that is "new" in earlier works however often these works have been previously examined (Merton 1968: 37).

To a limited extent, this sort of cognitive interaction between the printed page and the searching reader in which the cognitive content of the page changes character as one returns to it resembles the cognitive interaction between the lecturer and the searching listener. But only to a small extent. Drawing upon materials in point from the following chapters and elsewhere, I shall suggest various patterned differences of form, substance and function between learning from books and learning from teachers. And to the extent that such differences are found to obtain, the sociological puzzle of the persistence of university lectures, brought to our attention by that fifteenth-century chronicler (one Jacob Fillippo Foresti, Eisenstein informs us) and by Aldous Huxley, may be unravelled if not solved.

Along with possible cognitive differences between oral and printed publication are differences of social interaction. I shall propose that the significant aspect of oral publication is found in distinctive networks of social relations between teachers and students, masters and apprentices and collegial peers at every phase of academic life which feed back to affect the kinds of cognitive development resulting from the oral transmission of knowledge.

It will also be proposed that it is *the cognitive interaction between printed and oral publication,* of the kind hinted at in the preceding quotation, that is central to the transmission of knowledge between generations and within them just as it is central to the further advancement of knowledge. What students learn from teachers affects what they learn from books and journals just as in turn what students learn from books and journals affects what they learn from teachers. And alerted by Simmel who taught us all that every social relationship, however asymmetrical in rank, power, authority and influence it may be, is two-sided, we should be prepared to find that interactions between teachers and students have reciprocal cognitive consequences.

THE LECTURE AS SOCIAL ACT

As a major form of oral publication, the lecture is a more or less formal discourse upon a given subject presented to an aggregate of hearers (literally: an audience). The lecture is thus an ongoing social act, variously engaging speaker and audience in direct interaction. I adopt the common term audience but, or course, until the advent of radio,[3] that interaction was typically aural *and* visual. Strictly speaking, then, with due regard to the complex social interactions involved in the on-site lecture, the term audience is inadequate. It needs to be supplemented by another term referring to the visual aspect of the interactions; perhaps we need to resurrect from the nineteenth century that ugly, nearly unpronounceable, but exact nonce-word, spectatory, as the only word which refers to "a body of spectators" or onlookers. For as I shall indicate, it is both the visual and the aural components of social interaction which distinguish the perception of content in oral publications even—to take the limiting case—from the ostensibly same content in printed publications. And this may help explain how it is that people still voluntarily attend public lectures which they know will appear in print, just as it may help explain how it is that some academics prefer publication through lectures before putting their ideas into print.

With oral discourse as with written discourse, there is great variability of type and style. Those dronings and brayings about which Huxley complained are not of course the only mode for the oral transmission of knowledge and correlative skills in universities. In roughly graded sequence, running from the most formal to the least, the familiar forms range from (1) the formal lecture read without interruption from beginning to end, followed by the abrupt departure of the lecturer from the room; (2) the lecture based on notes or unaided memory without, however, further interaction with students, then and there; (3) the lecture punctuated by questions and discussions; (4) Socratic dialogues; (5) research and reading seminars which,

---

[3]The cant but analytically perceptive idiom "the unseen audience" of radio—and, one should add, "the unseeing audience"—provides the pristine case of assembled audiences *sans* spectators. Those audiences are of course commonly dispersed rather than assembled. Assembled audiences *sans* spectators are also found nowadays in some universities where huge overflow "classes" of students are located in several rooms and halls, there able to hear but not to see "their instructor." For early suggestions about the significance of such purely oral transmission as compared with transmission in print, one would be well served by turning to the early book by Lazarsfeld [1940] 1971.

involving interaction between members of the group, differ in structure and perhaps function from the give-and-take between teacher and student in private conference; (6) work in laboratories and research organizations, again involving interaction extending beyond the dyad of master and apprentice in which knowledge and skills are both created and transmitted through sustained example and much ongoing critical talk; and (7), in this truncated and advisedly less than systematic inventory of various types, individual private sessions centered on the instructor's and student's critical assessment of the student's work in progress.

Within each of these forms of oral transmission, there is further variability in the personal style of operation. Attending primarily to the lecture as a general form, we find variability in the sociocognitive matrix in which lectures are imbedded: in the network of social relationships and kinds of social interaction between instructor and students and in the cognitive orientations of the instructor, both of which interact with the style of lecturing itself.

The following chapters provide abundant evidence of both kinds of variability. Lecturing without notes, Leonard Cottrell informs us,[4] George Herbert Mead preferred to present his thoughts without interruption, not welcoming "questions and comments" from his classes. Granted that different styles of presentation may serve much the same functions, this does suggest that, for Mead, the uses of lectures differed substantially from the uses ascribed to them by his contemporary and colleague at the University of Chicago, Robert Park. For, as Helen MacGill Hughes reports, Park engaged in a kind of "participatory teaching," with instructors and graduate students engaged in a "joint enterprise" of inquiry, and the classroom providing the locale for only part of his frequent interaction with students. That style of intensive interaction outside the classroom contrasts with the instructional style of Robert MacIver who, in the words of Robert Bierstedt, was "not easy for a graduate student to know" and who "never talked 'shop' outside the classroom."

In juxtaposition, these accounts provide further variations in teaching and lecturing style. Robin Williams describes the lectures of Pitirim Sorokin from the twin positions of audience and, metaphorically speaking, spectators:

> Within a single hour one heard [*n.b.*] the objective scientist and the fervent moralist, the sensitive humanist and the vituperative critic, the systematic analyst and the intuitive prophet. What one saw [*n.b.*] was not only a mind at work, but also a personality and character being expressed and a life being developed. When Sorokin lectured on changes in Western art, his presentations

---

[4]When drawing upon the following chapters in this volume, I shall not cite chapter and verse; this invites readers to search out the ample and significant details in those chapters.

were not finely-polished cameos but vastly disorderly paintings or sculptures in process—the room often seemed filled with flying paint and chips of marble.

A student of Park's, Franklin Frazier emerges in Franklin Edwards's account as a solitary scholar much like MacIver in his "reserve and sense of privacy," with few students coming to know him "as a person," while his teaching, chiefly of the undergraduates available to him, was peppered by humor, "shock treatments," and impromptu blackboard exposition.

Far removed from Huxley's imagery of university lectures is Jackson Toby's description of Samuel Stouffer working to shape and polish each lecture to have it express "his freshest and best thoughts" on the subject in hand, and then fixing the attention of students on his developing ideas by putting the blackboard to extensive use. Complementing the lectures to large classes of students were the joint seminars with Talcott Parsons which, in Stouffer's intention, would enable graduate students to see "professors at work" while engaging them as associates in a collective enterprise of sociological research. Again, one gets more than an intimation of diverse functions for the transmission of knowledge served by these several forms of oral discourse that differ in kind from functions of the printed page.

In the case of Paul Lazarsfeld, as becomes evident in James Coleman's pen portrait, his great intellectual influence on graduate students—to say nothing of colleagues and collaborators—"occurred wholly apart from his lectures." For him, it was the university-based research-and-training organization, made up of students and staff in various phases of development, which was indispensable to his style of intensive interaction focussed on progressively defined problems of substance and method.[5] As Coleman observes, together with his intense preoccupation with educating and training successors, Lazarsfeld

> was fully occupied with ideas, yet he himself had the time to investigate only a subset of them. So he was engaged in a continual search for *people*—people who, as extensions of himself, could take the problem and carry it further. Yet he continued *himself* to be occupied with the problem, with strong and definite ideas about *how* the problem should be solved. . . This was his personal style— he could not stand to have a bright person, whether colleague or student, whom he respected, in the vicinity and yet not working on problems *he* saw as important.

However much they differed in other respects, Park, Stouffer and Lazarsfeld, among the eight masters of the sociological craft, were evidently most alike in their sustained and intense interaction with graduate students who, as junior colleagues, learned chiefly by working on problems initiated

---

[5]As Lazarsfeld said of the Columbia Bureau of Applied Social Research in an interview granted to a Parisian journalist: "c'est l'oeuvre de ma vie et c'est ce que l'on gravera, j'espere, sur ma pierre tombale." For detailed accounts of the instructional style in the Bureau, see Glock, 1979 and Barton (1979).

by the master. Lazarsfeld was persuaded that this style of instruction required the sociocognitive matrix of a research-and-training organization if it was to be at its most effective. Nevertheless, his personal style of instruction was much like that of Park's which, as Helen Hughes shows, was derived in no small part from his early experience as a philosophically educated newspaperman.

Asked to speak in this symposium of his experience in the Heidelberg of the mid-1920s where the influence of Max Weber remained strong, Talcott Parsons could not tell at first hand of Weber's life as a teacher. But, as we learn from what Parsons described as "Marianne Weber's distinguished and charming *Max Weber Ein Lebensbild,*"[6] Weber's troubled life can direct us to basic differences between oral and printed discourse as this was experienced by a prime originator of both kinds.

If the formal lecture was for Mead by far the chief medium for conveying his developing ideas, it was for Weber an object of deep ambivalence throughout a great part of his life. At first, the preparation and delivering of lectures presented anything but a problem for him as he moved from a tenuous lectureship at the University of Berlin to a chair at Freiburg to a full professorship (*Ordinarius*) in political economy at Heidelberg where, at the early age of 32, "he became the colleague of his former teachers" (Weber [1926] 1975: 227). Early on, at the public examination of Weber's brilliant doctoral dissertation. *On the History of Trading Companies in the Middle Ages,* the great historian of Rome and destined Nobel laureate in literature Theodor Mommsen declared that "When I have to go to my grave someday, there is no one to whom I would rather say, 'Son, here is my spear; it is getting too heavy for my arm' than the highly-esteemed Max Weber" (Weber [1926] 1975: 114). But a dozen years later, Weber's lectures and writing alike came to a halt soon after the death of his father, an event highly traumatic for having occurred just weeks after an angry confrontation in which the "son sat in judgment on his father" for his autocratic mistreatment of his mother (*Ibid.,* 230). Weber then entered upon a prolonged time of psychic disturbance and periodic emotional exhaustion. After having alternately suspended, resumed, and again suspended his lectures, "he asked to be dismissed from his position." He was induced to withdraw that request and to accept a leave of absence instead, only to find the stress of his further heroic efforts to resume teaching altogether insupportable. In final despair, he resigned his professorship at Heidelberg, once and for all.

Of most immediate interest to us here is that Weber's psychic turmoil seems to have affected his self-assessed capacity for scholarly writing and for

---

[6]In *Structure of Social Action* (Parsons [1937], 1949, p. 503n). The quotations in my compressed account all come from this superb biography (Marianne Weber 1926), now available in English translation (1975). For a subtle psychological analysis of Weber's breakdown, see Chapter 4 of Arthur Mitzman's *The Iron Cage* (1970).

academic lecturing in quite different ways. He was able to take up his writing again after an enervating and dispirited lapse of somewhat more than four years but he did not—to his mind, could not—resume an academic course of lectures for almost two decades. Yet outwardly assessed, Weber had been as accomplished in one as in the other; he had acquired much experience and an early reputation as a grand, even charismatic lecturer.

The Marianne Weber biography supplies some hints of how oral and written modes of discourse may have differed for him. For one thing, a course of original lectures taken seriously—and Weber clearly took them most seriously ["every lecture was a free creation" (p. 236)]—in effect imposes a sustained and implacable series of deadlines. For Weber, this was no small series of demands. At Berlin, his teaching assignment called for some "nineteen hours of lectures and seminars" (p. 195) and as a full professor at Heidelberg, it called for two seminars and "three major lecture courses" running to another twelve hours a week (pp. 202-3). Moreover, Weber had come to find deadlines of any kind overtaxing. He could not cope with the necessity of pacing his developing thought to accord with a calendar of externally imposed obligations. When, after that lapse of four years, he once again took up his scholarly writing—what would turn out to be his first major methodological essay: "Roscher and Knies and the Logical Problems of National Political Economy"—he found, in the words of Marianne Weber, that "this difficult investigation of the modes of thought of his discipline and of history expanded as he worked on it, and yet. . . *had to be ready by a certain date. This soon turned it into a burden and a torment. . .* " (p. 260; italics added). Evidently, the series of deadlines that made up his courses of original academic lectures had become and long remained an even greater burden and torment.

There are ample indications that, in good times and bad, lectures made special demands on Weber. During his early struggles to continue with his lectures, Marianne Weber observes that "Max regard[s] any mental exertion as harmful. . . [but] *talking* in particular immediately has a disagreeable effect" (p. 237; italics in original). And Weber himself reports that "'my inability to talk is purely physical, the nerves break down, and when I look at my lecture notes, my head simply swims'" (p. 239). The stress of lecturing was long remembered. Some fifteen years later, when first asked by colleagues at Munich "whether he would be interested in a lectureship, he. . . rejected the idea and reacted strongly when he noticed that his wife regarded it as worth trying: 'Terrible that you should still entertain the notion that I could get on a lecture platform!'" (p. 603).

During his time of troubles, Weber's agonizing sense of inadequacy—even, at times, total impotence—in composing and conveying his disciplined thoughts evidently became all the more intense when experienced in public, as in the university lecture hall, than when experienced in private, as in his study at home. His efforts witnessed by many in the one context produced a reverberating effect of intensified self-denigration; his failed efforts in the privacy of the home could, at the least, be kept from all but an understanding few.

This can be put more generally. Beyond its demands for meeting rapidly recurring deadlines, oral publication which takes the form of a course of original lectures involves a mode of social and cognitive interaction differing from that of publication in print. The lecture involves direct *inter*action, not merely *re*action to what is being said. As we sometimes have to remind ourselves, the lecturer sees-and-hears a presumably evaluating spectatory-and-audience just as they see-and-hear the lecturer. This contrasts with the social character of critical responses by reference groups and individuals to publications in print. Whether in anxious anticipation or in the actual event, the latter do not have the same immediacy and interactive effects.

When Weber resumed academic lecturing after that hiatus of nineteen years, he once again, in accord with Meadian theory, responded to the visible and audible responses of those who, assembled before him, were in effect engaged in assessing his role performance. He proceeded to interpret changes in their size, composition, and behavior as cues to the perceived character and quality of his lectures. Marianne Weber tells us of the "tremendous effort" it took to resume his lectures and goes on to report:

> Under the title "A Positive Critique of the Materialistic View of History," he presented his research on the sociology of religion as well as his sociology of the state. It was a matter of getting accustomed to lecturing again, and he evaluated his performance as "middling" ['mittelgut']. Soon, however, the steadily increasing number of his students showed him that he had not lost his charisma as a teacher. After some time he lectured in the largest auditorium to an overflow audience, and about one-third of it consisted of mature people: politicians, civil servants, university teachers. His lectures were "events" (p. 604).

Weber himself draws inferences from the behavior he observes in the assembly before him:

> Well, the first lecture [at Vienna] is over. . . . About sixty to seventy students who will probably dwindle down to 30 or 40 (judging from the number of those who took notes). It "drains" ["schlaucht"] me terrifically! I'd rather give ten impromptu "talks" than a two-hour academic lecture! I'll have to see whether I can endure it. In any case, full-time teaching is unthinkable; my physical condition today shows me this. The students are quite attentive. I have no complaints on that score (pp. 611-12).

> Well, the second lecture (i.e. two hours, from 6-8) is over, too. . . . Attendance has picked up; in particular a number of *colleagues* came and busily took notes. My God, what an *exertion* that is. Ten informal talks are nothing compared to a two-hour academic lecture. Merely being tied down to an outline and making allowance for those taking notes—it is fantastic. I shall never be able to manage more than two to three hours a week. And yet I know exactly that my lecturing

is middling *at best*—despite, or perhaps *because* of, the preparation which is indispensable after all (p. 612; italics in orginal).

Then, having taken the size, composition, and note-taking behavior of the assembled students and colleagues as indicators of favorable response to his lectures, Weber discounts that enthusiastic response, continues to find the lectures wanting, and concludes that "I was born for the pen and for the speaker's platform, not for an academic rostrum" (p. 312).

Nevertheless, besieged by offers from a half-dozen universities that had gotten wind of his course of summer lectures at Vienna, Weber accepted appointment to the distinguished Lujo Brentano[7] chair at Munich on condition that he need no longer teach political economy and finance but could turn primarily to sociology instead. Again, the lecture halls are filled— "naturally the *auditorium maximum* again for both lectures: almost 600 students had registered for Socialism and almost 400 for Political Science" (p. 694)—and again, the strain of oral publication in contrast to publication in print is almost too difficult to endure. And so again, he comes to the stoic conclusion that "I am now a man of the *pen, not* of the rostrum. But what must be, must be" (p. 665). The following year of stress and scholarly accomplishment was Max Weber's last.

The biography of Weber and the vivid descriptions in this volume of teaching styles adapted by other sociological masters suggest diverse questions about variations in styles of oral transmission of ideas and skills with attendant variations in forms of social and cognitive interaction between teachers and students. What aspects of the concrete situation in which a set of ideas is first encountered affect the understanding of those ideas, their selective hearing or selective reading? How does that context affect the later incorporation of what was learned into the work of the onetime student? What differences in understanding and assimilation, if any, result from coming upon those ideas as auditors and spectators in a formal lecture course, in the company of few or many; of having these encounters supplemented by intensive personal interaction with teachers or student-peers as contrasted with virtually no such interaction at all; of having the ideas worked out in

---

[7]Violating Weber's norms governing the vocation of scientist and teacher, Brentano, as a "socialist of the chair," often "addressed his classes as he would have political meetings, and they responded with cheers and countercheers." As Schumpeter hastens to add in a restrained Huxleyan vein, "I do not mean to assert that German lectures or seminars were exactly fascinating. The two examples adduced [the other being the socialist Adolf Wagner] were exceptional. As a rule, the professor read from a manuscript that was often yellow with age. . . This is the scene American visitors beheld and their experience may be one of the causes of irreconcilable—and, I think, exaggerated—hostility to the lecture method of teaching which we observe in many American universities" (Schumpeter [1954] 1968: 802). As Talcott Parsons reports in this volume, his doctoral dissertation paid some attention to Brentano's concept of capitalism.

seminars or work groups or through a teacher's intensive critical examination of students' trial-run manuscripts; of having the master assign the apprentice scientific problems at the leading edge of the discipline? Do the cognitive substance and form of exposition in various kinds of oral publication differ significantly from their content and form in printed publication? These are matters variously touched upon in the pages of this volume.

THE LECTURE AS QUASI-PUBLICATION

Beyond all these questions, biographical evidence suggests that, at least for some academic minds and their students, the formal lecture serves distinctive and important functions. A hint that this is the case is provided by the persistent use of the lecture in circumstances that would appear unsuited to this form of presentation. A few clinical cases in point must serve for many more.

There is the case of Willard Gibbs, celebrated for his phase rule and other pathbreaking contributions to thermo-dynamics and related fields of mathematical physics and often described "as the greatest scientist the United States has ever produced" (a phrase with less meaning than appears at first glance). That publication by word-of-mouth and other private communication was important to his style of work is at least suggested by his having been appointed a professor of mathematical physics at Yale in 1871, two years before he put his first scientific paper into print (Klein 1972: 387a). (To be sure, the terms of that appointment were without salary for the first nine years but Gibbs was in a position to prefer it to a salaried post offered him at Bowdoin.) His first year in this newly established chair found Gibbs lecturing to a grand total of two students (both destined to become professors at Yale and members of the National Academy of Sciences). As one of these students remembered it, "In the choice of work for this little class he was absolutely untrammeled either by precedent or by expressed preferences of his pupils; hence the character of his teaching possesses a peculiar interest as an indication of the contemporary state of his scientific development which, perhaps, would be sought in vain elsewhere" (Hastings, 1909: 375). Particularly in point is that his lectures in the next year were based on a work of Clausius on entropy, and it was during the course of that year that Gibbs presented "before the Connecticut Academy the first of the papers on the mechanics of heat which have established his eminence for all time" (*Ibid.*, 375).

But Gibbs's feat of lecturing to a class of two pupils was outdone by the mathematician and philosopher, A. N. Whitehead. As Roy Harrod describes it in his magisterial biography of Maynard Keynes:

> In the next following Summer Term (1904) [Keynes] showed his predilection for the best. He attended a course of lectures by Alfred Whitehead, given three times a week, *alone*. Not an easy task! *Experto crede*. There is some tendency to stay away, even if only to spare the lecturer his pains. In a letter written to me some thirty years later, Whitehead cited Bertrand Russell and Keynes as instances of his best pupils. At the time it puzzled me to know how Keynes had been his pupil. This solitary attendance for three hours a week surely justified the description (Harrod 1951: 96-97).

Harrod, it will be noticed, alludes only to the student's motivation for continuing to turn up as a lone student. But for us it is equally in point to speculate on the teacher's decision to continue lecturing to an audience of one—albeit such a one as the 21-year-old Keynes, even then plainly destined to become the even more distinguished son of a distinguished father. We do know that this was the time when Whitehead had abandoned the idea of putting a second volume of his *Universal Algebra* into print just as Russell was abandoning the second volume of his *Principles of Mathematics* upon discovering that "our projected second volumes were practically on identical topics, so we coalesced to produce a joint work" (Whitehead 1941: 10). That joint and difficult work proved to be *Principia Mathematica,* which, expected to take a year or so, began to appear in print some seven years later. As with Gibbs and his class of two, so with Whitehead with his class of one: the seemingly strange spectacle of his lecturing to that irreducibly small class becomes the less strange if construed as helping him to formulate and air ideas before he considered them ready for print.[8]

Bertrand Russell's appearance in the Whitehead story practically requires us to note that he, in his turn, met with thinly populated classes during his teaching at Cambridge, including a class devoted to the *Principia Mathematica*. In 1913–14, that class boasted a membership of three students. As it happens, one of them was the eighteen-year-old Norbert Wiener, freshly equipped with a Ph.D. from Harvard. But this case of institutionalized commitment to the oral transmission of knowledge scarcely measures up to the special demands of formal lectures such as those by Gibbs and Whitehead since Russell's was a reading, rather than a lecture, course.

---

[8]This is not at all to suggest that Whitehead was lecturing to the twenty-one-year old Keynes on problems treated in *Principia Mathematica*. Nothing of the kind; trace-indications in autobiographical accounts by Whitehead, Russell, and Keynes are all to the contrary. Indeed, Keynes, stung by Whitehead's later strong criticisms of his dissertation as a candidate for a fellowship, ever after had a way of referring to *Principia Mathematica* as having been written by Russell. This led Russell to protest Keynes's practice in print, writing that "Dr. Whitehead had an equal share in the work, and there is hardly a page in the three volumes which can be attributed to us singly" (as quoted in Harrod 1951: 654n). I am only suggesting that whatever the lectures meant to Keynes, they served Whitehead to formulate ideas that he was trying out on this gifted single student.

Still, we know from Russell's own testimony, that his first two terms of teaching mathematical logic at Cambridge provided the occasion for "lectures [which] contained the outline of *Principia Mathematica*" (Russell 1967: I, 222). To a degree, this case provides evidence of the differing significance of oral and printed instruction. Having a reading course with an author of the pathbreaking *Principia Mathematica* evidently served the student in ways that having studied the book intensively had not. As Wiener tells us:

> I became shamefully aware of the shortcomings of my own doctoral thesis [A Comparative Study of the Algebra of Relatives of Schroeder and that of Whitehead and Russell]. Nevertheless, in connection with the course I did one little piece of work which I later published. . . [It] has come to occupy a certain modest permanent postition in mathematical logic. . . and represents my true introduction into mathematical thinking and writing (Wiener 1953: 191).

It is an appropriate irony that the mature Wiener, as mathematician and pioneering contributor to cybernetics and information theory, turned out to be a remarkably poor lecturer.

The creator of Boolean algebra rounds out this array of cases in point by providing what is perhaps the limiting case to show that lectures may have significant functions for the lecturer as well as for students. In the reminiscent words of his grandson,

> [George] Boole took a great deal of trouble to make his lectures clear and he published textbooks on differential equations and on finite differences which give an idea of his teaching methods. Ultimately his conscientiousness in this respect led to his death for he got wet on the way to a lecture and insisted on lecturing in soaking clothes, an act which gave rise to his last fatal illness in 1864. His pupils were devoted to him. One day he arrived in his lecture room before them and started walking up and down in front of his blackboard thinking out some problem. The students arrived and sat waiting for him to begin, not liking to interrupt his thoughts. After an hour, they left, Boole still walking in front of the blackboard. When he got home he said to my grandmother, "My dear, a most extraordinary thing happened today. None of my students came to my lecture" (Taylor 1956: 51).

Through this episode, Boole provides us with a limiting, almost experimental clinical case in several respects. First, unlike instances even of formal lectures, let alone seminars or work sessions, no symbolic or cognitive *inter*action between teacher and students evidently took place. Second, the body of students constituted a pure case of spectatory rather than audience, able to see but not to listen to the master at work. (There is no record of what they made of his musings.) And finally, with Boole wrapped up in his own private thoughts and wholly unaware of audience or spectatory, the class can only have been the occasion for his developing ideas that day—the occasion, not, as we shall see is often the case with lectures and seminars, the evocative source.

That these past masters of their disciplines should have proceeded to deliver lectures even to minuscule classes suggests anew that such oral discourse in quasi-public had collateral functions for them as scientists and scholars as well as having the manifest function of providing instruction to students—instruction of a kind which, it is institutionally assumed by universities, even mature students do not ordinarily get just as well by only attending to work in print.

THE LECTURE: VEHICLE OF COGNITIVE PERFECTIONISM

More than for any of the other masters of sociology and social psychology treated in this volume, it appears that for G. H. Mead, the lecture was the medium. Plainly preferring to develop his ideas in courses of lectures, he never wrote a book. Nor did he take easily to other forms of print: reviews, abstracts, and brief remarks apart, he published some 45 articles all told, surprisingly few of them on his basic ideas in philosophy and social psychology. His famous four volumes, listed by Cottrell, were all published after his death. These were based upon a composite of his own lecture notes—which, Cottrell informs us, he never brought to the lecture room—scattered manuscripts, and student notes (Shibutani 1968: 83-84). Cottrell, along with Charles Morris, the editor of *Mind, Self & Society,* in effect notes the distinctive function of oral rather than printed discourse for someone of Mead's turn of mind:

> I have had the distinct impression that a major reason for his never having committed his thought to a systematic written opus was his being so impressed by the ramifications, implications and needed elaborations of his theory that he could never find the time to stop and put it all down (Cottrell, this volume, p. 59).

From observations of this sort, it appears that for Mead print carried with it the unacceptable connotation of his having arrived at a final formulation, as though new printed editions and subsequent writings could not be counted on to keep pace with his developing thoughts. It is as if he *felt,* or actually believed, that with his ideas always in process of change and, one hoped, development, it would be downright misleading to fix them permanently in the black and white magic of print. And, in a way, Mead was of course right. One cannot count on a continuing succession of editions of books and, by unexamined convention, journals do not publish new editions of articles. (Indeed the very image of "editions of articles" may be taken as strange.) But in his *oral* publications, Mead could easily set out what amounted to revised editions in each of the thirty years of his lectures in social psychology and, over a longer span, in philosophy. In effect, if not in deliberate calculation, Mead confronted a choice between transmitting annual revisions of his ideas to a comparatively small audience at the University of Chicago and transmitting a particular version of those ideas to a much more numerous readership at the cost of fixing that version in print permanently or for years at a time. His life long, he exercised the first option.

Mead is scarcely alone in having adopted the lecture form as a vehicle for continuing development of his ideas. That practice has continued without much evolutionary change over the centuries. For a first example, Adam Smith typically formulated his ideas in moral philosophy and political economy in his lectures and only later, in print. Shifts in foci of intellectual interest first appeared in his sequences of lectures. As his contemporary, the polymath Dugald Stewart,[9] noted in a prefatory memoir to *The Theory of Moral Sentiments,* "the plan of his lectures underwent a considerable change. His ethical doctrines, of which he had now published so valuable a part, occupied a much smaller portion of the course than formerly, and accordingly, his attention was naturally directed to a more complete illustration of the principles of jurisprudence and of political economy" (Smith [1759] 1853, p. xli). Sixteen years after the appearance of *Moral Sentiments,* Smith finally published *The Wealth of Nations,* his masterwork which, drawing with effective selectivity upon a variety of predecessors, definitively established political economy as a distinct discipline and set out those fundamental ideas which remain influential to this day.

But it is perhaps Alfred Marshall who provides the archetypal instance of the pattern of *cognitive perfectionism* that calls for continual revamping and development of one's ideas in annual editions of lectures rather than allowing them to see public print in short order. As Maynard Keynes observed in his beautifully analytic biographical essay, "Marshall's reluctance to print the results of his earliest investigations is mainly explained by the profundity of his insight into the true character of his subject in its highest and most useful developments and [in immediate point] by his *unwillingness to fall short of his own ideals in what he gave to the world. . .* " (Keynes [1933] 1972, p. 188; italics supplied). Just as with Adam Smith before him

---

[9]Stewart, by the way, wielded a considerable influence as a teacher. His oral publications, it seems, were more consequential than his publications in print. Some idea of his versatility as lecturer is provided by his feat, while in his mid-twenties, of standing in as lecturer in moral philosophy for Adam Ferguson, and giving "a course upon morality, besides lecturing three hours daily upon mathematics, and giving for the first time a course upon astronomy. He lectured from notes, arranging his ideas while walking in the garden. He afterwards wrote for publication quickly, but altered much while his works were in press. These early lectures were very successful, and by some hearers preferred to his later efforts" (Stephen, 1898, Vol. LIV, 283). Upon reading this recitation of Stewart's prodigious labors as lecturer, we should scarcely be surprised to have Leslie Stephen report that "He had to rise at 3 A.M. on five days of the week, and was so exhausted by his labours that he had to be lifted into his carriage for a journey." Stewart's labors did not go unnoticed and, in due course, he succeeded to the chair of the grand historical sociologist, Adam Ferguson.

and with George Mead after him, for Marshall, the perfectionist pattern spelled long delay in confiding his ideas to the special medium of print.[10] Like many another of Marshall's students, Keynes regretted his master's unwillingness to let the larger world know of the basic ideas and doctrines he was discovering to the immediate world of his students and colleagues. But delay he did, for as long as half a century. Again in Keynes's words:

> Marshall's serious study of Economic Theory began in 1867; his characteristic doctrines were far developed by 1875, and by 1883 they were taking their final form. Nevertheless, no part of his work was given to the world at large in adequate shape until 1890 (*Principles of Economics*), and that part of the subject at which he had worked earliest and which was most complete by 1875, was not treated in a published book until nearly fifty years later, in 1923 (*Money, Credit and Commerce*).

It is only for reasons of space that I limit myself to Mead, Smith and Marshall as prime instances of that special form of cognitive perfectionism which is expressed in readiness for oral publication and resistance to printed publication. I do not venture any speculations here on the psychological roots of the generic practice of exacting of oneself (and, for that matter, of others) a higher quality of performance than is called for by social definitions of the situation. In the categorical terms of one psychologist, such self-demands can be provisionally attributed to the super-ego in its various conceptualized aspects as "depersonalized parent," or more generally as "internalized external authority," or correlatively, as a "vehicle of the ego-ideal" or a "vehicle of tradition" (Freud [1932] 1973: XXII, 64-67, 178-9). Alternative readings of generic perfectionism are of course also available in our common stock of psychological knowledge. But our interest here resides rather in the sociologically relevant contexts and aspects *of the situation* which provide for the socially patterned form of cognitive perfectionism presented to us by a Mead, Smith, or Marshall. What are the structural and normative contexts of the options that were open to these self-demanding scholars, whatever the sources of their individual tendencies toward such exacting demands in the world of the intellect?

Part of the context of this perfectionist behavior is provided by the norm of "organized criticism" which has been described as central to the normative structure of science (Merton [1942] 1973: 277-8, passim; Storer 1966: 77-79, 116-126). This norm calls for public criticism by scientists of claimed contributions to scientific knowledge, both their own contributions

---

[10]Cf. the quantitative analysis by Cole and Cole (1973, pp. 91 ff.) of four types of academic physicists described in terms of the joint quantity and quality of their printed research, these types including "the perfectionists" who publish relatively little but that little being of considerable scientific consequence.

and, more easily perhaps, those of others. This norm is not suspended in the thin air of merely ideological affirmation, deprived of support by the reward-and-punishment system of science. On the contrary, the dispersed organization of science operates as a system of institutionalized vigilance (on this, see Zuckerman 1977b, especially at pp. 90-98.) That system provides both motivation and reward for detecting flaws and outright errors in public claims to scientific knowledge. In such a system of institutionalized competition and rivalry, reinforced by competing theoretical orientations and paradigms, scientists are simultaneously motivated and rewarded for appraising new knowledge claims in the field of their immediate interest and special competence. It is not too much to say once again that "this unending exchange of critical judgment, of praise and punishment, is developed in science to a degree that makes the monitoring of children's behavior by their parents seem little more than child's play" (Merton [1968] 1973: 339). In such a system of organized skepticism, it is only after their claims to significant knowledge have been validated by competent others in the social system of science that most scientists can feel confident in the contemporary cognitive merits of these claims.

This composite normative and social structure of organized criticism provides sociological context for research scientists and scholars deciding when to make their work widely public. As with all systems of socially induced or socially reinforced aspirations and all systems of social control, this one introduces the risks of punishment for failing to live up to variously demanding standards of role performance as well as the promises of reward for meeting or exceeding those partly self-selected standards to judge one's work-in-progress by. It is within this systemic context that cognitive perfectionism appears to find both its psychological and sociological place. For whatever the psychological sources of variability among scientists with regard to the intensity of self-demands and correlative anxieties about critical evaluations by significant others, the system of socially organized criticism provides ample context for such anxieties among scientists whose personality and character structure make them particularly vulnerable.

Cognitive perfectionism in science can thus be thought of as an anticipatory adaptation to these system-induced or system-reinforced concerns with the evaluative responses of one's work by competent peers. The context of such anticipatory adaptations was described a good many years ago in these terms:

> Science is public and not private knowledge; and although the idea of "other persons" is not employed explicitly in science, it is always tacitly involved. In order to prove a generalization which for the individual scientist, on the basis of his own private experience, may have attained the status of a valid law which requires no further confirmation, the investigator is compelled to set up critical experiments [sic] which will satisfy the other scientists engaged in the same

cooperative activity. This pressure for so working out a problem that the solution will satisfy not only the scientist's own criteria of validity and adequacy, but also the criteria of the group with whom he is actually or symbolically in contact, constitutes a powerful social impetus for cogent, rigorous investigation. The work of the scientist is at every point influenced [not determined] by the intrinsic requirements of the phenomena with which he is dealing and perhaps just as directly by his reactions to the *inferred critical attitudes or actual criticism of other scientists and by an adjustment of his behavior in accordance with these attitudes.*

Thus, J. J. Fahie quotes Galileo as having written that "ignorance had been the best teacher he ever had, since in order to be able to demonstrate to his opponents [organized skepticism] the truth of his conclusions, he had been forced to prove them by a variety of experiments, though to satisfy his own mind alone he had never felt it necessary to make any" (Merton [1938] 1978: 219; italics supplied).

Socially organized criticism in science apparently provided at least part of the structural context which led such cognitive perfectionists as Marshall, Mead and Smith to delay or to withhold altogether publication of their current work in print. Keynes observed of the vulnerability of Marshall that he

was much too afraid of being wrong, too thin-skinned toward criticism, too easily upset by controversy even on matters of minor importance. An extreme sensitiveness deprived him of magnanimity toward the critic or the adversary. This fear of being open to correction by *speaking too soon* aggravated other tendencies. Yet after all, there is no harm in being sometimes wrong—especially if one is promptly found out (Keynes [1933] 1972: 199-200; italics supplied).

As Cottrell in this volume as well as Mead's editors have indicated, Mead was another who could not bring himself to put the substance of his evolving lectures into print because they were never quite ready. Otherwise put, Mead felt that the substance of his lectures did not yet meet his standards for printed disclosure nor, presumably, the standards of significant others.

Finally, in this trio of exemplary figures, Adam Smith had occasion to observe marked differences between oral and printed publication from the time of his studies at Glasgow where he matriculated at the then late age of 14. His teacher of moral philosophy, Francis Hutcheson, later described by Smith as "the never-to-be-forgotten," was a master of oral communication, it being observed that the "power and appeal" of his personality "was incommunicable to the printed words of his writings" (Scott 1937: 31). When, after further studies at Balliol, Smith returned to Glasgow first as Professor of Logic, then of Moral Philosophy, he evidently took great pains with his own lectures which, whether based on a manuscript or detailed notes, were daily worked out anew (*Ibid.*, 70). Smith not only long delayed printed publication of the ideas which eventually appear in *Moral Sentiments* and the *Wealth of Nations* but took the ultimate step in the pattern of cognitive perfectionism by enjoining his friends, to whom he had entrusted the disposal of his manuscripts, that, in the event of his death, they should destroy all the volumes of his lectures, doing with the rest of his manuscripts what they pleased (Dugald Stewart in Smith [1759] 1853: lxv).

Plainly Smith, like the other cognitive perfectionists, distinguished between what he was prepared to make public in a limited way through oral communication, either in lectures or in discussions with colleagues and students, and what he would allow to become more generally public in print. Having interpreted such behavior in its sociological aspects as a kind of anticipatory adaptation to organized skepticism in science and scholarship, we are ready to consider distinctive structures and functions of oral compared with printed publication.

SOME FUNCTIONS OF ORAL DISCOURSE

Within the narrow scope of this introductory essay, we cannot, of course, attempt a systematic comparative analysis of the cognitive and social functions of oral discourse in academic contexts. That would require, at the least, a methodical examination of the various forms of oral publication in the differing contexts we have identified, ranging from the formal lecture through seminars to collaboration in ongoing research. Instead, I only extend and elaborate upon some functions that have been touched upon in the preceding pages and are more fully exemplified in the papers that follow. Our own discussion will be severely delimited by centering on selected functions of the lecture, first for the lecturer and then for the student.

Functions for the Lecturer. As has been suggested, certain functions of a course of original academic lectures for the lecturer stem from its commonly representing an early phase in the development of ideas. It provides a conventionalized medium for developing private thoughts into semi-public exposition before assigning them to fully public print, subject to scrutiny by peers in the larger community of science and scholarship. It is important that oral publication at this stage is conventionally subjected to less exacting critical demands than publication, both by the audience and by the lecturer (with occasional exceptions as we have seen). Half-baked ideas that would be ruled out by public critics (such as referees for journals) can be examined for their possible cognitive interest before the quasi-public audience of students, who have been led to understand the incomplete and provisional status of those ideas. Cooley speaks for many a teacher both before and after him, when he reports that

> all through my teaching, I was giving to my students what I was in process of thinking out for myself. This, I think, is a good way to teach, in spite of the crudeness of the matter thus offered, for one is apt to conceive an idea with

more zest when it first appears to him than he ever will again: and it is zest and sincerity, quite as much as intrinsic worth, that gets the idea across (Cooley 1930: 9-10).

Sociologically considered, this feature of oral publication which allows for airing crudely formulated, early thoughts depends upon the provisional suspension of critical disbelief which is provided in social definitions of the lecture situation in contrast to formal exposition in print. Within that social framework, the teacher is free to set forth partly baked ideas, meticulously labelled for what they are, some of which may become fully baked ideas. Or, to change the figure abruptly, as a result of shared conventional definitions of the situation, the lecture can allow for examining interesting but seemingly questionable conceptions in semi-public rather than quashing them at once in the primordial crime of ideational infanticide. In this context, neither lecturer nor audience need suffer foolish ideas gladly but the ideas are not indicted as foolish until they have earned the right to be so characterized.

The lecture situation also provides for more than a rehearsal of thoughts previously thought through. It can make for more than the semi-public disclosure of those interior monologues that take place in the solitude of preparing the lecture. It can provide for the discovery of thoughts barely conceptualized before they were put into so many words before an evocative group. Evocative interaction between lecturer and (at least selected members) of the perceived audience-and-spectatory can result in the formulation of entirely new ideas which had not been brought into the lecture room. Often enough, these special moments in the course of the lecture can be recognized by the oral expressions of tone, pitch, and phrasing of the lecturer, as he listens, with surprised interest, to the unexpected ideas which he finds himself putting into so many words. These are the moments, evoked by the lecture situation, in which the speaker becomes part of his audience, thus exemplifying E.M. Forster's memorable dictum: "How can I tell what I think till I see what I say?" Sociologically amplified, the dictum would go on to state: And how can I more fully discover what I think till others help me say what at first I did not say to myself?

The extent of such spontaneous discovery of latent ideas in the course of lecturing understandably differs according to lecture styles. And, as the following accounts of sociologists in this volume make evident, those styles vary greatly, ranging from the virtual reading of carefully prepared manuscripts to much extemporizing based upon a scattering of notes. In the absence of any overview of lecture styles adopted by scholars, a brief example may serve to bring out certain cognitive functions. Thus, to judge from the account of Adam Smith's lecture style by one of his most consequential students, John Millar—the later author of the sociological classic, *Observations Concerning the Distinction of Ranks in Society* [(1771) 1960][11]—Smith combined both careful preparation and improvised formulation in the lectures which eventuated in *The Theory of Moral Sentiments* and *The Wealth of Nations:*

> In delivering his lectures, he trusted almost entirely to extemporary elocution. . . as he seemed to be always interested in the subject, he never failed to interest his hearers. Each discourse consisted commonly of several distinct propositions, which he successively endeavoured to prove and illustrate. . . In his attempts to explain them, he often appeared, at first, not to be sufficiently possessed of the subject, and spoke with some hesitation. As he advanced, however, the matter seemed to crowd upon him, his manner became warm and animated, and his expression easy and fluent. . . By the fullness and variety of his illustrations, the subject gradually swelled in his hands, and acquired a dimension which, without a tedious repetition of the same views, was calculated to seize the attention of his audience, and to afford them pleasure, as well as instruction, in following the same object, through all the diversity of shades and aspects in which it was presented, and afterwards in tracing it backwards to that original proposition or general truth from which this beautiful train of thought had proceeded (Millar in Smith [1759] 1853: xvii-xviii).

The ingredients needed for a comparative textual analysis are of course missing from this eighteenth-century account: Smith's original "distinct propositions" in his prepared lecture notes and a transcript of the lecture as it was actually spoken to identify the extent, character and substance of the "extemporary elocution" so that these might be compared with the formulations that appeared in Smith's vastly influential works in print. Still, there are intimations in the initial hesitancies and apparent uncertainties that in the course of oral exposition the subject grew and developed, at times in unexpected directions. To some unknown extent, the oral publication evidently served to shape the publication in print.

Like many another scholar, from his time to ours, Adam Smith was himself able to transmute at least part of his lectures into a form he considered fit for print. But, as we know from the case of George Mead, and an indefinitely long line of scholars before and after him, the printed texts available to us are often prepared not by their authors but by others, drawing wholly or in part from student notes (with these seldom being stenographically verbatim as they were with Mead). To say nothing about the ancient texts of an Aristotle, significant works of Leibniz, Kant, Fichte, and Hegel derive from materials prepared for or evolved in a teaching context (Moore

---

[11]It is symbolically apt that Millar, who amplified Smith and somewhat anticipated Marx in deriving inequality from private property, should have based his own great work on years of partly extemporized brilliant lectures.

1936, viii). At times, versions of lectures are put in print by others during the author's lifetime, as with the great codification of Willard Gibbs's lectures on *Vector Analysis* by his last student and later polymathic physicist-mathematician, statistician, and social scientist, E. B. Wilson (who became affiliated with the Harvard Department of Sociology in the 1930s). In such cases, the author-lecturer can vet the manuscript for accuracy before it sees print, as did Gibbs with what remained the standard text in the subject for many years (Hunsaker & Mac Lane 1973: 287).

Often, however, as in the case of Max Weber's lectures entitled "Outlines of Universal Social and Economic History," which were put into print after his death as *Wirtschaftsgeschichte,* 1923, and translated by Frank Knight as *General Economic History,* the text, largely reconstructed from student notebooks, is vulnerable to criticism on various counts. As Parsons observed some time ago, this book "cannot be considered an adequate statement of the results of his researches in economic or institutional history, to say nothing of sociological theory and the methodology of social science" (Parsons 1949: 67; *cf.* Merton [1938] 1978: 100n). So, too, with other even more consequential works. A major example is provided by the posthumously compiled and printed *Cours de linguistique générale* ([1916] English translation 1959) by the prime forerunner of structural linguistics, Ferdinand de Saussure. A perfectionist who published a total of some 600 pages in his lifetime, Saussure's cognitive influence derives in no small part from this small volume based upon the notebooks of a few students in his famous three courses in general linguistics. Ever since, much debate has centered on the extent to which the printed publication faithfully reproduces the essentials of Saussure's own oral publication (*cf.* Godel, 1957). The sociologically oriented linguist Joseph Greenberg (1968) has noted that "in some instances 'fruitful misunderstandings' of Saussure's ideas have exerted an influence on the development of European linguistic theory."

In such cases, one finds the composite autobiographical-and-historical irony that perfectionists, concerned to perfect their evolving ideas through continued oral publication, in the end succeed in leaving behind distinctly imperfect versions of those ideas, in the form of posthumous reconstructions in print. This is not the only dysfunction of oral publications which are not periodically translated into printed publications.

Dysfunctions for the Lecturer. Along with its various functions, oral publication, like other socioculture patterns, has its distinctive dysfunctions, limitations, and costs. It has the defects of its qualities. If it provides for the quick exchange of ideas, it does not allow for the detailed pondering of complex ideas. If it is flexible in providing for the continuing development of ideas before their full public disclosure, it is also fugitive, unless it is set down in more permanent form than speech allows. If conventional definitions of the situation calling for the partial suspension of disbelief in the classroom provide for the open exploration of interesting though risky ideas, they also make for less exacting quality control in the form of sustained critical judgments. In sum, oral like printed publication has its comparative advantages and disadvantages.

In the course of proposing a new form of communication in science, the EUGRAM,[12] the biologist Joshua Lederberg maintains, in psychological cognitive terms,

> the essentiality of writing for complex cognitive performances. . . A glance through the pages of [a scientific] journal is evidence enough of the impossibility of assembling complex scientific arguments without the use of the written record. The manipulation of recorded symbols is a pale shadow of an internal cognitive imagination we hardly understand, but our most intricate intellectual exercises rely heavily on these external marks, (Lederberg 1978: 1316).

This serves to remind us that what we sometimes describe as "oral traditions" in science in fact involve the commingling of complex written documents and face-to-face interactions.

In its sociocognitive aspects, oral publication appears comparatively fugitive, though not as much so perhaps as was claimed by the one-time dean of historians of science, George Sarton, when he observed that "Teaching at its best is ephemeral; from the point of view of posterity the only thing that really matters is a man's published work, for his teaching dies with him while his publications live after him forever" (Sarton 1947: 42). From the time perspective of a Sarton, directed toward a posterity measured in terms of centuries and millennia, even the oral publication that deeply influences students must indeed seem ephemeral. And, in any case, it is demonstrably less widely accessible than print. But an exclusively hypermetropic angle of vision is no more defensible than a myopic one in comparing modes of transmission of knowledge. As Keynes observed, for example, "it is through his pupils, even more than his writings, that Marshall is the father of economic science as it exists in England to-day" (Keynes [1933] 1972: 224). Or, as has been said of Wittgenstein, "He published very little. . . but the problems he discussed with a small group of pupils are now aired in universities throughout the world. 'Philosophers who never met him,' Gilbert Ryle

---

[12]". . . a system that accomplishes efficient transfer of digitally encoded information in near-real time among terminals that interface both to human users and to computer-manageable files. The economic integration of user, file, processor, and distance-indifferent communication link is the novel capability of what I shall call a EUGRAM system. EUGRAPHY thus embraces not only electronic dispatch of mail but also a panoply of computer-augmented text-handling tools and protocols" (Lederberg 1978: 1314).

wrote at the time of his death in 1951, 'can be heard talking philosophy in his tone of voice; and students who can barely spell his name now wrinkle up their noses at things which had a bad smell for him'" (Kenny 1973: 1). The following accounts in this volume bear varied witness to ways in which the cognitive influence of masters of the sociological art—not, clearly, in the form of uncritical imprinting—takes distinctive form among their immediate students, as compared with readers-at-a-distance. But, from the very long-term perspective of a Sarton, when simply or largely mediated through students, that influence is relatively short-lived and progressively obscured.

There are other costs of this mode of transmitting new knowledge. For almost by institutional prescription, oral publication is far less consequential than printed publication within the reward system of science. This derives from the seemingly paradoxical character of intellectual property in the domain of science: that the more freely scientists give that property away (by publication), the more securely it becomes their private property. For, as we have repeatedly noted, science is public not private knowledge (Ziman, 1968). Only when scientists have published their ideas and findings can they be said to have made a scientific *contribution*—as the telling phrase has it—and only when it has thus become part of the public domain of science can they lay claim to that contribution as truly theirs. For that claim resides only in the recognition accorded the work and its author by peers in the social system of science through reference and use of that work. Since such recognition of the worth of one's work by qualified peers is, in science, the basic form of reward (all other rewards deriving from it) and since it can only be widely accorded when the work is widely known, this provides institutionalized incentive for the open publication, without necessarily *direct* financial reward, of scientific work. Such open publication, in turn, allows for the ongoing evaluation and correction of claims to knowledge within the social system of science. Finally, for present purposes, since peer recognition is the basic coin of the scientific realm, and since the cognitive structure of science makes for multiple independent discoveries, this social and cognitive complex motivates scientists to get there first and to establish their claims to priority of discovery by certain forms of open publication. (On this model of the distinctive structure and functions of the interrelated cognitive, communication and reward systems of science, see Merton [1942] 1973: Chapter 13; also Chapters 12, 14; Price 1978: 79-81; Merton 1979: 47-49.)

In the course of historical evolution of the reward system of science, claims to priority of discovery or conception have become institutionally validated only by one form of publication. As Lederberg (1978: 1315) puts it succinctly: ". . . no piece of work, no claim to priority, is authentically recorded until it has appeared in public print in a respectable refereed journal.''[13] This widely adopted institutional rule tilts the reward system against oral publication in at least two respects beyond the manifest one of not allowing the oral communication of new and significant ideas or findings to qualify for recognized priority. First, it takes no notice of the possibility of such orally reported work becoming, without deliberate misappropriation on the part of any one involved in the process of diffusion, the basis for more developed versions of it being first put into print by others. And second, the rule takes no account of the independent appearance of essentially the same discovery in the interval between oral and printed publications by the originating scientist.

Once again, Alfred Marshall provides a prototype case in point. As we have noted, thanks to Keynes, much of Marshall's basic work was orally published. Part of this did not find its way into print at all; another major part in the form of the then ubiquitous *Principles of Economics* did so only some twenty years later, and the earliest part on the theory of money, only half a century later. Keynes goes on to observe,

> Meanwhile he had not kept his ideas to himself, but had shared them without reserve in lecture and in talk with friends and pupils. They leaked out to wider circles in privately printed pamphlets and through the writings of his pupils, and were extracted in cross-examination by Royal Commissions. [And then Keynes notes a cost of this sustained preference for oral over written publication:] Inevitably, when the books themselves appeared, they lacked the novelty and path-breaking powers which would have been acclaimed in them a generation earlier. . . (Keynes [1933] 1972, pp. 179-180).

This generic cost of oral publication was compounded in the specific case of the ideas centered on the fundamental notion of marginal utility. Multiple independent discovery and the rule that only printed, not oral publication, is to count, combined to rob Marshall of his priority:

> The publication of [Jevons's *Theory of Political Economy]* must have been an occasion of some disappointment and annoyance to Marshall. It took the cream of novelty off the new ideas which Marshall was slowly working up without giving them—in Marshall's judgment—adequate or accurate treat-

---

[13]See, for example, a formal and more specific version of the rule adopted by the American Council of Biology Editors: ''An acceptable primary publication must be the first disclosure containing sufficient information to enable peers (1) to assess observations, (2) to repeat experiments, and (3) to be susceptible to sensory perception, essentially permanent, available to the scientific community without restriction, and available for regular screening by one or more of the major recognized secondary services [e.g. currently, Biological Abstracts, Chemical Abstracts, Index Medicus...] in the United States and similar facilities in other countries'' (Cook 1970: 1286). In the physical and biological sciences, and somewhat less often in the social sceinces, first publication in print is typically in journals; much the same rules governing priority hold for publication in books.

ment. Nevertheless, it undoubtedly gave Jevons priority of publication as regards the group of ideas connected with "marginal" (or, as Jevons called it, "final") utility. Marshall's references to the question of priority are extremely reserved. He is careful to leave Jevons's claim undisputed, whilst pointing out, indirectly, but quite clearly and definitely, that his own work owed little or nothing to Jevons. (Keynes [1933] 1972: 183 ff; see Schumpeter [1954] 1968: 837-840).

In that last sentence, Keynes implicitly directs us to a final, and altogether ironic, possible cost of oral publication. The earlier originator may not only lose priority but may be taxed with having derived from the later independent discoverer by the many who had no access to the original formulations presented orally to a comparatively small audience.

It is perhaps the consummate perfectionist of twentieth-century philosophy focussed on the connections between language, mind and reality, who most crisply exemplifies the several perceived costs of oral publication. Reluctant for much of his life to put his continually evolving ideas into hard-and-fast print, Ludwig Wittgenstein was finally driven to prepare the manuscript of his *Philosophical Investigations* for publication. In the preface, he reports with characteristic candor:

> Up to a short time ago I had really given up the idea of publishing my work in my lifetime. It used, indeed, to be revived from time to time: mainly because I was obliged to learn that my results (which I had communicated in lectures, typescripts, and discussions), variously misunderstood, more or less mangled or watered down, were in circulation. This stung my vanity and I had difficulty in quieting it.

First, then, we have the intended turn to printed publication as presumably less subject than oral publication to misunderstanding and varied distortions of imputed exposition. Then, the not-so-oblique allusion to the further cost of losing priority by having his diffusing ideas reflected in the writings of others:

> For more than one reason what I publish here will have points of contact with what other people are writing today.—If my remarks do not bear a stamp which marks them as mine,—I do not wish to lay any further claim to them as my property.

And finally, the perspective of the skeptical perfectionist:

> I make them public with doubtful feelings. It is not impossible that it should fall to the lot of this work, in its poverty and in the darkness of this time, to bring light into one brain or another—but, of course, it is not likely. . . . I should have liked to produce a good book. This has not come about, but the time is past in which I could improve it (Wittgenstein 1968: ix-x).

It is perhaps this configuration of Wittgenstein's responses to certain consequences of oral publication which Ayer apparently detected a dozen years before, in noting that

Wittgenstein had already moved away from the position which he held in the *Tractatus,* but his current views were imparted only to the narrow circle of his Cambridge pupils. He was at pains to keep any report of them out of general circulation, from a morbid fear of their being misrepresented or plagiarized. It was not until the late nineteen-thirties that one or two copies of notes taken from his lectures, the celebrated Blue and Brown Books, somehow managed to find their way to Oxford (Ayer 1977: 120; *cf.* 130).

Still, like Mead, Wittgenstein remained loath to publish. Even the *Philosophical Investigations,* which he set down in manuscript in the middle and late 1940s, was in the end published only after his death, as were ten or so other volumes of his work. Indeed, the only philosophical book he published in his lifetime was the *Tractatus Logico-Philosophicus* (Kenny 1973: 3). One of the more recently published of the posthumous works, *Lectures & Conversations on Aesthetics, Psychology and Religious Belief* (Wittgenstein 1972), based on notes taken by a handful of his carefully selected students, contains the kind of prefatory remark which has grown increasingly familiar to us:

> The first thing to be said about this book is that nothing contained herein was written by Wittgenstein himself. The notes published here are not Wittgenstein's own lecture notes but notes taken down by students, which he neither saw nor checked. [And then with the informed candor one expects of Wittgenstein's students:] It is even doubtful if he would have approved of their publication, at least in their present form (Wittgenstein 1972: preface).

It comes as no great surprise that, somewhat like the less demanding Adam Smith in his time, the most severe perfectionist Ludwig Wittgenstein should have ordered most of his notebooks to be destroyed upon his death.

So much for this bare sketch of attributes, contexts, functions and dysfunctions of oral publication for the originating scholar, particularly in the case of lectures which have been transmuted into print by other than the author. Since the chapters of this book allude in abundance to the functions and dysfunctions of oral communication for students, even less will be said about them here.

Functions for the Student. From the following accounts and similar sources, it appears that the cognitive micro-environments composed of selected teachers and fellow students greatly affect the extent to which the potential functions of learning directly from the master are actually realized. Not least is the "climate of enthusiasm" and excitement generated and maintained by the sense that something of great cognitive interest is happening, then and there, and that one is lucky to be on hand. Not to anticipate the accounts that follow with regard to such great moments in the recent history of American sociology, one readily calls to mind cases drawn from other departments of science and learning. There is the well-known time of exciting advances in chromosome theory through which Edmund B. Wilson stirred up enthusiasm among Columbia students, leading a fair number of them to become participants in Morgan's *Drosophila* research group (Carlson 1966: 94-95). So, too, with the students of a William Osler in the lecture room, the medical dispensary, or on the wards, led into new directions of inquiry and practice not so much by the substance of what was patently being learned but by the tone and method with which problems calling for solution were being approached (MacNider 1953: 95).

At the extreme, the collateral functions of intensifying the cognitive interests of students and directing their attention in previously unconsidered directions can apparently take effect almost to the exclusion of what is being said substantively. Both the strength and the weakness of the spoken word may reside in its being fugitive. Less than with the written word which, being recursive, can be scanned again and again, one often remembers having been moved or instructed or excited or disturbed in productive ways without being able to identify precisely what was said. The effect rather than the substance remains. This theme recurs in accounts about a wide variety of scholars and scientists. As clear and strong a formulation as any I know was set forth by the author of the long consequential *Lectures on the Relation between Law and Public Opinion in England during the Nineteenth Century,* the jurist and political philosopher Albert Venn Dicey, writing of his experience as a pupil of Benjamin Jowett:

> A man may be a good teacher in the sense of stirring one up at the right moment and guiding one in the right direction, and [*n.b.*] say nothing in lectures which remains by one. This, as far as I was concerned, was the case with Jowett. To no man do I owe more. He made in many ways a difference in the whole course of my life both at College and after I left it, but I can't say that I remember much of his lectures (Dicey 1925: 27-28).

Other collateral functions of oral instruction involve what can be described as the Machlup Paradox: "The teacher's performance that prompts witnesses to say he is a good teacher is not always equivalent to good teaching if good teaching is what produces good learning" (Machlup 1979: 376). On this view, a good teacher can achieve such lucidity of exposition that students fail to recognize the complexities of the subject, develop a premature sense of having mastered it, and therefore neglect the further intensive study that would have brought them further along. Whether these assumed processes obtain generally remains moot. But almost as if he were supplying case material for the Machlup Paradox more than thirty years before it was enunciated in so many words, the great physicist and director of the Cavendish, J. J. Thomson, in effect described it in telling of his teacher W. D. Niven from whom he

> derived great benefit. Niven was not a fluent lecturer nor was his meaning always clear, but he was profoundly convinced of the importance of Maxwell's

views and enthusiastic about them; he managed to impart his enthusiasm to the class, and if we could not quite understand what he said about certain points, we were sure that these were important and that we must in some way or other get to understand them. This set us thinking about them and [*n.b.*] reading and re-reading Maxwell's book, which itself was not always clear. This was an excellent education and we got a much better grip of the subject, and greater interest in it, than we should have got if the question had seemed so clear to us in the lecture *that we need not think further about it.* The best teacher is not always the clearest lecturer but the one who is most successful in making his pupils think for themselves, and this Niven by his enthusiasm certainly did (Thomson 1936: 41-42; italics supplied).

It is only appropriate that Thomson in his turn should have been recognized as "an unsurpassable lecturer."

So, too, it is sometimes the incidental remark turning up spontaneously in the lecture which, for some hearers, remains memorable and consequential through much of their later lives. I think of one such thought-evoking aside by L. J. Henderson in his famous seminar on Pareto's general sociology at Harvard in the early 1930s: "It's a good thing to know what you're doing." I have found myself turning to this fine dictum repeatedly as a goad to searching out hidden assumptions that, once identified, often make a hash of a seemingly interesting idea. And, expressly modifying it to read: "In general,[14] it's a good thing to know what you are doing," I have passed it on to generations of my own students, some of whom bear witness similar to my own.

The foregoing repeated allusions to the lecture and seminar only remind us again that these are not the only or the most consequential forms for the oral transmission of knowledge in the academy. The most intensive form is evidently the "master-apprentice pattern" (Zuckerman 1977a, Chapter 4 by that title). This involves frequent and close interaction between the master and the novice in every phase of research and inquiry, from the time of formulation of problems, on through the phases of data collection and theoretical elucidation, as the case may be, to detailed analysis and writeup of the research materials.

One gains the impression that, except during the crucial phase of writing a dissertation, lectures play a greater part for students in the humanities than in the physical and life sciences, with the social sciences

---

[14]The qualifying phrase, "in general," was added, of course, to warn against the *premature* pressing for clarity during those early phases of thought which allow for creative chaos, searching for elusive idea, providing for Max DelBruck's "principle of limited sloppiness." L. J., by the way, did put his aphorism into print, in his masterly little book, *Pareto's General Sociology* (Harvard University Press, 1935), p. 73, where it reads: "It is a good plan to know what you are doing." I have never seen a reference to the printed version of the aphorism but, as I report overhead, I have seen to it that it was transmitted to hundreds of my students over the decades.

being poised between. One sign of this difference appears in the central and longstanding place of post-doctoral work in the natural sciences which contrasts with its virtual absence in the humanities and its still limited place in the social sciences. Still, there remains ample room for variation in instructional styles *within* each of the major divisions of knowledge. As I have briefly noted and as the following chapters make vividly clear, the eight master sociologists preferred one or another of two distinct styles. Weber, Mead, MacIver, and Sorokin (the last particularly in his Harvard years), who were primarily oriented toward the humanities, tended to make the lecture their prime vehicle of instruction (supplemented by seminars and direction of dissertations). So, too, with Frazier, who was constrained by having few graduate students altogether. In sufficient contrast to be noticeable, Park, Stouffer, and Lazarsfeld adopted a teaching style more nearly like the dominant mode found in the other sciences. Park, who made the city his laboratory and trained his students in that laboratory; Stouffer who has worked as an apprentice on the family newspaper before doing his doctoral work at Chicago followed by a post-doctoral year with Karl Pearson and R. A. Fisher; Lazarsfeld who, having received his doctorate in applied mathematics in Vienna and having been trained at the Bühlers' Psychological Institute, remained committed throughout his life to a master–apprentice style of teaching within the framework of a university-based research bureau which could provide for both pre-doctoral and post-doctoral instruction through participation in collaborative research.

Such observations can direct us to types of further systematic inquiry designed to gauge the kinds and magnitudes of differences in the education and socialization of scientists and humanists, both with regard to the dominant modes of oral transmission of knowledge and their consequences. Such research still waits in the vestibule. Nor, for that matter, can we be more than hypothetical in assessing the extent to which significant differences of outcome result from learning through direct and sustained personal interaction with teachers and through print. But, at their least, the chapters that follow provide materials bearing on both sets of questions.

* * *

It is now abundantly plain to me, as it must be plain to other readers, that this orienting piece can serve only to open up a few questions about the distinctive place of oral communication in the education of scholars and scientists and in the advancement of knowledge. Many correlative questions and problems dealing with the historical, social, and cognitive contexts of oral transmission must remain altogether untouched as I reach the outermost limits of space assigned to me by the editors.

REFERENCES

Note: Dates in brackets refer to time of first publication.

Ayer, A. J. *Part of my life: The memoirs of a philosopher.* New York & London: Harcourt Brace Jovanovich, 1977.

Barton, Allen H. "Paul Lazarsfeld and applied social research." *Social Science History,* 1979, 3, 4–44.

Carlson, Elof A. *The gene: A critical history.* Philadelphia, Penn.: W. B. Saunders, 1966.

Cole, Jonathan R. & Cole, Stephen. *Social stratification in science.* Chicago: University of Chicago Press, 1973.

Cook, Ellsworth B. "Biology editors' definition." *Science,* 12 June 1970, 168, 1286.

Cooley, Charles H. *Sociological theory and social research.* New York: Holt & Co., 1930.

Dicey, Memorials of Albert Venn. Edited by Robert S. Rait. London: MacMillan, 1925.

Eisenstein, Elizabeth L. *The printing press as an agent of change: Communications and cultural transformations in early-modern Europe.* Cambridge University Press, 1979. Two volumes.

Freud, Sigmund. *New introductory lectures on psycho-analysis and other works. Standard edition of the complete psychological works,* ed. by James Strachey, Vol. XXII. London: Hogarth Press, 1973.

Glock, Charles Y. "Organizational innovation for social science research and training." In Robert K. Merton, James S. Coleman and Peter H. Rossi, eds. *Qualitative and quantitative social research: Papers in honor of Paul F. Lazarsfeld.* New York: The Free Press, 1979, 23–26.

Godel, Robert. *Les sources manuscrites du Cours de linguistique generale de F. de Saussure.* Geneva: Droz, 1957.

Greenberg, Joseph H. "Ferdinand de Saussure." In David L. Sills, ed., *International encyclopedia of the social sciences.* New York: Macmillan & The Free Press, 1968, Vol. XIV, pp. 19–21.

Harrod, R. F. *The life of John Maynard Keynes.* New York: Harcourt, Brace, 1951.

Hastings, Charles S. Josiah Willard Gibbs. *Biographical memoirs.* Washington, D.C.: National Academy of Sciences, 1909, VI, 375–393.

Henderson, L. J. *Pareto's general sociology.* Cambridge, Mass.: Harvard University Press, 1935.

Hunsaker, Jerome & Saunders Mac Lane. Edwin Bidwell Wilson, 1879–1964. *Biographical memoirs,* National Academy of Sciences. New York: Columbia University Press, Vol. XLIII, 1973, 285–320.

Huxley, Aldous. *Proper studies.* London: Chatto & Windus, 1949.

Kenny, Anthony. *Wittgenstein.* Cambridge, Mass.: Harvard University Press, 1973.

Keynes, John Maynard. *Essays in biography.* London: Macmillan, [1933] 1972.

Klein, Martin J. Josiah Willard Gibbs. *Dictionary of scientific biography.* New York: Charles Scribner's Sons, 1972, Vol. V, 386–393.

Lazarsfeld, Paul F. *Radio and the printed page: An introduction to radio and its role in the communication of ideas.* New York: Arno Press, [1940] 1971.

Lederberg, Joshua. "Digital Communications and the Conduct of Science: The New Literacy." *Proceedings of the IEEE,* 1978, 66, 1314–1319.

Machlup, Fritz. "Poor Learning from Good Teachers." *Academe,* October 1979, 376-380.

MacNider, William deB. *The good doctor.* Chapel Hill, N.C.: University of North Carolina Press, 1953.

Merton, Robert K. *Science, technology and society in 17th-century England.* New Jersey: Humanities Press and Sussex: Harvester Press, [1938] 1978.

Merton, Robert, K. *Social theory and social structure.* New York: The Free Press, 1968, enlarged edition.

Merton, Robert, K. *Sociological ambivalence.* New York: The Free Press, 1976.

Merton, Robert, K.. *The sociology of science: An episodic memoir.* Carbondale, Ill.: University of Southern Illinois Press, 1979.

Millar, John. "The Origin of the Distinction of Ranks." In William C. Lehmann, *John Millar of Glasgow: His life, thought and contributions to sociological analysis.* Cambridge: Cambridge University Press, [1771] 1960, 165-322.

Mitzman, Arthur. *The iron cage: An historical interpretation of Max Weber.* New York: A. A. Knopf, 1970.

Moore, Merritt H. "Prefatory Note and Introduction." In George H. Mead, *Movements of Thought in the Nineteenth Century.* Chicago: University of Chicago Press, 1936, v-xxxvii.

Parsons, Talcott. *Essays in sociological theory, pure and applied.* New York: The Free Press, 1949.

Parsons, Talcott. *The structure of social action.* New York: The Free Press [1937] 1949.

Price, Derek de Solla. "Toward a Model for Science Indicators." In Yehuda Elkana, Joshua Lederberg, Robert K. Merton, Arnold Thackray and Harriet Zuckerman, eds. *Toward a metric of science: The advent of science indicators.* New York: John Wiley & Sons, 1978, 69-95.

Root, Robert K. "Publication before Printing." *Publications of the Modern Language Association,* 1913, xxviii, 417–431.

Russell, Bertrand. *Autobiography.* Boston: Little Brown; New York: Simon & Schuster, 1967-69. Three volumes.

Sarton, George. "Paul, Jules, and Marie Tannery." *Isis,* 1947, 38, 33–51.

Saussure, Ferdinand de. *Course in general linguistics.* New York: The Philosophical Library, [1916] 1959.

Schumpeter, Joseph A. *History of economic analysis.* New York: Oxford University Press, [1954] 1968.

Scott, William Robert. *Adam Smith as student and professor.* Glasgow: Jackson, Son & Co., 1937.

Shibutani, Tamotsu. "George Herbert Mead." *International Encyclopedia of the Social Sciences,* 1968, 10, 83–87.

Smith, Adam. *The theory of moral sentiments, an essay towards an analysis of the principles by which men naturally judge concerning the conduct and character, first of their neighbours, and afterwards of themselves.* New edition, with a Biographical and Critical Memoir of the Author, by Dugald Stewart. London: Henry G. Bohn, [1757] 1853.

Stephen, Leslie. "Dugald Stewart." *Dictionary of national biography.* London: Smith, Elder, & Co., 1898, LIV, 282–286.

Storer, Norman R. *The social system of science.* New York: Holt, Rinehart & Winston, 1966.

Taylor, Sir Geoffrey. "George Boole, 1815-1864." *Notes and Records of the Royal Society of London,* 1956, 12, 44–52.

Thomson, J. J. *Recollections and reflections.* London: G. Bell & Sons, 1936.

Vansina, Jan. *Oral Tradition: A Study in Historical Methodology.* Chicago: Aldine Publishing Company [1961] 1965.

Weber, Marianne. *Max Weber: A biography.* Translated by Harry Zohn. New York: John Wiley & Sons, [1926] 1975.

Weber, Max. *Wirtschaftsgeschichte.* Munchen und Leipzig: Duncker & Humblot, 1923 (translated by Frank H. Knight, *General Economic History.* New York: Free Press, 1950).

Whitehead, A. N. "Autobiographical Notes." In P. A. Schilpp, ed., *The philosophy of Alfred North Whitehead.* New York: Tudor Publishing Co. [1941] 1951, 3–14.

Wiener, Norbert. *Ex-prodigy.* Cambridge, Mass.: The M.I.T. Press, 1953.

Wittgenstein, Ludwig. *Lectures & conversations on aesthetics, psychology, and religious belief.* Cyril Barrett, ed. Compiled from Notes taken by Yorick Smythies, Rush Rhees, and James Taylor. Berkeley & Los Angeles: University of California Press, 1972.

Wittgenstein, Ludwig. *Philosophical investigations.* New York: Macmillan, [1953] 1968.

Ziman, John. *Public knowledge.* Cambridge: Cambridge University Press 1968.

Zuckerman, Harriet. *Scientific elite.* Chicago: University of Chicago Press, 1977a.

Zuckerman Harriet. "Deviant Behavior and Social Control in Science." In Edward Sagarin, ed., *Deviance and social change.* Beverly Hills: Sage Publications, 1977b, 87–138.

2

The Circumstances of My Encounter with
MAX WEBER

Talcott Parsons

[Talcott Parsons died on May 8, 1979 in Munich, the city where Max Weber had died almost sixty years before. The end came only a few days after he had been honored in Heidelberg on the fiftieth anniversary of his having been awarded the degree of D. Phil. by that most ancient of German universities. It was a degree, incidentally, which he invariably took pains to distinguish from the more demanding Ph.D.

On the day Talcott Parsons and his wife Helen left for Germany, we talked with him about his plans for expanding this piece for publication. He planned, among other things, to work out the ways in which Weber's continuing influence had been mediated through the writings of Simmel, Toennies, Sombart and von Wiese. He wanted to enlarge upon the influence of "the Weber circle," to elucidate the impact of *The Protestant Ethic* on his own thinking and to examine the theoretical ideas in that monograph which crystallized into the concept of capitalism as it was later developed in the literature of German social science. He wanted to give some idea of the substantive and theoretical questions he had brought back with him from his studies at Heidelberg and to expand the account of Weber's specific influences on his own early years of thought at Harvard. He intended to provide a fuller account also of the ways in which his own theoretical interests had moved from treating the concept of capitalism as a socio-economic system to making that concept the basis for examining the relations between economic theory and the yet-to-be-developed theory of the social system. He especially had it in mind to identify some "Weberian insights" which he thought had continuing relevance for sociology today.

We can now only imagine the richness of what he may have gone on to write. As his former, and continuing, students, we thought long and hard about possibly piecing together fragments from his writings that relate to themes in his intended revision of the paper—not least, passages from the two public lectures on Weber which he delivered virtually in the shadow of Weber's statue in Munich on the two evenings before the day of his death. But it soon became evident that any such effort would be altogether inadequate. It would, moreover, be alien to the intent and the character of this collection of essays. This short paper therefore provides only the unelaborated, largely unedited essentials of what Talcott Parsons said to a captivated audience at the Philadelphia meeting of the Eastern Sociological Society on March 31st, 1978.]

Unlike the other contributors to this symposium, I never knew my subject, Max Weber, in person. He died in April of 1920 and I never even knew of his existence until June of 1925. In view of the importance of his impact on my own career, however, and partly through me, though involving much broader channels, on the development of sociology and other sciences, I think it is worth recounting these circumstances. He served, in a very real sense, as my teacher.

My first year of graduate study was spent at the London School of Economics in the academic year 1924-25. I was fresh out of college and I would say a distinctly callow graduate student whose interests in an undefined way bridged the relations between economics and sociology. I had no clear-cut training plans and was open to the suggestion, as the London year drew to a close, of going to Germany on a German–American exchange fellowship program, which had been instituted just during that year and was meant as a gesture of reconciliation after the first World War. One of my Amherst teachers, Professor Otto Manthey-Zorn, was a member of the American committee and informed me about the program, suggesting that if I were interested I should apply. I did so and was awarded a fellowship and without having any personal say in the matter, was assigned to Heidelberg.

Studying in Germany required a reasonably good command of the German language and, though I had some background, I did not feel mine was adequate. I went to Vienna for the summer of 1925 with the primary purpose of improving my German in preparation for the fall semester at Heidelberg. However, Heidelberg was right on the way between London and Vienna so I decided to stop off there and announce myself and leave a few things. I did so in the month of June. I am quite confident that when I left London after a full academic year at L.S.E., I had never heard the name of Max Weber. To be sure, R.H. Tawney was at that time working on his book *Religion and the Rise of Capitalism*. Though I attended Tawney's lectures, they were on other topics and I do not remember him mentioning Weber. It was perhaps more surprising that I did not hear Weber's name from Morris Ginsberg. A fairly recent talk with Professor Donald MacRae of L.S.E. elicited the opinion that Ginsberg had probably not yet read Weber at that time, though of course he was fully conversant with the German language.

However that may be, on my arrival in Heidelberg I was immediately briefed on the important theoretically-inclined social scientists with whose work I ought to familiarize myself. It was quite clear from the beginning that Weber led the list. There were, of course, others such as his brother Alfred Weber, who became one of my teachers, Georg Simmel, Ferdinand Toennies, Werner Sombart, and Leopold von Wiese. My principal briefing agent was Dr. Arnold Bergstraesser, who later became a figure of considerable stature.

However, my summer occupation in Vienna was such that I did not undertake any reading of Weber until my return to Heidelberg to settle in, the following fall. I don't think it was mere chance that the first of Weber's works which I read was his study, *The Protestant Ethic and the Spirit of Capitalism*. I don't know how surprising it will be for others, however, that this reading had an immediate and powerful impact on me. It gripped my intense interest immediately and I read it straight through—that is, subject to the limits of library hours, since I did not yet own a copy—as if it were a detective story. This reading had much to do with the crystallization of a dissertation project in the months that followed. When I first went to Heidelberg, I had no plans to be a degree candidate there. Indeed, I scarcely had plans of any sort. Various people I met, however, inquired about my intentions and I soon discovered that it was possible to get a degree without impossibly difficult conditions. For example, I had only to accumulate residence credit for three semesters and to write a dissertation. The idea seemed attractive, and in consultation with a young economist-sociologist, Edgar Salin, I formulated a plan for a study of the concept of capitalism in German social science literature. This was to deal with three main figures, Karl Marx, Werner Sombart, and Max Weber, in addition to several not quite so prominent ones such as Lujo Brentano. The plan was carried out. In due course I submitted my dissertation, it was accepted and I received a Heidelberg doctorate. I still feel compelled to point out that this was a Dr. Phil., not a Ph.D. in the American style. Ever since I have been listed in various connections as a Ph.D. and have finally given up protesting. It appears to be totally fruitless but the two types of degree are of course far from being the equivalent of each other.

To accent this difference, I should report that, in addition to the dissertation, and putting in three semesters of residence, I had to face oral examination in four fields. These examinations took place in the summer semester of 1927. The four fields and examiners were: two "major" fields, namely economic theory with Salin and sociological theory with Alfred Weber, and two "minor" fields, modern European history with special reference to the French Revolution, with Willy Andreas, and modern philosophy, with special reference to Kant, with Karl Jaspers.

The influence of Weber in the Heidelberg of my day was not confined to library and classroom. I may mention two notable experiences of a more informal nature. First, Weber's widow, Marianne Weber was living in Heidelberg in the same house, overlooking the river Neckar and the Heidelberg castle, that she had shared with her husband. She carried on a tradition which had been initiated during his lifetime, of holding what were called "sociological teas" on Sunday afternoons. A considerable group gathered in the large living room, and after tea there was a presentation by an academic notable, often a visitor, and then a discussion. I was fortunate enough to be invited to a number of these occasions and found them most stimulating.

Secondly, Else von Jaffé-Richthofen, the widow of Weber's successor as editor of the *Archiv für Sozialwissenschaften,* and a special friend of the Webers' lived in Heidelberg and I had the good fortune to be invited to her house a number of times. Indeed, it could probably be said that the "Weber circle" was the main center of Heidelberg academic society at that time. Among the younger people I also came to know were Karl Mannheim and Alexander von Schelting.

It was during the summer of 1927 that I conceived the idea of translating Weber's *Die Protestantische Ethik und der Geist des Kapitalismus* into English. At that time none of Weber's works was available in English, though I learned subsequently that Frank H. Knight, the Chicago economist, was translating Weber's *General Economic History,* which appeared shortly before my translation. At any rate I went to Marianne Weber with my suggestion and she welcomed it wholeheartedly. She kindly put me in touch with the German publisher, Mr. Siebeck, of the Tübingen firm which had published almost all of Weber's works. I went to see Siebeck and worked out the arrangement. He in turn arranged publication of the English version by Allen and Unwin of London. It appeared, after a few vicissitudes, in the early summer of 1930.

On my going to Harvard as instructor in economics in the fall of 1927, my first concern was to finish my dissertation, in which Weber was the centerpiece. By that time, however, I had conceived the idea of shifting my emphasis, in a future study, from the idea of "capitalism" as a socio-economic system, to that of the relations between economic *theory* and the *theory* of the social system. Indeed, it was with that in mind that I came to Harvard, especially to learn more about economic theory than I had gleaned at London and Heidelberg.

There were a variety of features of the Harvard situation which I did not know about when I decided to go there, and which turned out to be important to me intellectually and in terms of my career. For example, I did not know of any plans for the development of sociology there, nor had I heard of L.J. Henderson, though I had heard of Pareto and was determined, when I had the time, to become acquainted with his work.

In considering this new project, however, it seemed that a particularly suitable starting point was to take the work of at least one prominent, theoretically oriented economist and to subject it to a kind of "sociological study." This is to say that I wanted to work out the framework in the larger theory of the general social system within which he had developed his economic analysis. For this purpose I chose the figure who was the most prominent figure in English-language economics of his generation, namely Alfred Marshall. To put it in somewhat cliché form, I was interested in the sociological framework within which Marshall worked out his economic analysis. This study of Marshall, which was published independently before the *Structure of Social Action,* gave much food for further thought. In those same early years at Harvard, and not only through L.J. Henderson, I became aware of the work of the Italian economist-sociologist, Pareto. He was a particularly important figure for my purposes, because he was both an economic theorist of a high order and wrote a massive work in the field of sociology. I was therefore particularly concerned with the ways in which Pareto linked the two subjects as theoretical disciplines. Finally, there had been much discussion about that time of the work of Emile Durkheim and I undertook a serious study of that work. It turned out that it fitted into my plan exceedingly well and gradually the plan to write a general study of this problem in the work of European authors of that generation took shape. I am quite sure that without the exposure to Weber's work, which occurred from the beginning of my Heidelberg experience, I would never have undertaken anything like the *Structure of Social Action.* Whatever its impact on American sociology may have been, and beyond America as well, it was that book, of course, which established something of a position for me personally. Had I not written it, heaven knows what kind of a career I might or might not have had.

Though the four chapters in *The Structure of Social Action* constitute the most extensive study of Weber's work that I have undertaken, this was by no means the end of my concern with that work. Of course, the translation of Part I of *Wirtschaft und Gesellschaft* came along some years later, as did the writing of the long introduction to it. I have had further occasion, however, to come back repeatedly to Weber in a variety of ways. This was very much the case with my teaching as well. Indeed, given the course on which I had embarked, it did not seem likely that, as long as I remained intellectually active, I would ever cease to be concerned with Weber's work. However, a few of the subsequent highlights may be of interest.

First my involvement with the translation of Weber did not end with *The Protestant Ethic*. There may be some interest in the story of how I became involved in the translation of Part I of *Wirtschaft und Gesellschaft*. I think it was early in 1939 that I received a letter from Friedrich von Hayek, the Austrian economist, who was then at the London School of Economics. He said that a draft translation of the first two chapters of *Wirtschaft und Gesellschaft* had been made under his supervision by a young English economist named [A.R.] Henderson, and wondered whether I would be willing to review the draft. He sent it to me and I replied first, that the Henderson draft was in need of, not merely substantial, but drastic revision and, secondly, that it would be a serious mistake to publish a translation of the first two chapters without including others, especially Chapter 3, *Die Typen der Herrschaft*.

This correspondence ended with Hayek requesting me to undertake the revision of the Henderson draft. Just at that time, the second World War broke out, and Henderson was called into the British armed services so that his further participation was out of the question. The upshot was that not only did I undertake a very thorough and far-reaching revision of the Henderson draft, but translated Chapters 3 and 4 myself. In Chapter 1, I was greatly helped by a mimeographed draft translation which had been worked out by Edward Shils and Alexander von Schelting. Robert Merton was in on my decision-making about this project and I imagine he remembers it well.

The importance of Weber's work for me was, of course, by no means confined to the opportunity to serve as its translator. As I have said, the translation of *Wirtschaft und Gesellschaft* served as the occasion for me to write a quite long analytical introduction—one which came to 83 printed pages. This, however, was at a rather late stage of my interest in Weber. Perhaps I may mention four still later occasions. The first of these was that attending an English translation of Weber's general monograph entitled *The Sociology of Religion* which was originally published as part of *Wirtschaft und Gesellschaft*. I was asked to write an introduction to it. This turned out to be a rather long and comprehensive survey of Weber's work in that field. It was published in 1963. The second occasion followed closely after that. 1964 was the centenary of Weber's birth and to mark the occasion, the German Sociological Association organized a large meeting in Heidelberg. On that occasion, which was a very complicated affair both intellectually and politically, I chose to deal, in my paper, with what I regard as some of the central themes in Weber's work, namely, the relation first between evaluation and objectivity in social science, and the relation of this in turn to the structure of Weber's substantive interests in the field. I put forward the not-widely-shared view that Weber's substantive centerpiece was the study of law, the discipline in which he was originally trained, and that his economic and political sociology should be placed on one side of this centerpiece, with the sociology of religion on the other side.

The other two encounters I have had with Weber's work have been recent, indeed the results in both cases are still unpublished. The first of these was at a conference held in September of 1977 under the auspices of the University of Konstanz in West Germany, dealing with Rationality and Rationalization in the thought of Max Weber, an altogether central topic. I gave the lead-off statement of the problem for the conference.

The last encounter was at least an initial fulfillment of an ambition I have cherished for a good many years. This was to attempt to bring the thinking of Weber and Freud into closer articulation than has usually been done. To attempt this, I took the occasion of being asked to speak, last October, at a meeting of the Psycho-Historical Society.

My personal concern with Max Weber's work thus extended well over fifty years, and I see no sign that my experience has been idiosyncratic in the sense that I have concerned myself with things of only secondary interest to the theoretical development of the field. As in the case of other great minds who have turned their attention in the direction of sociology, Weber's thought constitutes an inexhaustible mine of insight and suggestiveness. In this sense he belongs to the small number of "immortals" in our field.

3

GEORGE HERBERT MEAD
The Legacy of Social Behaviorism[1]

Leonard S. Cottrell, Jr.

There may be special point in having one of his relatively few surviving students reflect upon the ideas of George Herbert Mead and upon the ways in which they came into being and were communicated to a succession of student-cohorts at the University of Chicago. As I shall soon tell, I write only from the vantage point of having sat in his famous course, Advanced Social Psychology, almost half a century ago and from a subsequent deep interest in what I take to be the essential Mead. On that basis, I shall try to convey a sense of Mead the teacher. I shall examine his theoretical orientation as I understood it then and as I have come to understand it since. I shall then go on to say something about the continuing relevance of his ideas and I shall report on that influence as I know it best—upon my own work. And, finally, I shall suggest some promising lines of inquiry for the further development of Mead's seminal ideas.

All of us tend to revise the past to fit our current beliefs and the imperious realities of our lives. It is a hazardous undertaking, therefore, to try to parcel out the details of how I, as a student, saw Mead's work and how I understand him today. To reduce the hazards of reading the present into the past, I shall move freely between them and, not infrequently, check my own estimates against those of others.

[1]It is a pleasure to acknowledge my indebtedness to John W. Riley, Jr. whose numerous notes, suggestions and queries were most welcome and evocative stimuli; to Anita Cottrell for her critical editorial help and to Anna Tyndall, research assistant and secretary, whose help so generously given made possible the completion of this undertaking.

DISCLAIMERS AND CAVEATS

At the outset I wish to enter certain disclaimers lest I appear to be sailing under false colors.

In the first place I never experienced the close working relationship with Professor Mead that so frequently occurs between a graduate student and a teacher whom he greatly admires and is strongly influenced by. He was in the Philosophy Department and I was in the Sociology Department, and, while there was a reasonably good working relationship between the two departments, there were few occasions of interdepartmental contacts. I took only the one course I have mentioned with Professor Mead, the large lecture course, Advanced Social Psychology, in the winter quarter of 1930. There was no class discussion, and I never had a personal conference with him. I can recall no contact with him outside of class. It has been a matter of keen regret and a sense of loss that has increased over the years that I did not seize the opportunity to take additional courses and seminars with him and thus gain a firmer grasp of his thought and a more intimate acquaintance with him as a person. But remote and transient as the contact was, there is no question that Professor Mead has had a profound impact on my thinking and on my career as a social psychologist.

Secondly, I wish to make clear that I do not qualify as a Meadian scholar. He was a philosopher of central importance as well as a social psychologist. His writings and lectures cover a wide range in pragmatic philosophy and social psychology as well as in practical matters such as education, crime and punitive justice, problems of the urban community, the societal functions of play and recreation, war and international relations. Nor do I pretend to an adequate grasp of Mead's philosophic position, though with the prodding of my young friends David Lewis of Notre Dame and Richard Smith of Charleston College (1978), and Charles Varela of Union College (1973 and 1978) I am only now beginning to get some glimpse of Mead's central importance in the current drive for a more adequate metaphysic for social theory and philosophy of science.

However, it is as a social psychologist that I am fascinated, not to say obsessed, by the social behaviorism of Professor Mead. And if I, as I shouldn't, do say so myself, I believe I have a better understanding of Meadian social behaviorism and have used his system more consistently in my research and theorizing than most contemporary behavioral scientists, and certainly more consistently than most symbolic interactionists. Having voiced such a deplorably immodest sentiment, let me hasten to balance it with the admission that I find many regrettable instances in some of my own work of what I now recognize as misperceptions and misinterpretations of Mead's conceptualizations. Let me then, with all due apologies, urge the caveat that what I report here is Mead as perceived and experienced by Cottrell the 1930 student and not necessarily as he is understood by his more learned and competent students.

With disclaimers and apologies out of the way we can now turn to consider Mead's impact on my thinking and career and my assessment of his place in our discipline.

BIOGRAPHICAL NOTE

As background, it will be helpful to have some idea of Mead as a person. Within the limitations of space the best that can be done here is to provide a capsule history of his career. As students, we somehow knew a great deal about Mead's background, although I never did understand how this information was gathered and distributed. On the other hand, it was, of course, incomplete and sketchy. In outlining this brief history, I shall therefore draw upon David L. Miller (1973), one of Mead's outstanding students in philosophy, for much of the biographical detail. Those interested will find much more, plus references to other biographical sources, in Miller's treatise, *George Herbert Mead: Self, Language, and the World.*

George Herbert Mead was born at Hadley, Massachusetts on February 27, 1863; he died in Chicago on April 26, 1931.

Mead came from a well-established middle-class intellectual background with a substantial Puritanic orientation. His father was descended from a line of New England farmers and clergymen and was himself a Protestant minister who in his late career taught homiletics at Oberlin Theological Seminary. Mead's mother came from a prominent New England family and after her husband's death taught at Oberlin College and was, for ten years, president of Mount Holyoke College.

Mead's own educational career was marked by a persistent drive to free himself from what he regarded as the stultifying restraints of doctrinal theological beliefs and practices. While an undergraduate at Oberlin, he and his roommate, Henry Castle, called themselves the "conspirators" and frequently occupied themselves with proving to their own satisfaction that various basic religious doctrines and beliefs were in error, that is, quite inconsistent with scientific findings. Seeking still greater intellectual freedom, he studied philosophy at Harvard and was strongly influenced by Royce and his interpretation of Hegelian romantic idealism. From his later teaching and writing, I suspect that the interactional emphasis in Hegelian dialectics was of special interest to him. Still feeling somewhat cramped by the strong components of religious doctrine in American higher education, Mead decided to seek a more naturalistic philosophy by way of science. He worked toward a doctorate in physiological psychology at Leipzig and Berlin and was strongly influenced by the work of Wilhelm Wundt and by Darwinian theory. Wundt's analysis of the evolutionary significance of the "gesture" and Darwin's work on the expression of emotions in animals and men were important steps in Mead's behavioral analysis of communication, interaction, and social integration and the emergence of mind and the self.

Before he completed work for the doctorate, Mead was persuaded to join the faculty at the University of Michigan, where he became acquainted with Charles Horton Cooley's elaboration of Adam Smith's concept of the "looking-glass self" and the role of "sympathetic imagination" in social interaction and social integration (Miller, 1973). There, also, he became a close friend of John Dewey and was much interested in Dewey's conception of the instrumental functions of mind and thinking. He thus came early into fruitful contact with American pragmatic philosophy. Although they represented somewhat different philosophic orientations within the pragmatic tradition, Dewey and Mead were close friends and were able to communicate quite freely. There is strong evidence of their close relationship: when Dewey was asked to join the Department of Philosophy at the University of Chicago, he accepted on condition that he could bring Mead with him. The condition was met. In 1894 Mead joined the University where for the ensuing 37 years he was to pursue his goal of a naturalistic philosophy consistent with what scientific research was revealing about a universe of interactive processes.

What was of special interest to us as students was Mead's elaboration of an interactive social psychology that he called social behaviorism. In this highly creative conceptual elaboration, he attempted to give a behavioral process account of the emergence of mind and thinking, of consciousness, of the self, of the person, of communication, and of the integration of individual selves into functioning collectivities. Throughout this work, Mead imposed the requirement that it be consistent with and descriptive of the processes of evolutionary adaptation as well as with his broader philosophic framework.

MEAD AS TEACHER

There is a widely held but mistaken impression today that Professor Mead's philosophical position and his social behaviorism were central in providing the intellectual foundations of "The Chicago School" of sociology. Professors Lewis and Smith (1978) have undertaken to challenge this view. It does appear from their analysis that there was a rather sharp difference in philosophic orientation between those whose basic approach was primarily nominalistic and those who, like Mead, were social realists. Whether the philosophic cleavages were as clear-cut as these authors report, the record of the number of sociology students who took Mead's courses, the references by their professors to Mead's work, the citations of Mead in the writings of the professors and the students—even those who took his courses—fail to support the belief that he was a central figure for most Chicago-trained sociologists. Nevertheless, most of the students during my days at Chicago felt that something very important was "going on" in Mead's classes. It is also true, of course, that a good many students in psychology and sociology, some of whom became the principal architects of "The Chicago School," took courses with Mead during his first 25 years at Chicago. The sociologists included W. I. Thomas, C. A. Ellwood, L. L. Bernard, E. S. Bogardus, E. W. Burgess, E. H. Sutherland, S. A. Queen, J. F. Steiner, F. W. Znaniecki, R. D. McKenzie, E. B. Reuter, D. Sanderson, F. M. Thrasher, K. Young, W. B. Bodenhafer, C. R. Shaw, and F. B. Karpf, to mention only a few. The striking fact is, however, that most of these students-become-masters rarely cited Mead's teachings and writings in their research and teaching.

It was not until Professor Ellsworth Faris joined the sociology faculty in the early 1920s that students in the department were regularly exposed to systematic presentation of Meadian theory and to routine counselling to take his courses. Faris held a Chicago Ph.D. in psychology and had been a student of Mead's. By the time I took Mead's course, Advanced Social Psychology, in 1930, any sociology student with an interest in the processes and products of personal or collective interaction was expected to take work with Professor Mead. This expectation was expressed more through word-of-mouth and informal discussions among students than through formal advice from the faculty. It is of interest to note that after 1920 practically no graduate students in psychology took any of Mead's courses and only two or three ever cited his work (Smith, 1976).

For me, the course with Professor Mead was a unique and unforgettable experience. The class was large. We met in the moot courtroom of the Law School. Professor Mead was a large, amiable-looking man who wore a magnificent mustache and a Van Dyke beard. He characteristically had a benign, rather shy smile matched with a twinkle in his eyes as if he were enjoying a secret joke he was playing on his audience. He always entered the classroom at the stroke of the bell, tossed his overcoat, cap and long copious scarf on the railing in front of the judge's bench and took his seat in the swivel chair behind the bench. He then reached behind him and picked up a good-sized piece of chalk from the blackboard that covered the wall behind the bench. He cast a benevolent smile over the heads of the class, who sat with notebooks and pencils ready, and without more ado launched into his lecture. His lectures always started with a summarization of what had been previously presented. As the course moved on, these summaries took a substantial segment of the class hour, but they seemed useful as a way of giving him a running jump into the new material.

As he lectured—always without notes—Professor Mead would manipulate the piece of chalk and watch it intently. From time to time he would scribble something on the bench, look at it and rub it out with his sleeve. When he made a particularly subtle point in his lecture he would glance up and throw a shy, almost apologetic smile over our heads—never looking directly at anyone. His lectures flowed and we soon learned that questions or comments from the class were not welcome. Indeed, when someone was bold enough to raise a question there was a murmur of disapproval from the students. They objected to any interruption of the golden flow. I have mentioned Professor Mead's intent focus on the gyrations of his piece of chalk as he lectured. One day an irreverent miscreant removed all the chalk from the chalk shelf. Professor Mead came in, tossed his cloak, etc., etc. on the rail, sat down and reached for his chalk. Not feeling any, he turned around to look. Not finding any, he momentarily lost his benevolent expression and appeared a bit disturbed. He obviously had difficulty in getting his lecture underway and it was only after a rather labored ten or twelve minutes that he hit his usual stride. For some time after that I carried some chalk in my pocket and as I entered the classroom glanced over to see that chalk was in the proper place.

His expectations of students were modest. He never gave exams. The main task for each of us students was to write as learned a paper as one could. These Professor Mead read with great care and what he thought of your paper was your grade for the course. One might suppose that students would read materials for the paper rather than attend his lectures but that was not the case. Students always came. They couldn't get enough of Mead.

By the time I became a student in Professor Mead's course I considered myself a behaviorist. J. B. Watson's experiments in conditioning so-called instinctive responses of infants were for me quite convincing evidence of the modifiability of human behavior. My undergraduate major had been in biology where genetic determinism was stressed, and when I ran head on into the sociological challenge to that perspective I found it quite exciting. However, the sociological evidence lacked explicit description of the processes by which human behavior patterns were implanted. J. B. Watson's behaviorism seemed to point the way to closing the gap. But I had serious reservations about his dismissal of what he called mentalistic phenomena as irrelevant to the objective analysis of behavior. It seemed to me he was ruling out much that was distinctive of and essential to an understanding of human behavior. Imagine, then, my excitement and delight to discover a thoroughgoing behaviorist, trained in physiological psychology, who proceeded to treat intrapersonal processes such as empathic responses, the self, mind, thinking and all their elaborations as behavior and legitimate objects of behavioral analysis. Early in the course, Mead (1934) sharply distinguished between his social behaviorism and the behaviorism of Watson (1919). The juxtaposition of these two positions, however, was one of the highlights of my student days with Mead.

As some of you know, Watson had studied, did research and taught at the University of Chicago during the period of 1900-1908. He took several courses in philosophy—some of them with Professor Mead. During the first 15 years or so of his career at Chicago, Professor Mead had taught courses in general psychology, comparative psychology and methodology of psychology, in addition to his course in social psychology. Watson also took some of these courses and I believe that for a time he was Mead's assistant. There can be little doubt that he got a good deal of stimulation from Professor Mead to make behavioral research his focal interest. While, as Watson reported in his autobiography (1961), he could never make much sense out of Mead's philosophy courses, the two men were good friends and spent many Sunday afternoons in the animal psychology laboratory discussing Watson's experimental work with rats and monkeys. The young behaviorist apparently found peace of mind away from the confusion and ambiguity of philosophic discourse when he could make objective observations of the behavior of his animals. Unfortunately, in this interaction, Watson either rejected or never grasped the possibility and crucial significance of behavioral analysis of the covert processes that are of such central importance to the understanding of human behavior.

To leap from my student days to my current estimate of Mead's behaviorism, Watson, of course, was not alone in his failure to grasp the significance of Mead's system. By and large the American psychological establishment has neither understood nor cared to understand or test Meadian social behaviorism. Sociologists likewise have largely failed to grasp the full significance of Mead for their discipline. I believe it can be shown that these disciplines are paying and will continue to pay a high price for their failure to make full use of Meadian social behaviorism. An inability to achieve a satisfactory theory of the distinctive nature of the human being and of the integration of human societies is a substantial part of this price. In my opinion there are rather strong practical, ideological, economic and political reasons for this strange resistance to Meadian theory. I shall touch briefly on these later in this paper.

BASIC CONCEPTS OF MEADIAN SOCIAL BEHAVIORISM

But what is this Meadian mystery that I claim so many are failing to comprehend and utilize? While we cannot here undertake a complete examination of Meadian social behaviorism, I must clarify what appear to me to be certain unique and critical features of his system. In attempting to do this, I shall rely heavily upon my own recollections and upon my own student notes, although I shall not hesitate to draw upon the critiques and writings of others. In that way, I hope to substantiate to some degree my estimate of Mead as of central and enduring importance for achieving a more adequate social science (Mead, 1913, 1922, 1932, 1934, 1938, 1964).

Social Interaction: The Central Process

Even those having only a limited acquaintance with Mead's work will know that the central focus of his theory is the analysis of the processes and emergent products of social interaction. Obviously a key to understanding Mead is to know what he means by social interaction. Not many have an adequate grasp of the term and its implications. It is ironic that, as Charles Varela (1973) has so well demonstrated, sociological theorists have pretty generally failed to give a satisfactory behavioral account of the concept of social interaction. Thus what is regarded as a central concept and assumed to be universally understood, remains a rather ambiguous catch-bag of doubtful theoretical or practical value.

The term *interpenetrative interaction* indicates more precisely an essential part of the process as conceived in the Meadian (1934) theory. It points to the crucial assumption that, behaviorally speaking, in any given social interact the participants become parts of one another. Thus a basic proposition can be stated as follows:

> When two human organisms A and B become involved in a series of reciprocally interdependent interacts, each participant in the interaction not only learns his own act part, but also learns the act part of the other *as he perceives or experiences that other.*

This learning of the act part of the other as it is perceived is usually learned covertly and not manifested overtly. It should be emphasized that this is not a metaphorical statement. The act parts covertly acquired are assumed to be actually enacted behaviorally in incipient neuromuscular or attitudinal mobilizations. The interchanges may be in gestural form, verbal or nonverbal. These are covertly learned and the actions they signify are assumed to be evoked in incipient form. It should also be recognized that misperceptions and distortions of various kinds may complicate the process. However, continued interaction will move the perceptions toward greater shared commonality. The proposition stated above is addressed to the dyadic situation.

It can be extended to apply to more than two participants and to symbolized collectivities or "generalized others," as Mead (1934) called them. As Mead's student in 1930, I can remember these arguments coming through to me with little or no ambiguity.

If, then, one can get a firm grasp on this basic process and see social behavior in terms of it, one will have no trouble in understanding the rest of Meadian social behaviorism. Otherwise, one will not get to first base—assuming that one wants to get to first base.

At this point, you are undoubtedly asking how does Mead or Cottrell or anyone else know what goes on in this so-called interpenetrative interaction? A good question. You should also be impressed by now by the difficulties confronting any attempt to demonstrate experimentally that what the theory claims does in fact happen.

Those whose perceptions are sensitized by a reasonably good understanding of the concept of interpenetrative interaction will find a certain amount of confirmatory evidence in observational, anecdotal, clinical and other qualitative case-study material. (For illustrations see Cottrell, 1933; Burgess & Cottrell, 1939; Cottrell, 1941, 1942, 1969.) Much rarer are controlled experimental demonstrations such as these: An exploratory study by Cottrell and Dymond (1949) in measuring variations in role-taking accuracy, reported in Dymond (1949); an experimental study of role-taking by O'Toole and Dubin (1968 & 1976); an electromyographic study of covert role-taking in interpersonal interaction by Cottrell (1971); an experimental study by Richard Smith (1971) of Mead's treatment of vocal gestures; a study of electrophysiology of mental activities by Jacobson (1932). A helpful summary and discussion of these and other experimental studies will be found in O'Toole, Smith and Cottrell (1978). Also relevant to this type of research is David Lewis's discussion of the social behaviorist's conception of the Meadian "I" (1979).

As technology for precise observation and recording of overt as well as covert behavior improves, more experimental testing of the central concepts of social behaviorism can be undertaken. Considerable progress is being made in this technology by those interested in nonverbal communication. Unfortunately, most of the research on this kind of interaction is being done without regard to the kinds of questions posed by the hypothesis of interpenetrative interaction. For example, Duncan and Fiske (1979) in their study of face-to-face conversational interaction, have developed precise methods of observation and recording of even the most detailed bits of verbal and nonverbal behavior. Although their identification of regularities in action sequences is of considerable interest, their results indicate to me that their theory and method need to be greatly enriched by the conceptualizations of Meadian social behaviorism and methods which permit observations of covert behavior if they are to make much progress in understanding social interaction. It is, incidentally, ironic that these investigators, based at the University of Chicago, write as if they had never heard of George Herbert Mead.

I have spoken at some length about the concept of interpenetrative interaction as I understood it as a student and as I have perceived its development since then because, in my opinion, it is the central component in Meadian social behaviorism. If the processes indicated by that central concept can be shown to be real, then the remaining components of the Meadian system follow as natural behavioral emergents. Obviously, this is not the place for a detailed examination of the entire conceptual framework, but I do propose to touch briefly on the essential elements in an effort to show why I regard it as a coherent, straightforward and strategic formulation, well worth careful and persistent testing and application. Of critical significance are the following:

1. The emergence of what Mead calls the significant symbol and its function in communication
2. The self process and the nature of identity
3. Thinking and the mind as a social behavioral process
4. Social integration

All these can be shown to be behavioral processes and emergent products of the basic process of interpenetrative interaction. As Mead's student, I glimpsed all these processes and products. While my understandings have obviously developed and deepened since 1930, the foundation was clearly laid down during those early years in Chicago.

Act, Gesture and the Significant Symbol

Complex social interaction is greatly facilitated by the fact that small movements in the early stages of an act come to stand as signs or signals of the oncoming act. These signals, which we call gestures, evoke responses to the whole act that the gesture signals. These responses themselves, in turn, are indicated by gestures of the respondent. Thus, complex social interacts can be conducted in shorthand, as it were, by a conversation of gestures. In these gestural transactions, taking the role of the others is accomplished by responding to one's own gestures with the gestured responses of the others. Now, when an actor is able to respond to his own gesture with the response of the other, that is, in the role of the other, Mead (1922 & 1934) states that the gesture has become a significant symbol. It has the same meaning to both participants. The meaning of a gesture is the response it evokes. It has a common meaning to the extent that it evokes the same response in the actor and his respondent. Vocal gestures have a special efficiency for significant communication since the participant who makes the sounds that evoke responses in the hearer also hears his own vocal gesture and can take the role of his hearer and respond to his own gesture as the other responds to it. Thus, when we speak, we know what we are saying to the degree that we can respond to our words in the role of the hearer. It is only when this condition is met through interactive learning that we communicate meaningfully. It is regrettable that much contemporary communication theory and practice is relatively weak and sterile because of failure to utilize this kind of Meadian contribution to the understanding of communicative behavior.

But the social behaviorist concept for the significant symbol is not only relevant for understanding communication; it is also of critical importance in the analysis of basic intrapersonal behavioral processes: the self, identity and mind.

The Self and Identity

Over the years, the self has, by and large, been something of an embarrassment to most psychologists. They use the term, but when called upon to define it they resort to tautologies or catch-bag lists of descriptive attributes that tend to become so extended as to be unmanageable. The so-called objective psychologists prefer to do without the concept altogether.

The social behaviorists, on the other hand, regard the self as an emergent of the interpenetrative interact. Actions of participant A are responded to by actions of participant B. A takes the role of B and responds to his own acts with the incorporated responses of B. A's acts become objects to himself, or he knows or experiences their meaning through reacting to them in the role of B. It is this reflexive behavioral process that constitutes the experience of self. A self, therefore, is not a given, an endowment of the organism, but an emergent. The subjective experience of what we refer to as *myself* or *me* arises when an action in its initial or incipient or attitudinal stage evokes the incorporated attitudinal responses of the relevant significant others. Thus, the self is a dynamic process rather than a static morphological entity.

Describing the self in this way may make it appear ephemeral and of no substance. However, we know that the person's very sense of being depends on incorporation of this dyadic process. As the human being matures and experiences broader, more stabilized interactive contexts or situations in which he achieves roles or positions, he develops what we call identities. An identity, as subjectively experienced, is an established pattern of anticipated other-responses to one's acts. If these anticipated acts are not confirmed in reality or at least in fantasy, the person suffers the pain and panic of a disastrous loss of identity or sense of self. The self-conception or identity becomes more stabilized as the person interacts in stable group settings that make up his life situations. In these he develops what Mead (1913 & 1934) refers to as "generalized others" with whom he interacts. Thus I heard it said in 1930.

Language as a system of significant symbols facilitates both the overt interaction of the person with respondent-others and the intrapersonal covert interaction processes through which the person finds his concept of himself and his self-evaluations.

Mind and Thinking as Social Interaction

Professor Mead once remarked in a lecture to our class that, "Mind is the presence in behavior of significant symbols." This rather enigmatic comment had me stumped for quite some time. It is unintelligible unless one goes back to a social behavioral statement of what a significant symbol is. Remember what was said about it? A significant symbol is a gesture—a bit of behavior that signals an oncoming act—that evokes in the maker of the gesture the responding gestures of the other to whom the gesture is made. Now, keeping in mind that these gestured acts can be experienced as covert act mobilizations or attitudinal postures, we can say that thinking is a social interactional process conducted by means of significant symbols. Mind is not, therefore, something apart from behavior. So far as we know, the human organism is unique in its capacity to import the social interactional process and thus be capable of the behavior we experience and describe as thinking. This enables the organism to anticipate responses of the environment to alternate proposed lines of action and to select those which permit resolution of the problematic situation and completion of the blocked social act.

Social Integration

A social interactional account of how aggregates of separate organisms become an integrated collectivity capable of functioning as such was one of Mead's early theoretical concerns. For his students it was a challenging problem, indeed. Among nonhuman species, there are numerous instances of the precise and intricate integration of complementary actions necessary for the life of the collectivity. But in these species, the separate collaborating actors appear to be genetically programmed for their parts in the communal act. No such principle of integration appears to be operative in human social units except in the bisexual and parent-offspring relations, and here only in a rather limited determination of specific behavioral patterning.

From the foregoing discussion, I am sure you will anticipate that the processes of interpenetrative interaction and the capability of the human organism to incorporate the roles of the other participants in the interact were seen by the social behaviorists as making possible the integration of functioning collective entities. The individual member's action can be guided by his expectations of the acts of the others and his perception of their expectations of him. Moreover, in the course of collective activity and in the course of determining and achieving group goals, the individual develops a generalized concept, a personification of the group or community. As we have seen, Mead (1934) termed this a "generalized other" and regarded it as functioning as a symbolically represented "other" in the interactional situational field as perceived by the participant. Thus, the person's reference to what his family would say or what his platoon or his community would do is a reference to a behaviorally real, generalized other—whose role can be taken in response to his own acts and intentions. Can you imagine the excitement of Mead's lectures when he dealt with such topics?

Alternative Interpretations of Social Behaviorism

So here we have what, in my view, is an elegantly lucid and coherent account of the behavioral processes through which emerges that amazing creation, man—the human person and the human society. Through their capacity for interpenetrative interaction, by incorporating the responses of the objects of their environment, these organisms become objects to themselves, develop reflexive selves, symbolic communicative processes, minds and societies. These profoundly important realities are not given; they are emergents of an ongoing process. I hold that Meadian social behaviorism still offers a far more promising conceptual framework for a basic social psychology than any of the currently competing conceptualizations.

The widely utilized conceptual framework of the various conditioning theories and the practices based on them can in no way account for or produce the emergence of the basic and distinctive human characteristics that must be of central concern to any adequate social psychology. This is not to underestimate the highly effective technology of conditioning and its behavior-modification procedures. Man is an animal and like rats, pigeons, monkeys, etc., his overt behavior can be conditioned by procedures developed by highly competent scientists (Skinner, 1953). But behavior molded in this manner will not result in significant symbolic communication, reflexive selves, minds or societies based on interpenetrative interaction. The conditioning procedures can produce an aggregate of individuals appropriately conditioned to respond to controlling stimuli. But such mass-conditioned behavior is more like that of mindless lemmings than of collaborative-minded participant-selves. Indeed, it is a matter of serious concern that the rapid rise of electronic technology has put the means of widespread mass conditioning, manipulation and control in the hands of powerful interests. To the extent that persons and groups become subject to such conditioning they become dehumanized. Fortunately, the social behavioral capabilities and processes continue to operate sufficiently to constitute a threat to the manipulative controls and make possible a recovery of the important human competencies. Sometimes this recovery is a slow, painful and costly process, for example, after the apathy and nonparticipation in political processes which appear when people feel they have been taken for a ride by their government, or, to take another example, after the costly loss in productivity by workers following the perception that their employers have manipulated them through various simulations of concern for their welfare. For an interesting discussion of the recent literature on this problem, I recommend Richard Sennett's (1979) article entitled "The Boss's New Clothes" in the *New York Review of Books*. Speaking as one who has always regarded himself as a student of Mead, I can assure you that we were innocent of all such questions in 1930.

I do not propose to review here the other competing conceptual frameworks used by sociologists as social psychological foundations of their discipline. It would be an interesting exercise to use the Meadian system as a touchstone for examining the more widely used theoretical systems to determine their relative adequacy for use as the social psychological foundations for sociological theory. In my own limited efforts in this respect I have, as you will anticipate, become quite convinced that Meadian social behaviorism comes closer to meeting the requirements of our discipline than any other system of social psychology. It is disconcerting, therefore, to realize that most sociologists appear to prefer almost any conceptual framework except that of Meadian social behaviorism.

In 1940 I was quite optimistic about the signs of a trend in the behavioral disciplines toward an interactional orientation; my colleague, Ruth Gallagher, and I (Cottrell & Gallagher, 1941) predicted an acceleration of that trend for the next decade with the result that Meadian social behaviorism would be a predominant theoretical base. We were wrong. In recent years, however, it has been encouraging to note the apparent renaissance of Meadian theory and research among an increasing number of sociologists who refer to themselves as symbolic interactionists. This increasing interest has provided the impetus for the formation of a Society for the Study of Symbolic Interaction. Unfortunately, the term symbolic interaction has become something of an umbrella covering a rather wide range of theoretical orientations. The literature (Manis & Meltzer, 1978) being generated frequently describes attempts to effect syntheses of some aspect of Meadian theory with operant conditioning theory, psychoanalysis or some of its offshoots, cognitive theory, phenomenology and numerous others.

Now while one must applaud these efforts to broaden the theoretical base of a social psychology fit to serve as a foundation for sociological theory and practice, it is also the case that, by and large, this literature is quite confusing and sometimes actually misleading for anyone seeking to comprehend Meadian social behaviorism. Even when the objective is to clarify Meadian theory there is frequently evidence of a lack of grasp of significant aspects of the theory. I have found it advisable to caution students to avoid this literature until they have gained a firm hold on Mead's own ideas.

In this connection, I find it somewhat disconcerting that I have never felt clear about or satisfied with Professor Herbert Blumer's interpretation of Meadian social psychology. Some of his discussions (Blumer, 1969) seem to me to be somewhat ambiguous mixtures of Mead's social behaviorism and a nonbehavioral subjectivism that is more akin to European phenomenology than to Meadian behaviorism. He, of course, has every right to construct any theoretical framework he finds useful for his purposes, but it is, in my view, unfortunate that the result should be a rather confusing dilution and obscuring of Mead's clear and straightforward social behaviorism. This is not the place for exegesis and polemics, which in any case cannot carry us much further toward our goal. At this stage, we desperately need explicit hypotheses and their rigorous testing.

Indeed, if my advice were asked, I would strongly recommend that a solid core of talented symbolic interactionists should strive to develop a clear, thoroughgoing consensus as to the basics of social behaviorism. From this center of understanding, deficiencies of the theory can be identified and a coherent strategy of research and conceptual elaboration, developed. Relevant aspects of other theories can be utilized where necessary. An illustration of what I am suggesting is found in my recent discussion of the possibility of a partial synthesis of Meadian social behaviorism and the interpersonal psychiatric concepts of Harry Stack Sullivan (Cottrell, 1978). I fear that, unless some such strategy as I have indicated is vigorously pursued, symbolic interactionism will remain an ambiguous mishmash from which no coherent and strong social psychology is likely to emerge.

MEAD'S CHALLENGE: NEW RESEARCH HORIZONS

My enthusiastic advocacy of Meadian social behaviorism could, with some justification, lead some to suspect that I consider Mead the alpha and omega of social psychology. Although I sometimes suspect myself, let me hasten to disavow that untenable position. Mead himself would reject any such idea. Indeed, he clearly regarded his formulation as an open system and he consistently pressed this view on his students. Most certainly, I took him seriously. I have had the distinct impression that a major reason for his never having committed his thoughts to a systematic written opus was his being so impressed by the ramifications, implications and needed elaborations of his theory that he could never find the time to stop and put it all down. As the editor of *Mind, Self and Society,* the distinguished philosopher, Charles W. Morris, states in the Preface, "that [Mead] was not the writer of a system is due to the fact that he was always engaged in building one'' (Mead, 1934). Actually, social behaviorism as formulated by Mead in his lectures gives rise to an incredibly rich agenda of empirical research. One reason for the theory not having made more of an impact is that so many of those regarding themselves as followers of Mead have avoided the empirical testing and concrete application of his ideas. This avoidance has led to a failure to develop an appropriate research methodology, a serious handicap in communicating the system to disciplines with well-developed methodologies.

It is not possible here to set out a comprehensive agenda of research suggested by the Meadian system, but I can briefly indicate some areas that promise stimulating and significant research results.

Obviously, the first order of business is a greatly stepped-up program of empirical testing of basic elements in the theory. Such a program would include experimental studies utilizing the rapidly developing technology for detailed observation of interactive behavior, both overt and covert. Earlier in this paper I referred to a few such studies that yielded significant findings clearly consistent with the interpenetrative and role-taking hypotheses. These studies barely scratch the surface but do point the way to a promising line of research.

Depth case studies guided by the Meadian orientation represent another line of empirical testing which needs to be much more fully exploited. I have pointed to this fruitful field elsewhere in the analysis of marital interaction and in suggesting the utility of Meadian theory in interpersonal psychiatric analysis as developed by H. S. Sullivan (Cottrell 1933, 1941, 1978). This approach offers almost unlimited opportunities for testing the validity of social behavioral concepts.

The problems of developing competence in interpersonal relations can also be profitably studied from the perspective of social behaviorism (Foote & Cottrell, 1955).

Research on variations, aberrations and complications in the interactive processes serves not only to test the theory but leads to extensions and modifications of it. Studies of empathic or role-taking behavior usually reveal differences in the degree of accuracy with which it takes place (Dymond, 1949a). Cultural, situational, developmental and organic factors appear to be related to the variations, but more systematic research is needed to understand how they operate. As persons interact in different contexts they develop different self-systems or identities. Some of them are conflicting. How are these conflicts managed and the different selves integrated into a coherent personality? The social behavioral analysis of intrapersonal pathologies, loss of identity, apathy and alienation has hardly been touched. The social behavioral equivalent of the unconscious behavior explored by psychoanalysis is a significant and fascinating field of inquiry (Varela, 1973).

What is referred to as group psychology—the achievement of group identity, interaction in terms of group symbols, the conditions of group competence to function as such, disintegration of the group—presents challenging problems to the social behaviorist.

The increasing awareness of the need for a more adequate metaphysical foundation for social science has led some students to take a fresh look at Meadian social psychology as helping to provide a bridge between positivism and a new metaphysic better adapted to a science of human behavior. Some of these revisionists see the behaviorally based social realism of Mead as a welcome alternative to the sterility of the predominant nominalism of psychological theory. In any case, here is an exciting area of scholarly research for those attracted to the philosophy of science and the metatheoretical problems of the science of human behavior (Varela 1973, 1978; Lewis & Smith, in press).

Much more could be said of the research agenda implicit in the Meadian theoretical framework, but enough has been indicated to make the point that Mead presents us with a tremendous and exciting challenge.

MEAD IGNORED—WHY AND WITH WHAT CONSEQUENCES?

If you have concluded from the foregoing remarks that, in my opinion, Professor Mead is of central importance to any sociological theory worthy of serious consideration, you are one hundred percent correct. This centrality that some of us thought we perceived fifty years ago has been ignored, misunderstood and all but forgotten by the psychological and sociological establishments. But I do not fear that the theory will disintegrate and fade away. Rather, I am concerned for the viability of efforts to concoct theories of personal and collective behavior without the potent Meadian insights and concepts. Such theoretical efforts will, I fear, continue to drift toward ambiguity and triviality.

At this point I am reminded of one of my more talented students who, at the end of one of my lectures on Mead, raised his hand and asked the embarrassing question:

"If Mead is all that important, why is he so generally ignored?"

Saved by the bell, I made a hasty exit, promising the student to discuss his question at the next meeting of the class. I did not then nor do I now have a fully satisfactory answer. I will, however, list briefly the principal points I tried to make in my explanation—some of them factual; others more speculative.

The most general and fundamental condition making for nonacceptance of Meadian theory is the basic philosophical cleavage between nominalism and realism. The predominant orientation in American psychology is nominalist while Mead was a thoroughgoing social realist. This difference has made it practically impossible for most psychologists to grasp the emergent realities of social behaviorism. Even in sociology with many of its traditional roots in social realism such as that found in Durkheim, theorists fall back on some nominalist psychology when they come to deal with the psychological foundations of sociology. Conditioning theory and psychoanalytic theory have been the most popular of those nominalist conceptual frameworks. This tendency is found even among those symbolic interactionists who consider that they derive from Mead. An extensive discussion of this problem is in the manuscript by Lewis and Smith (in press) to which I have referred.

A second factor that contributed to a widespread lack of interest in Mead was the tidal shift in sociology from qualitative research on behavior to quantification and statistical analysis. Mead died in 1931 so that his courses ceased to be offered just about the time this shift in focus was rapidly taking place at Chicago. Meadian concepts do not lend themselves readily to quantification, the collection of mass data and statistical manipulations. For a time I was caught up in this shift in fashion, and in our study of the prediction of adjustment in marriage, Professor Burgess and I were the first sociologists to apply L. L. Thurstone's factor-analytic procedures to sociological data (Burgess & Cottrell, 1939). However, I did hold onto Meadian theory in analyzing role interaction in marriage (Cottrell, 1933), and actually found it to be in several respects a better predictor than our statistical prediction (Cottrell, 1941). The rush to number crunching, aided tremendously by computer technology, has continued, and departments of sociology have placed major stress on virtuosity in manipulating mass data rather than on the understanding of social behavior. This dominant trend has encouraged so-called macrosociology with the accompanying disposition to avoid anything that looks like psychological analysis. The tendency is to regard "all that stuff" as in the domain of psychology and thus to get rid of it. I do notice, however, that when the computer results drop into the lap of the clever but unsuspecting student and he has to give some meaningful interpretation of them, he tends to sneak in some home-made *ad hoc* psychological explanation or tries to fit the findings into some nominalist psychology framework, usually with rather sterile results.

A third factor leading to lack of interest in Meadian theory is the far greater facility with which the simpler nominalistic stimulus-response conditioning psychologies can be applied to the control of mass behavior. The modern centralization of economic and political power calls for effective large-scale techniques of control and manipulation. The rapid growth of the technology of mass media has made possible widespread conditioning of the desired economic, political, and other mass behavior. While this may be highly profitable to big business, big labor, big government and, be it said, big psychology, it has its ominous side. There are signs that populations constantly subjected to such "scientific" management will tend increasingly to display mindless lemminglike behavior and become less and less competent to act in a minded, deliberate and autonomous manner. In the longer run, the controls will break down as the awareness of having been exploited dawns. Apathy and alienation ensue (Sennett, 1979) frequently followed in turn by various explosive forms of behavior.

Add to these three underlying factors, the practical difficulties of designing empirical research relevant to the complexities of social behaviorism and the further difficulties of making practical application of the theory to the problems of social life (Cottrell, 1976) and one can readily understand why it is so much easier to ignore Mead than to take him seriously.

Quo Vadis?

At the request of the organizers of the sessions on *Sociological Traditions from Generation to Generation* I have attempted to convey to you my personal experience of Professor Mead's teachings and writings as I understood them and as a onetime student of his, I have given my assessment of the significance of his system of social behaviorism for our discipline. As you can see, I consider his contributions of central importance, not only to social theory and research, but to our society as well. I am well aware that in holding this view, I and a relatively small number of behavioral scientists differ sharply from the substantial majority of our colleagues. So where are we headed and what does the future hold for the Meadian perspective? I must confess that I am much less optimistic than I was forty years ago when, as I have reported, Ruth Gallagher and I tried to appraise the trends in social psychology during the 1930–40 decade (Cottrell & Gallagher, 1941). And today when I consider the wide ideological and philosophical differences between Meadian social realism and the nominalism of predominant psychological and sociological theories—the greater simplicity of their models of behavior, research design and implementation; their greater usefulness to economic and political power groups in providing efficient means of short-run control and manipulation of behavior—I see little basis for anticipating a general turning to Meadian social behaviorism, certainly in the near future. Finally, the current confusion and contradictory state of interpretation of Meadian theory found in the ranks of the symbolic interactionists does not afford much basis for optimism.

Regardless of the difficulties, however, I am convinced that to ignore Mead's social psychology is seriously to imperil any hope we may have of building a viable science of human behavior. And lacking such a science, we seriously endanger our chances of building a competent democratic society of minded participant citizens.

REFERENCES

Blumer, H. *Symbolic interaction: Perspective and method.* Englewood Cliffs, N.J.: Prentice-Hall, 1969.

Burgess, E.W. & Cottrell, L.S., Jr. *Predicting success or failure in marriage.* Englewood Cliffs, N.J.: Prentice-Hall, 1939, Chapter 11.

Cottrell, L.S., Jr. "Roles and Marital Adjustment." *Publications of the American Sociological Association, 1933, 27,* 107–115.

Cottrell, L.S., Jr. "The Case-Study Method in Prediction." *Sociometry,* 1941, *4,* 358–370.

Cottrell, L.S., Jr. "The Analysis of Situational Fields in Social Psychology." *American Sociological Review,* 1942, *7,* 370–382.

Cottrell, L.S., Jr. "Interpersonal Interaction and the Development of the Self." In D.A. Goslin (ed.), *Handbook of socialization theory and practice.* Chicago: Rand McNally, 1969, 543–570.

Cottrell, L.S., Jr. "Covert Behavior in Interpersonal Interaction." *Proceedings of the American Philosophical Society* Vol. 115 No. 6 1971, 462–469.

Cottrell, L.S., Jr. "The Competent Community." In B.H. Kaplan, R.N. Wilson, and A.H. Leighton (eds.), *Further explorations in social psychiatry.* New York: Basic Books, 1976, 195–211. Also found in R.L. Warren (ed.), *New perspectives on the American community: A book of readings.* Chicago: Rand McNally, 1976, 546–560.

Cottrell, L.S., Jr. "George Herbert Mead and Harry Stack Sullivan: An Unfinished Synthesis." *Psychiatry,* 1978, *41,* 151–162.

Cottrell, L.S., Jr. & Gallagher, R. *Developments in social psychology 1930–1940.* New York: Beacon House, Inc., 1941.

Cottrell, L.S., Jr. & Dymond, R.F. "The Empathic Responses: A Neglected Field for Research." *Psychiatry,* 1949, *12,* 355–359.

Duncan, S., Jr. & Fiske, D.W. "Dynamic Patterning in Conversation." *American Scientist,* 1979, *67,* 90–98.

Dymond, R.F. *Empathic ability: An exploratory study.* Unpublished Ph.D Thesis, Cornell University, 1949 (a)

Dymond, R.F. "A Scale for the Measurement of Empathic Ability." *Journal of Consulting Psychology,* 1949(b), *13,* 127–133.

Foote, N.N. & Cottrell, L.S., Jr. *Identity and interpersonal competence.* Chicago: University of Chicago Press, 1955.

Jacobson, E. "Electrophysiology of Mental Activities." *American Journal of Psychology,* 1932, *44,* 677–694.

Lewis, D. "A Social Behaviorist Interpretation of the Meadian 'I'." *American Journal of Sociology,* 1979, — , 00-00.

Lewis, D. & Smith, R.L. *American sociology and pragmatism: Mead, Chicago sociology, and symbolic interaction.* Chicago: University of Chicago Press, in press.

Manis, J.G. & Meltzer, B.N. *Symbolic interaction: A reader in social psychology.* Third Edition. Boston: Allyn and Bacon, Inc., 1978.

Mead, G.H. "The Social Self." *Journal of Philosophy,* 1913, *10,* 374–380.

Mead, G.H. "A Behavioristic Account of the Significant Symbol." *Journal of Philosophy,* 1922, *19,* 157–163

Mead, G.H. *The philosophy of the present.* Chicago: Open Court, 1932.

Mead, G.H. *Mind, self and society.* Chicago: University of Chicago Press, 1934.

Mead, G.H. *Movements of thought in the nineteenth century.* Chicago: University of Chicago Press, 1936.

Mead, G.H. *The philosophy of the act.* Chicago: University of Chicago Press, 1938.

Mead, G.H. *Selected writings,* A.J. Reck (ed.). Indianapolis: The Bobbs Merrill Co., 1964.

Miller, D.L. *George Herbert Mead: Self, language, and the world.* Austin, Tex.: University of Texas Press, 1973.

O'Toole, R. *Experiments in George Herbert Mead's 'Taking the role of the other' II: Sidedness.* Unpublished manuscript, 1976.

O'Toole, R. & Dubin, R. "Baby Feeding and Body Sway: An Experiment in George Herbert Mead's 'Taking the Role of the Other'." *Journal of Personality and Social Psychology,* 1968, *10,* 59–65.

O'Toole, R., Smith, R.L., & Cottrell, L.S., Jr. "Interpenetrative Interaction: Some Implications of a Neglected Approach." Unpublished manuscript, 1978.

Sennett, R. "The Boss's New Clothes." *New York Review of Books,* 1979, *26,* 42–46.

Skinner, B.F. *Science and human behavior.* New York: Macmillan, 1953.

Smith, R.L. *Reflexive behavior: An experimental examination of George Herbert Mead's treatment of vocal gesture.* Unpublished M.A. dissertation, University of South Carolina, 1971.

Smith, R.L. *George Herbert Mead's sociology graduate students: A case of restricted access.* Unpublished manuscript, 1976.

Varela, C. *The crisis of western sociology: The problem of social interaction, the self, and unawareness for sociological theory.* Unpublished Ph.D. dissertation, New York: New York University, 1973.

Varela, C. *How is sociology impossible?: The distrust of reason and the conceptual reformation.* Unpublished manuscript, Cranford, N.J.: Union College, 1978.

Watson, J.B. *Psychology from the standpoint of a behaviorist.* New York: J.B. Lippincott, 1919.

Watson, J.B. "Autobiography." In C. Murchison (ed.), *A history of psychology in autobiography.* New York: Russell and Russell, 1961.

4

ROBERT EZRA PARK
The Philosopher-Newspaperman-Sociologist

Helen MacGill Hughes

I first met the sociologist, Robert Ezra Park, in 1924 when I was a student at the University of British Columbia. On graduating I went to the University of Chicago, became his student and wrote my Master's dissertation under him, and, after a long interval, my Ph.D. thesis. I believe I was his last doctoral candidate. I continued to know him for 25 years and was well acquainted with his family. Since in the 1920s it was customary for a university student, especially for a Canadian university student, to refer to his teachers respectfully, I always called him "Dr. Park." Because I think of him this way, I will refer to him so in the account which follows of some of his major ideas, including especially the idea of ecology, and the pedagogical devices by which he communicated them to his students.

ENCOUNTERS WITH LIFE AS SOCIOLOGY

Recalling his state of mind when he was devising his first course at the University of Chicago, called "The Negro in America," Dr. Park, years later, wrote that he had come to the conclusion that he ought, as he put it, "to stick around and see if I could work out in the classroom the more theoretical problems which have arisen, as far as I was concerned, out of my own encounters with life."

Certain of his encounters which seem to have focused his attention and imagination—determining, in the end, his sociology and how he taught it—are introduced here in a short *ad hoc,* flagrantly eclectic and incomplete account of his career.[1]

Born in 1864 in a farming family in Pennsylvania, while his father was fighting in the Union Army, he followed in due time the standard practice of the day, described in the Alger books and the dime novels to which he was addicted: He ran away from home. At the age of eighteen, he ran away to the University of Minnesota, where he planned to study engineering. But his mother always knew his whereabouts, and when she told his father, Hiram Park, who had gone into the grocery business in Minnesota, that their son was a student in the state university, Hiram sent back word by the maternal grapevine that he would pay the fees if the young man would transfer to the more esteemed University of Michigan.

Dr. Park confesses that he was a poor student until, when studying with John Dewey at Michigan, he became infected with his notion that learning is exciting. And when he graduated in 1887, filled with the determination to quaff deep draughts of "life," he became a newspaper man, or "newsman," as we say now. In the next eleven years he worked on papers in five lively cities: Minneapolis, Detroit, Denver, New York and Chicago. He had the good fortune to be a reporter on the city desk and the police court precisely in the decade when the American newspaper was taking radically new form as the outcome of the heroic rivalry of Pulitzer and Hearst. On the front pages of their papers competing editors tried to outdo each other in dramatizing the news. And for features the metropolitan dailies bought syndicated material, but they also played up pieces composed by their own staffs, for those gave them exclusive attractions. So, like an explorer, Dr. Park tramped about the city, looking for story material to work up for the afternoon and Sunday editions.

Through Professor Dewey he met an unusual character, Franklin Ford, a man obsessed with a conception of the stock market as a mechanism of communication between public opinion and Wall Street. Prices, as Ford saw them, were news, stripped down to parsimonious quantitative expression, and he argued that movements of thought should lend themselves to a comparable reduction. The three, Dewey, Ford and Park, actually got out an experimental first issue of a proposed newspaper, *The Thought News.* But they had exhausted their capital with the first issue and, as Dewey said, "people weren't ready for it." (This raises the interesting question: "Are we readier for it now?")

In a discussion of Dr. Park as a teacher, the relevance of his newspaper years is that early in his career, while he was deep in the drama of real life, he

---

[1]For biographical facts I have drawn upon Rauschenbush, Winifred—*Robert E. Park: Biography of a Sociologist,* Durham, NC, Duke University Press, 1979.

was seeking to organize concrete experience into scientific propositions, to draw knowledge of human behavior from his down-to-earth, disjunctive assignments and explorations. Reporting was his real apprenticeship to sociology. From Dewey, he says, he got his first great assignment; to study the newspaper itself. He became a city man, urbane, knowledgeable, and insatiably curious.

In the further pursuit of familiarity with life, he gave up reporting and in 1889, with wife and three children (the fourth was born in Germany), went to the University of Berlin. Here, for the first and only time, he attended a course in sociology. It was given by a Dozent, Georg Simmel at the Friedrich University. He took Simmel's courses also in ethics and in nineteenth-century philosophy. He became a student of the philosopher, Windelband, and followed him from Strasburg to Heidelberg, where he took his doctor's degree in 1903 with a thesis on *Masse und Publikum: Eine methodologische und soziologische Untersuchung* (Crowd and Public: A Methodological and Sociological Inquiry). In Heidelberg he grew enthusiastic over the lectures of the political scientist, Professor Hettner, and was persuaded that every student of human society should know geography.

On his returning to the United States in 1904, Dr. Park was appointed as "assistant" (which did not mean assistant professor) in philosophy at Harvard. But, determined not to be sequestered in the ivory tower, he took a job as press agent of the Congo Reform Association. This changed the focus of his career. He was writing public relations pieces on Belgian atrocities in Africa, but his generalizing bent persisted. He grew curious to learn the sequence of change which sets in when Europeans invade tribal villages, turn local raw materials into commodities, and wring from the land products for world trade, with, as a rule, the involuntary labor of primitive peoples. He noted the constant disposition of Westerners to identify commerce with soul-saving and, willy-nilly, to slip from economic contacts into moral relationships, typically confused and contradictory.

In the Congo Reform Association he met Booker T. Washington and was won over to the latter's belief that industrial education, as carried on by Washington at the Tuskegee Normal and Industrial Institute, was the means whereby the blacks could improve their status in American society. Leaving African reform, Dr. Park became attached to the Institute and for seven years, during which he also did a great deal of writing for magazines, he travelled, lectured, and wrote with Washington. It was from this connection that he developed his understanding of the mulatto and his concept of the marginal man. The American Negro, he wrote, may be seen as offering a social laboratory, exhibiting all the historic phases of development from the primitive tribesman to the polished cosmopolite.

Also at Tuskegee Dr. Park made the acquaintance of William Isaac Thomas, professor of sociology at the University of Chicago. They were greatly drawn to each other. Through Professor Thomas, they became colleagues in the department in 1913. Dr. Park was fifty years old when his career as sociologist began. He remained at Chicago until his retirement in 1934.

THE DEVELOPING AMERICAN SOCIOLOGY

When Dr. Park joined the department of sociology in Chicago, he was not tilting against orthodoxy. Sociology at that time often took the form of do-goodism, and certainly there was no such thing as an orthodox American sociology. Indeed, there was not very much sociology in the United States, anyway, and the great eminences, like E.A. Ross of Wisconsin, William Graham Sumner of Yale, Albion Small of Chicago, and Lester F. Ward of Brown claimed squatter's rights in it to suit themselves. Dr. Park, too, was an independent, and went his own way.

A few American scholars were lecturing in sociology, it is true, but there were almost no sociologists by training; the pioneers, in the nature of the case, were explorers from some other sphere. Small had a degree in divinity and took his Ph.D. in welfare economics. Ward, who conducted with Small an interminable debate on the scope and nature of sociology in the pages of the *American Journal of Sociology,* was a botanist and geologist. Ellsworth Faris, a former missionary, had become a psychologist at Chicago, and Charles Cooley of Michigan was an economist. Dr. Park, himself a philosopher, student of Windelband, was well acquainted with the works of his European predecessors in philosophy and sociology—Hobbes, Spencer, St. Simon, Comte and Durkheim—and of his own contemporaries at home, W.I. Thomas, William James and John Dewey. He was one of a very few path-breakers. With Professor Ernest Burgess, a young man with a doctor's degree from the Chicago department, he gave to American sociology its first sophisticated, non-normative conceptual scheme since Sumner's *Folkways* (1906). Their monumental book, *Introduction to the Science of Sociology* (1921) for many years had no effective rival.

Dr. Park set out from the premise that society contained uniformities; they could be classified as types and formulated as general statements; thus society could be scientifically studied. His conception of society and of sociology was plainly evident in his course in Human Ecology when he offered it for the first time in the spring quarter of 1926. My notes on those lectures and on his courses on Social Forces and The Newspaper have providentially survived the half-century, and I will talk of Dr. Park as he taught in them. In particular, I will advert to the lectures on Human Ecology for, being a new course, it had an exploratory character.

Rereading these classroom jottings, I am struck with how abstract the lectures were and, at the same time, how concrete. The focus was sometimes on *Form* and sometimes on *Inhalt,* two concepts which were introduced early in the term. We students learned of them by way of Dr. Park's copy of a lecture he had heard in Berlin given by Dr. Georg Simmel, who held the modest academic post of Privatedozent. My classmate, Everett Hughes, and I translated the lecture from his copy. One theme was the independence of *Form* and *Inhalt,* seen in the fact that like forms of social life appear with different content, and also that like content is contained in unlike forms. Dr. Park made Simmel's concepts central to an emerging American sociology in adopting the latter's definition of the forms of social relationships as the stuff of society: society is the sum of ways in which human beings act with or against each other.

Necessary to this paradigm, as Dr. Park recognized, was the concept of social distance. From it his former student, Emory Bogardus, of the University of Southern California, devised a scale and then fitted it into the race-relations cycle. And the race-relations cycle was an instance of natural history. The theme of natural history was, in fact, pervasive in all of Dr. Park's courses, while evolution was a term he used sparingly. A process of natural history does not continue until some termination, some final phase. It is continuous. In the race-relations cycle, for instance, there is no ultimate phase. Change disrupts a temporary equilibrium and some other racial pattern is reached, consistent with the established order of the time and place. But this, too, passes, and the cycle runs on. One phase and its appropriate structures may prevail in one place, while in another location the phase may be quite different. He implied this once in asking, "Can there be any racial peace before there is racial justice?"

For rubrics under which to generalize ecological relationships, Dr. Park drew upon economic history and geography and from studies of flora and fauna. The *Introduction to the Science of Sociology* (the 1923 edition was the one then in use), does not index the word, "ecology." But Chapter Three, "Society and the Group," includes extracts from studies of plant and insect communities (which are not societies) as well as of the symbiotic relationships between human beings and the beasts, some of whom they have domesticated. The individuals in the plant or animal community are bound to each other by a division of labor, or symbiosis of some sort, while those in a society are more intimately held together by communication, consensus, and custom. It was postulated that the natural biological kingdoms were sufficiently alike for knowledge of one of them to shed light on the others.

Like W.I. Thomas, from whom, he says, he learned a great deal, Dr. Park broke intellectual boundaries and, being an essentially unconventional thinker, invaded and appropriated other realms of thought. Under his prodding and probing, he and we graduate students built human ecology *de novo.*

The classroom became the theater of gestation. Concepts were borrowed, analyzed, adapted and exhaustively compared. Dr. Park wrestled with abstractions, theories, cases, as a terrier worries a slipper. For example: The examination at the end of the course required, as the first question, a comparison between Graham Wallas' Great Society and "our" concept of the World Community; in the second question, the students were asked to compare "our" conception of the city with that of his former student, R.D. McKenzie; in the third question, distinctions were to be made between a number of concepts which we had met with in botany, biology and kindred disciplines—among them competition, invasion, succession, dominance. And in lectures, Dr. Park reverted constantly to the difference between, on the one hand, economic history and economic geography—which inquire into what happened and where—and, on the other hand, human ecology— which seeks out forces and processes that keep things in their relative positions in space.

FIELD WORK AND THE HONING OF CONCEPTS

In teaching students to observe and analyze, Dr. Park turned to the concepts, *inter alia,* of the continuum and the marginal case. In the course on Social Forces, for example, when Norman Hayner was reporting to the class his study of the hotel, Dr. Park had us draw up a continuum of institutions providing shelter, ranked according to how long the occupants stayed. This made for a great gamut, from the ancestral castle to the "mobile" home and on to the gypsy's tented wagon. The game could be prolonged by playing it all over again, but with some other variable. It was a pedagogical tactic which always led to spirited debate, as we tried to pin each other down to some statement of exactly what made a hotel of the hotel.

The fine honing of concepts was part of each student's assignment. In the course on Social Forces we heard each other's reports on a variety of urban institutions. One of these was given by Ruth Shonle (known later, as Cavan, for her studies of the family and delinquency), who discussed the delicate distinctions drawn between professional and amateur in the Little Theater Movement. We had a report by Clark Tibbitts, who was to be one of the earliest of the gerontologists, on the city's settlement houses and the differential distribution of the types of patron and client. W.O. Brown, who later became an authority on the peoples of Africa, described types of missions to homeless men. And Louis Wirth, who was already deep in studies of the ghetto, contrasted the institutions in Chicago's immigrant areas of first settlement with those in the areas of second settlement. We sought what was essential and common to all these institutions. The projects were designed to sharpen the notion of institutions as modes of organized behavior, to add to the accumulating data on Chicago, and, in doing so, to familiarize us with scientific method.

Research in this highly theoretical framework was anchored and held solidly down to earth by field work. To begin with, Dr. Park incorporated observations and deductions from his own experiences into his courses. His first course was on The Negro in America; the second was on The Newspaper; then he offered a course on The Crowd and Public, the subject of his doctoral dissertation. In The Survey, he organized his theories of urban behavior; it soon was renamed The City. Human Ecology and Human Migrations covered much of the ground of an earlier course, Social Forces. Each course testified in some measure to the attainment of his original goal: to restate particular perceptions as generalizations.

To teach his students to do the same for themselves, he assigned empirical work, in which he insisted on methodical observing and recording. He urged us to keep journals, to train ourselves to see minutely and accurately—and then to write it all down. Throughout, he rejected, of course, the precedent of some of his American colleagues, who preached and deplored. It must be remembered that many sociologists of his day came into sociology from social work or the parsonage, and continued to think in the hortatory mood. What he was teaching us was an American sociology which was becoming one of the social sciences.

In the course on Human Ecology the substantive matter was phenomena treated as indices of social processes. Visible, quantitative, measurable, the movement of population in space, for instance, as well as various other behavior patterns, were interpreted as evidence of less visible social change. We who were Local Community Research Fellows—of whom I shall speak later—each had a research project based on some aspect of urban behavior, and each worked on indices of it. We plotted our indices on huge street maps, where the boundaries of Chicago's seventy-five local communities had been entered.

Thus Andrew Lind, later known for his analyses of racial intermarriage in Hawaii, studied streetcar traffic at important intersections. He needed a measure of the volume of traffic in terms of which the spatial mobility of populations at various locations could be compared, and found that measure with the help of the streetcar company. From the company he got great bundles of transfers, all issued for a certain day and time, at certain places. But it was out of the question to count the thousands of flimsy, dog-eared, little strips of dirty paper, and I believe that in the end Andy weighed them. It took imagination to discover what was an index of what. And was *post hoc propter hoc?* Or simple contemporaneity?

The graduate students' spot maps showed by superimposition how certain indices would appear in some places in clusters, while in other localities they trailed off, or were entirely absent. The indices signalized types of community about which the sociologists could then postulate certain kinds of behavior. For example, the patterns of the distribution of alcoholics, suicides and homicides were almost identical—and that very urban creation, the storefront church, found its natural habitat in the same localities—so that personal pathology indexed community disorganization.

The indices behaved as waxing or waning gradients, running along the important thoroughfares. An account of how the concept of the gradient was arrived at will, at the same time, demonstrate that learning was a cooperative enterprise of instructors and students. One evening the graduate students' organization, the Social Research Society, then a young and very small affair, was addressed by the University of Chicago neurologist, Professor C.M. Child, who depicted the nervous system of an organism (in this case an insect of some sort). Its brain was the receiving center, whereon the outer world impinged. Impulses radiated from the brain center along the nerve pathways to all parts of the organism in a starlike pattern of gradients, the impulses weakening as distance from the center increased. Dr. Park and Dr. Burgess, who were at the meeting, almost on the spot adapted the Child scheme of impulse pathways to the city, where the system of big "through" streets was the analog of the nervous system. Life in the city, as in the organism, is most intense at the center and least intense at the periphery. At the periphery, however, the index may begin to respond to some rival adjacent center. In that case a decreasing gradient might begin to increase. I might add that Charles Newcombe, one of the Fellows, provided a beautiful case of just such ecological competition for "turf." By plotting the sources of retail advertising in the *Chicago Daily Tribune* and in the local newspaper of the small neighboring city of Aurora, he was able to demonstrate the limits of the economic dominance of each of the competing centers.

The Child lecture also suggested a model of the mode of urban growth. Like an organism, the city responds to stimulation *as a whole.* It grows outward from the center along the radials of transportation; that is, not by simple additions at the perimeter, but by invasions at the center, where new things, new styles, new populations, and news and information meet least resistance, entering there most easily and then spreading out. When needing more space, the center (in the city it is "downtown") expands into the next zone, the "zone in transition," penetrating it by way of the radial streets. In turn, this second zone spills over into the next and the process of expansion and spillover is repeated until the outer suburbs are reached.

THE FRUITS OF PARTICIPATORY TEACHING

This particular item of urban theory originated, as I have said, in a discussion engaging graduate students, two professors of sociology, and one professor of biology. Our instructors were, in effect the senior partners in a joint enterprise with the students. Dr. Park's own role was certainly that of initiator, but he says his model was Dewey. He once wrote:

> One thing I now recall as characteristic of Dewey's method of teaching is that his students always seemed to have had the notion that he and they were somehow engaged in a common enterprise. With him, learning was always, so it seemed, an adventure; an adventure which was taking us beyond the limits of the safe and certified knowledge into the realm of the problematic and the unknown.

Today we might call it participatory teaching.

But classroom lecturing was not adventuresome at the expense of logical rigor. In the Preface to the first edition of the *Introduction,* Dr. Park conveys a sense of the taut organization of proposition and concrete case in describing the book as "no mere collection of materials, but a systematic treatise," in which the excerpts—there were nearly two hundred of them—are not simply illustrations, but stimulants to embolden students to derive social theory from their own lives and lives encountered in their reading.

Dr. Park's style of teaching was on the bespoke model, tailored to fit his graduate students. Among them six or eight belonged to a special category, the holders of a Laura Spellman Rockefeller Local Community Research Fellowship. On quite generous subventions they worked toward graduate degrees. Their theses were on aspects of city life, with Chicago as the laboratory. In actuality, much of their research was on problems raised by Dr. Park as long ago as 1915 in a paper in the *American Journal of Sociology* called "The City: Suggestions for the Investigation of Human Behavior in the Urban Environment" (XX, pp. 577-612). I believe there were holders of these fellowships in the departments of history, economics and political science, and in those departments, as in sociology, certain faculty members worked very closely with the Fellows. It is surely safe to say that no city was being studied as Chicago was being studied then.

Of the Fellows in the department of sociology, all but me had their undergraduate study at least two or three years behind them and had been employed in some sort of work, typically teaching or community or social work. There are differences in the norms of teaching graduate students fifty years ago and those of today. For one thing, in the earlier decades an instructor could not assume that the graduate student had had undergraduate courses in sociology. Today, the graduate student will probably have majored in sociology, and may even have had some experience in research while in college. But there were compensations to facilitate communication: the instructor of the earlier time could count upon a common fund of allusion—quotations from the Bible and Shakespeare, lines from the poets everyone had read in school, certain familiar hymns and popular songs. For this reason, teaching may have been brighter and more imaginative.

Few though we were, we graduate students had our own club: in fact, two clubs. The oldest was a true fraternity: when there were at most two women candidates for membership, it resolutely set its face against them. That gave the *raison d'etre* for the second, which took in all two of us. Programs in the two clubs were likely to be the exploration of some marginal subject—an informal talk at dinner by Professor George Herbert Mead, for example, or an account by a student from California of a history course given there by Professor Frederick J. Teggart, or a review of Vaihinger's *Die Philosophie des Als Ob,* by one of us who had read it. As students we were serious and professional. We drew upon the faculty in and out of season, and the faculty responded.

Classes in the 1920s and 1930s met every day from Tuesday to Friday for an hour during the twelve-week quarter. On Saturdays and Mondays, when there were no classes, we went out into the field, and we wrote up our field notes. Dr. Park, who offered two courses each term, always had one of them at eight o'clock in the morning. The Local Community Research Fellows also met twice a week in a two-hour seminar with him and Dr. Burgess. Classes and seminars, as I have already said, were often turned over to students, to render to their classmates an account of their research. We knew each other's work and were interested auditors of the instructors' comments. In effect, we played a part in each other's thesis conferences. None could complain that the faculty were occupied with their own research; to a great extent we did the same research. All being focused on urban modes and manners as witnessed in Chicago, the research reports were related to each other to some degree.

To these relatively sophisticated students I never knew Dr. Park to *read* a lecture. He launched into his subjects from notes, developing his own conceptions before our eyes. He was also much given to sharing with the class excerpts from whatever he was reading at the time. I remember once it was Aristotle on entelechy, and once Bergson on *l'élan vital;* once it was a missionary's diary, and once it was William James's essay, "On a Certain Blindness in Human Beings"; once it was Whitman's verses on wishing to go and live with the animals, and once an incident from a novel of George Meredith. He told anecdotes from his newspaper days. An inveterate and indefatigable field worker, he would report his current observations: for instance, that on Memorial Day he had gone to a Bohemian cemetery on the

West Side of Chicago, where there was a crematorium for socialists and atheists. Here, he noted, people were laying wreaths on the urns, following the American Memorial Day custom, and he commented, "Free-thinking is not the lack of religion. It is itself a religion, an extreme form of Protestanism, and its function is solace." At that point it would have been in character for him to have us set up a continuum of institutions, ranked as to, perhaps, the repudiation of authority.

Perhaps what I am trying to say is that he treated students like colleagues. He was continuously in touch with them and their research on campus. With one of us whose job plus field work was particularly time-consuming he arranged to have luncheon once a week throughout the term. And he kept up an active correspondence with those who, having attained their degrees, had gone out to become professors of sociology at home or abroad—in Hawaii, Africa, India, Japan, China. They were his antennae. After he retired, he made two trips around the world, doing stints as a visiting professor, and at the same time keeping alive the network connecting his former students with him and with each other.

When Lloyd Warner was working on what later became the Yankee City Series, and wrote Dr. Park for advice on how to classify news in the local Newburyport newspaper, he received in reply a six-page analysis of the nature of news. That letter encompassed the whole theoretical framework of the course on the newspaper. At the end of this full-dress performance Dr. Park wrote:

> I have perhaps burdened you with an essay when you expected merely a letter; but I am interested, as you surmised, in this matter, particularly as one of our graduate students is writing a paper on the classification of news.

Dr. Park sent me a copy of the letter for in all this he was building, around a mutual interest, a community of scholars whom he expected to be the next generation of academic sociologists.

I see now that he sought to inspire in us, the graduate students, the notion of a thesis topic as a lifelong preoccupation, something about which we would organize thought for years to come. And he encouraged a conception of one's self as a person in process of becoming an authority. He would write: "[Your book] can open up for systematic study a field that has hitherto been in the hands of the philosophers and the literary men."

DR. PARK'S RELEVANCE TODAY

The Park and Burgess text and Dr. Park's articles spoke for themselves. Beyond that, what I myself gained from being his student was some appreciation of the well-rounded and truly scholarly mind, but one with no trace of the snob or the highbrow. When the daughter of André Maurois, on a visit with her father to the University, asked Dr. Park to name a purely American literary production, he responded by introducing her to "Casey at the Bat," which he read in proper declamatory style. Lively and gregarious, he gave free rein to his robust enthusiasms. At breakfast he would read aloud from the front pages of the *Chicago Tribune,* with gestures, the lusty, gusty stories of the brazen buccaneers in City Hall. He knew city life revealed in the night courts and the late police beats. It did not occur to me at the time how extraordinary was this combination of the philosopher's habit of abstract thought and the newspaper reporter's familiarity with the more disreputable features of city life, the one orientation surprisingly illuminating the other.

Were he here now, he would certainly enter the lists with the sociobiologists. He was always alert to new things and seemed able to anticipate the currents of public and popular interests. Exploring and defining the field was his role in the study of human ecology, as it was also in the study of the American Negro and the newspaper. In these fields research seems never to have quite caught up with him. The widely debated zonal description of city growth survived criticism by Professor Robert MacIver of Columbia, and his student, Milla Alihan, and by Professor Maurice Davie of Yale. Dr. Park staked out this intellectual turf. He introduced to the newly emerging American ecologists the names and works of geographers, economists and others, many of them European scholars, thereby endowing the discipline with its theoretical base. His student, Roderick McKenzie, was associated with him in studies of the world community, and McKenzie's student, Amos Hawley, is active in urban studies, including research in occupational mobility. The Park papers on human ecology speak to today's investigators of the subject.

The Park papers on the newspaper, too, are still relevant. Current studies of the mass media are largely focused upon the most popular of them, television. But in his lifetime television was not the force it has since become. However, in the '30s he was pioneering studies of the newspaper as entertainment and as carrier of popular culture. Many of his observations on the subject of news-based divertissement are reappearing in print, but equipped with new authors, while the concepts, though renamed, are virtually unchanged—a situation reminding one of the saying that history is rewritten in every generation.

Dr. Park gave his final eight years to Fisk University. Race relations dominated his intellectual interest then and his last published paper was an ecological statement of race relations. Entitled "Missions and the Modern World" (*American Journal of Sociology, L,* pp. 177-183), it was found on his desk after his death in 1944, a week before his eightieth birthday. Here he brought together two universes of discourse which had engaged his attention for the greater part of his life: In the Great Society, though time and space are nearly annihilated as impediments to communication and commerce, moral unity, he observed, has not yet been attained. The achieving of it, to the extent it is so, is in the hands of unrelated specialists. But missionaries, who, he had found, were "always right on race," here and there have been able to bring into existence a limited local moral solidarity between widely unlike peoples. His studies of missions are, in effect, local pilot studies of the translation of symbiosis into consensus.

5

ROBERT M. MacIVER
Political Philosopher and Sociologist

Robert Bierstedt

It was not easy for a graduate student at Columbia to know Robert MacIver. The few meetings that one might have with him in his office, to discuss a procedural point or two on the way to the degree, were always brief and marked by embarrassment on both sides. MacIver was a private man, diffident and reticent, and one who never talked "shop" outside the classroom. In fact, he had no "small talk" at all. He was himself conscious of his diffidence, as he discloses in his *Autobiography,* and did not regard it as a virtue. In contrast, Robert S. Lynd had a breezy, Midwestern air about him, an open style that encouraged everyone to call him "Bob." Few would have thought of calling MacIver "Robert," and a nickname was even more unthinkable. I did not get to know my future father-in-law until the day of my comprehensive oral examination for the doctorate in 1938. It occurred to me, while preparing for that tribulation, that I really ought to look into his *Society* before presenting myself to the "delivery room," as the examination room in Fayerweather Hall was called. Graduate students do not ordinarily read textbooks, and I had been no exception. Accordingly, the night before the examination I began to read *Society*. I was entranced by it. Here was a man who could write the English language as few sociologists could, whose conception of the order that society exhibits was superior to any I had previously known, whose account of the sustaining forces of code and custom seemed to me to be by all odds the best in the literature, and who had achieved a level of abstraction that, in my opinion, was just right for sociological inquiry. My respect for MacIver took a quantum leap upward and on the following day, during the examination, it was apparent to both of us that some spark had been struck between us, that we shared in some ineffable way the same intellectual traditions and tastes.

MacIver often described himself as a "scribbler." Indeed, he piled sentence upon sentence every day of his adult existence, until the result was an impressive row of books. Like Bertrand Russell, and unlike lesser mortals, he never needed to revise.[1] Except for the change of a word or two or the interlineation of a more felicitous expression, his first draft was his last. No one outside the family ever caught him at work. But every day without exception he wrote his two pages of manuscript. He was thus a steady worker rather than a hard one, a trait in which he took some pride. Even as a student he invariably—and as a matter of principle—spent the day before an important examination on the golf course rather than at his desk.

THE STUDENT DAYS

MacIver was born in 1882, in Stornoway, Scotland, the port and principal city of the Isle of Lewis, in the Outer Hebrides. It is the center of the Harris tweed industry, in which his father participated as a successful merchant. His primary education in a local school, The Nicholson Institute, was marked by mediocre teachers and by at least one headmaster whose favorite method of discipline was to stuff snuff up the noses of his unruly pupils. His father's library contained the standard classics of Victorian literature—the Brontes, Scott, Dickens, Thackeray, Ruskin, Tennyson, and Browning. But the ambience of his home—indeed that of his culture—was one of a joyless and oppressive Calvinism, in which prayers before and after meals and endless Sunday sermons played a ubiquitous role and in which parental and religious authority frowned on any activity that did not contribute to a stern and earnest rectitude. It was an atmosphere from which he freed himself at an early age, at first intellectually and then emotionally, but one that he continued to resent throughout his life.

Like most of those who later win a degree of success in the academic profession, MacIver was an outstanding scholar in his school and won the bursary competition which offered him a choice of one of the four Scottish universities—St. Andrews, Aberdeen, Glasgow, or Edinburgh—for his higher education. He chose Edinburgh, "the Athens of the North," and encountered there for the first time the world of museums, libraries, concert halls, and theaters. After three years at the University, and a record of

---

[1]Bertrand Russell remarks in his *Autobiography* that he once revised an article he had written and the revision was so far inferior to the original that he never tried it again.

distinction in classical studies, he went on to Oriel College, Oxford, where he found a trancelike world, "a serene remoteness from the world of affairs." There were two kinds of students there, more than half of them "commoners," the sons of privilege, who tooks a "pass" course, and the others, the so-called "scholars," who took an "honors" course. MacIver himself took a double first in *Litterae Humaniores,* also known as "Greats," a curriculum that required two examinations, one in classical literature and the other in philosophy. At one point, in addition, he won an award for the best showing in the entire University in an examination on the literature of Greece, Rome and England.

The heavy emphasis upon the classics, however, began to trouble him. His tutors, it seemed, were more interested in the *Republic* of Plato, the *Politics* of Aristotle, and the *Letters* of Cicero than they were in the subjects in which Plato, Aristotle, and Cicero themselves were interested—namely, economics, political science, and sociology. There was an occasional lecture on political philosophy, but for the most part MacIver educated himself in the literature of the social sciences, often at the British Museum, where he notes particularly his discovery of Simmel, Durkheim, and Lévy-Bruhl. Of his Oxford tutors he mentions only his fellow Scot, W. D. Ross, the great Aristotelian scholar, and two provosts or Oriel whose names are otherwise unknown to history.

Three years at Edinburgh and four at Oxford made, as he says, a long apprenticeship. About it he writes:

> I owe much to it. I am grateful for what it did for me and for the opportunity I was given to go through with it. But gradually the conviction has been borne in on me that our established mode of training scholars is wasteful and roundabout. Oxford was better in one important respect than most universities. It didn't harass you with a multiplicity of niggling examinations, and it did make some effort to assure quality and evoke initiative. But for many of us who went there, the process was needlessly long. Later, when I taught in a postgraduate faculty at Columbia University, I was conscious of the same needless lag. Lecturing *at* students is the traditional way. It is not enough and it is not good enough. Nor is there any merit in the laborious process necessary to arrive at the goal of a doctorate, often resulting in the lapse of several years before the candidate has completed all the requirements. We should teach our abler students to educate themselves. (MacIver, 1968, p. 63)

FIRST APPOINTMENT

MacIver received his first academic appointment at the University of Aberdeen, as a Lecturer on Political Science. Not long afterward the Professor of Latin invited him to transfer to his department, but by that time he was fully committed to the social sciences. Unfortunately, the social sciences were no more conspicuous at Aberdeen than they had been at Edinburgh and Oxford. There was a little economics, doubtless attributable to the respectability of Adam Smith, a little political science, consisting entirely of the history of political philosophy from Machiavelli to Hegel, and no sociology. Sociology in fact was snobbishly regarded as the sort of subject that would "catch on" only in such uncivilized parts of the world as the American Middle West. Persuaded nevertheless that the state did not exhaust the reality of society, and attributing such a notion to Plato and Aristotle themselves, MacIver asked for and received permission to introduce a course in sociology and from 1911 to 1915 he was lecturer on Political Science and Sociology.

As a lecturer, without vote in faculty, MacIver served under the imperious authority of the Professor of Moral Philosophy, J. B. Baillie, the translator of Hegel's *Phenomenology of Mind*. The relationship between them was a cordial one until MacIver published a highly critical review of Bosanquet's *The Philosophical Theory of the State,* a neo-Hegelian work, which Baillie, although his name was not mentioned, interpreted as an attack upon himself. The situation at Aberdeen was then untenable and MacIver had to seek another appointment. By this time he had published a number of articles in prestigious journals and the manuscript of his book *Community* had been awarded a prize by the Carnegie Trust for the universities of Scotland. When the University of Toronto offered him an appointment as associate professor of political science, therefore, he was glad to accept.

Mention of MacIver's *Community* in a book devoted also in part to Robert E. Park reminds me that the two of them had no appreciation of each other's work. In his *Autobiography* MacIver writes that he is not "much elated by approbation or deflated by adverse criticism," and that he prefers to be his own judge of the quality of his work. The facts belie the claim. No man is immune from praise nor insensitive to criticism. When *Community* was published in 1917, Park wrote a review of it in *The American Journal of Sociology* that was entirely negative. He damned the book, as MacIver reports it, with the words "thin, vague, insubstantial, and 'jejune'" (MacIver, 1968, p. 87). It was the word "jejune" that MacIver pondered and apparently could not forget. Actually—so fragile is memory —Park did not use that word. His adjectives were "vague, thin, plausible, and innocuous" (Park, 1918). On the other side of the Atlantic the reviews were unanimously favorable. The *Athenaeum* called it "a masterly book," The *Times Literary Supplement* referred to it as a work of "unmistakable originality," George Unwin said "it ought to mark an epoch in English sociology and political science," and no less a person than Lord Bryce wrote that he was reading it "with great interest and profit." But Park's review ruined it on this side of the Atlantic and it had little circulation among American sociologists.

THE DEPARTMENT AT COLUMBIA

In 1927 MacIver accepted an invitation to head the Department of Economics and Sociology at Barnard College and two years later became chairman of the Columbia Department of Sociology with the title Lieber Professor of Political Philosophy and Sociology. In 1929 the Department of Sociology was in an unsatisfactory condition. After the departure of Giddings it had fallen into a state of decay, with no single outstanding figure, and its repute was far less than that of the Department at Chicago. At one point a faculty move to abolish it, led especially by the historians, was successfully resisted by MacIver and an accomplice named John Dewey. The depression years of the '30s, however, were not conducive to departmental growth and MacIver encountered difficult and often insoluble problems. With the help of his own high reputation, however, a reputation approaching its apogee, to say nothing of the reputation of the University, he was able to recruit for the staff such men as Robert S. Lynd, Willard W. Waller, Bernhard J. Stern, Theodore Abel, a little later Paul F. Lazarsfeld and Robert K. Merton, and such visitors for variable periods as Florian Znaniecki, George A. Lundberg, and Alexander von Schelting. It was, as can be recognized, a kaleidoscopic group. If I fail to include William Casey, Mirra Komarovsky, and, a later arrival, C. Wright Mills, it is either because they were not members of the Graduate Faculty or, in the case of Mills, not recruited by MacIver.

Although MacIver had been drawn to Columbia because of his ambition to participate in the development of sociology, his attitude toward the discipline was always an ambivalent one. On this matter he wrote the following confession'';

> Sociology has always been for me a kind of beloved mistress with whom I seemed unable to get on really comfortable terms. I regarded, and still regard, it as a great and challenging subject. I fought lonely battles to get it accepted in Scotland and in Canada. Yet I was never happy with my accomplishment in that field. My own books in sociology did not give me anything like the degree of satisfaction I got from my books in political science, *The Modern State, The Web of Government,* and *Power Transformed.* The popular texts of the time I regarded as diffuse, lacking definition, sprawling over into genetics and anthropology and ethics, whereas I wanted to offer a systematic account of the structure of society (MacIver, 1968, p. 109).

This "systematic account" he was to provide in *Society: Its Structure and Changes,* published in 1931, and for which he, along with sixty-two other scholars of world renown, received an honorary degree at the Harvard Tercentenary of 1936, with the citation, "An inquirer into the structure of society, a learned systematizer of our social theories." Incidentally, he was the most "decorated" sociologist of his time. In addition to Harvard, he held honorary degrees from Columbia, Yale, Princeton, The Jewish

Theological Seminary of America, The New School for Social Research, Toronto, Edinburgh, and Aberdeen, the last of which, in exception to a rule, conferred *in absentia*.

MacIver held his Columbia post until 1950, at which time he was given emeritus status. He had, however, an unusual post-retirement career. He continued to be active as director of several research projects, one an evaluation of the work of the various and often competing Jewish agencies in the country, another on academic freedom, another on the United Nations, and still another on the prevention and control of juvenile delinquency in New York City—all of which resulted in books. Among the board memberships he held in New York, including The New York School of Social Work, the Russell Sage Foundation, and the American Civil Liberties Union, was the board of The New School for Social Research. As chairman of a committee of the board to select a new president for the School, he and his colleagues suffered several disappointments. To his surprise, his associates suggested that he assume the presidency, at least for a short period. He was then eighty-one years old and had no administrative ambitions. Indeed, he had often declined consideration for university presidencies. He was so devoted to the educational enterprise that The New School represented, however, that he accepted the assignment. Accordingly, he served with conspicuous success first as president and then, honorifically, as chancellor. He retired finally in 1966 at the age of eighty-four and died on June 15, 1970, four years later, of the complications of old age. During the years following his retirement from Columbia he also wrote nine more books, including three of philosophical reflections. His bibliography contains twenty-one books of sole authorship, twenty-five edited volumes, three reports, and ninety-seven articles.

During MacIver's stewardship the Department of Columbia suffered more than financial difficulties. In 1930 MacIver offered Robert Lynd a full professorship and a Ph.D degree on the strength of *Middletown,* which had appeared in 1929 to the acclaim of almost everyone, literate citizen and sociologist alike. It is a commentary on the times, incidentally, that Helen Lynd, the co-author of *Middletown,* received neither an appointment nor a degree in recognition of the accomplishment. In any event, MacIver hoped that Lynd would continue in New York the general kind of research and writing he had done in Muncie, Indiana. Unfortunately, when he took up his duties at Columbia, Lynd's interests turned in other directions, especially to problems of the consumer and to the distribution of power in society. In the late '30s he was doing research also on the impact of the depression on families in the upper-middle-class suburb of Montclair, New Jersey, a study that was never published. Although MacIver, of course, never exerted any pressure upon anyone, he was nevertheless disappointed that Lynd did not pursue his urban studies, and it was not until many years later, as President of The New School, that MacIver was able to establish a Center for New York City Affairs, now a thriving enterprise.

Unfortunately, MacIver and Lynd did not become friends. Indeed, they were so different in interests, temperament, personality, and purpose that friction was inevitable. MacIver was the philospher, Lynd the practioner. MacIver wanted to focus his attention, and that of the Department, on the significance of sociology as an inquiry into the structure of society. Lynd, on the contrary, saw sociology as a practical endeavor, one that would prepare students for a service profession. When, upon the death of Robert E. Chaddock, the elderly statistician of the Department, a new appointment became possible, MacIver and Lynd clashed over the selection of the most appropriate person to fill it. MacIver's choice was Robert K. Merton, then at Tulane, whom he regarded as the most promising of the young sociologists in the country. Lynd wanted Paul F. Lazarsfeld, who regularly attended his seminar during the period of the Montclair research and who advised him on methodological matters. The Department was thus divided into two factions and an impasse became a crisis, a crisis finally resolved by the University's Solomon-like decision to appoint them both.

In the midst of this trying time MacIver committed an unwise act. He published a highly critical review of *Knowledge for What* (1939), the Stafford Little Lectures that Lynd had given at Princeton. He castigated it for its utilitarian view of education in general and of sociology in particular. In the book Lynd, an activist, deplored those who wanted "to lecture on navigation while the ship was going down," and there was no doubt that he had sociologists like MacIver in mind. We have had, of course, more recent echoes of this dispute. But it was an unfortunate episode in the history of the Department and in the relationship of two men who had adjoining offices in Fayerweather Hall.

While on the subject of reviews I might mention that MacIver and Sorokin also gave negative notices to each other's books. In the Preface to Volume IV of *Social and Cultural Dynamics* Sorokin had written, incredibly, "While the sweet theories of the critics are entirely washed out by the inexorable course of events, my diagnosis and the theory underlying it need no correction. History, so far, has been proceeding along the schedule of [my] *Dynamics*." In reviewing this volume MacIver, regarding the entire study as "apocalyptic," wrote "Happy Mr. Sorokin! He knows the secret of history," and again, "Thrice happy Mr. Sorokin! He has answered all the important questions" (MacIver, 1941, p. 904). And in a later review of Sorokin's *The Reconstruction of Humanity* (1948), MacIver referred to Sorokin's prophetic declamations and vehement italics and concluded that his prescriptions amounted to little more than a plea that man cease to be sensate and try to become ideational. Sorokin, in his turn, reviewed MacIver's *Social Causation* (1942) in the *Harvard Law Review*. The review was full of the familiar Sorokinian bombast. He not only indulged in *ad hominem* arguments, accusing MacIver of lacking the philosophical training to undertake inquiries that require a rigorous logic but accused him in addition of using arguments that were either incorrect or tautological. With regard to the reputed tautologies he concluded, "Happy MacIver and happy social sciences! They have already solved all their causal problems!" (Sorokin, 1943, p. 1026). These exchanges remind me of Gabriel Tarde who in his utopia, translated as *Underground Man,* made allowance, in accordance with Spencer's principle of "separation," for a city of painters, a city of sculptors, a city of musicians, of poets, of chemists, of psychologists—indeed, a city of specialists of every kind—except philosophers, explaining that "we were obliged after several attempts to give up the idea of founding or maintaining a city of philosophers, notably owing to the incessant trouble caused by the tribe of sociologists, who are the most unsociable of mankind." It should be said, however, that MacIver and Sorokin forgave each other their reciprocal indiscretions and indulged in cordial conversation when they later sat side by side on the dais at a meeting of the Eastern Sociological Society.

The atmosphere at Columbia was entirely different from that at Harvard where I was also privileged to be a graduate student. At Harvard we had a community, a genuine *Gemeinschaft.* The number of students in the Department in the mid-thirties was small, no more, as I remember, than eighteen or so; Merton was "section man" for Sorokin and tutor to most of us, and we saw one another not only in seminar but also outside the classroom. Talcott Parsons, who was then, improbable as it may seem, an assistant professor, was unusually generous with his time and attention, and held informal seminars with us in his rooms at Adams House, known of course as "The Parsonage," and there we plumbed the depths of problems that we could only touch upon in our regular classes. It was a grand and illuminating experience, and we were all deeply indebted to Talcott.

At Columbia it was difficult to know even the members of one's own graduate student cohort. One saw colleagues in class but seldom anywhere else. The sheer size of the city was one factor. Another was the much longer time period required to earn a Ph.D at Columbia. In the '30s the archaic provision remained that a dissertation had to be published and the candidate had to present it in galley proof at the time of his defense. (By contrast, Harvard then accepted even a handwritten dissertation.) In addition to every other obstacle to the Ph.D., therefore, there was a financial obstacle running from several hundred to one or two thousand dollars, a not insubstantial sum in those Depression days when starting salaries for assistant professors ranged from $2,000 to $2,500 a year. MacIver himself took the initiative in a movement to change this policy—again opposed by the History Department—and to bring Columbia into accord with the practice of other American universities. But in the '30s Columbia held the dubious record of exhibiting the longest average time-span for completing work for the Ph.D of any university. I remember a student in the History Department whose chairman asked him whether he was preparing for this life or the next one.

We did have, at Columbia, a periodic Sunday evening seminar at the MacIver apartment on Riverside Drive. Some of the graduate students were invited, and so were the faculty, to listen, usually, to a visiting speaker, and then to participate in the ensuing discussion. But the graduate students were awed by the faculty and the visiting speaker and the sessions had nowhere near the congeniality and informality of our group at Harvard. Nevertheless, as Harry Alpert (1953) has written, we "developed a common, unanimously shared respect for MacIver's intellectual acumen and his tolerant, but discriminating, regard for those with whom he disagreed."

If I were asked, as indeed I have been, about MacIver's developing sociological orientation during the time I studied with him I should have to respond, in all candor, that I suspect he was beginning to lose interest in sociology. There is an exception, however, to that observation. In 1937 he had done a revision of *Society,* with the new subtitle *A Textbook of Sociology*[2] and had then turned his attention to the problems of social causation, both logical and substantive, and produced his *Social Causation* in 1942, a book to which I have earlier referred. There are some who regard it as his most successful book. For my part I have to confess that I regard it as his least successful and agree with the long, respectful, but negative review of it by Ernest Nagel in *The Journal of Philosophy.* Even in the mid-thirties MacIver was offering more courses in political science than in sociology. For many years he gave the large lecture course on the history of political philosophy and in the early forties began to plan and to write his magisterial work, *The Web of Government* (1947), which won the Woodrow Wilson Prize of the American Political Science Association. Some of it is dated now—for example, MacIver's discussion of the totalitarian states at the time of World War II—but as a contribution to the sociology of government it has no peer. Of all of his books it is, with the exception of *Society,* the most eloquent.

[2]To be revised once more, with Charles H. Page, and published in 1949 with the subtitle, *An Introductory Analysis.*

MacIver founded no school of thought in sociology. He had no disciples and wanted none. His influence, as measured by the number of recent references to him, has clearly diminished. His work illustrates a phenomenon that I call "the depopulated Pantheon." There is a flux and flow in the reputations of the great men of our discipline—and other disciplines as well. Their statues may be seen in the Great Hall of the Pantheon for a decade or two and then they are removed to the basement to make room for others. Sometimes, after a period of neglect, they are dusted off and restored to their former place of honor. No one can predict whether or when this will happen in individual cases. I am reminded, for example, that Weber and Durkheim were not great names in this country until Talcott Parsons, almost single-handedly, gave them a posthumous fame. Sorokin, in his 1928 *Contemporary Sociological Theories,* gave more than twice as much space to Frédéric Le Play as he did to Weber and Durkheim combined. Herbert Spencer lived to see his own reputation disappear. Crane Brinton pronounced him dead again in 1933, and now once more we are listening to him. As a graduate student at Columbia and Harvard in the '30s I never heard the name of Cooley. And so it goes.

It is impossible, therefore, to predict the response that a future generation will give to MacIver's name. He will always, of course, belong to my personal Pantheon. On the occasion of his retirement, a date that is now more than twenty-five years in the rapidly receding past, a number of his students prepared ceremonial statements in his honor. In conclusion to this paper I can do no better than to quote my own, slightly edited and containing, on purpose, a number of his own most graceful expressions:

"It is not easy to assess in a few short paragraphs the contributions that Robert M. MacIver has made to sociology. Indeed, 'sociology,' even when broadly conceived, is almost too narrow a word with which to try. First of all, and perhaps in the long run most important, we note his unerring sense of the fundamental order that society exhibits, an order that pervades its every phase and sector. This is the order that makes the rational analysis of society possible and gives point to the existence of sociology as a separate discipline of learning. MacIver knows that 'The structure of any society is at best an elementary and somewhat clumsy arrangement,' but he knows too that in this 'vast intrinsic traffic of society' there are recurrences and regularities. 'Custom,' he says, 'is always at work turning example into precedent and precedent into institution.' Here, in a sentence, is a system of sociology.

"We may say, secondly, that MacIver's quest has never lost its focus, never strayed into the dark morass of methodology on the one hand or into the cerulean haze of the philosophy of history on the other. Community and society, their customs and institutions, and society's government, these have always been his first concerns. This is no small achievement in a period when so much of sociology has succumbed to strange lures like psychoanalysis, for example, at one extreme, and matrix algebra at the other. One need only compare the chaotic thing that sociology is in general with the disciplined system it is in MacIver's books in order to recognize the merit and magnitude of this accomplishment.

"Of MacIver's political theory it is similarly impossible to write in detail. Here, however, we appreciate him most of all when he insists, with a constant emphasis, that government is no mere legal phenomenon, no mere political phenomenon, but primarily and in a larger sense a social phenomenon. Government for him is no fictitious affair residing in the formal structure of the law or in the vague superstition of sovereignty. Government springs from the community and owes its source and practice to the society of men. And here, incidentally, lies the strength of democracy. Democracy recognizes that government is a limited institution, contrived for limited purposes, and democracy alone gives constitutional sanction to the distinction between the community and the state. In MacIver's own words, 'The authority of government does not create the order over which it presides and does not sanction that order solely by its own fiat or accredited power. There is authority beyond the authority of government.'

"But MacIver is not only sociologist and political theorist. If we attempt to characterize him in the ordinary academic terms we shall miss one of the most subtle qualities of this quiet scholar. Sociologist he is, and political theorist, too. But above all, and in a deeper sense, he belongs to an old and honorable—even Scottish—tradition, the tradition of moral philosophy. MacIver has never forgotten the importance of defining properly the relationship between the individual and society. In this respect he knows that 'The individual is never wholly absorbed in his society, wholly responsive to it, wholly accounted for by it.' He gladly teaches that 'It is in individuals that all social values are realized' and that 'We cannot, except by a flight into mysticism, attribute to this whole, society, any fulfillment except the continuing fulfillment of its members.' He has no patience with a social code so conservative, so rigid, or so authoritarian that it menaces 'the autonomy of judgment which is the prime condition of an enlightened adult morality.' He denounces the dogmatist who, 'secure in his own faith, would refuse other men the right to theirs.' And he is an enemy forever of the 'immoral intolerance which only the exclusive visionary possession of an unreasoned faith can inspire.'"

REFERENCES

Alpert, H. (ed.), *Robert M. MacIver: Teacher and sociologist.* Northampton, Mass.: Metcalf Printing and Publishing Company, 1953.

Bierstedt, R. In H. Alpert, ed. *Robert M. MacIver: Teacher and sociologist.* Northampton, Mass.: Metcalf Printing and Publishing Company, 1953.

Lynd, R. S. *Knowledge for what? The place of social science in American culture.* Princeton: Princeton University Press, 1939.

Lynd, R. S. & Lynd, H. M. *Middletown.* New York: Harcourt Brace, 1929.

MacIver, R. M. *Community: A sociological study.* New York: Macmillan, 1928. [First American edition]

MacIver, R. M. *Society: A textbook of sociology.* New York: Farrar & Rinehart, 1st ed. 1931; 2d ed. 1937; 3d ed., with C. H. Page, 1949.

MacIver, R. M. *As a tale that is told: The autobiography of Robert M. MacIver.* Chicago: University of Chicago Press, 1968.

MacIver, R. M. "Review of P.A. Sorokin, *Social and cultural Dynamics.*" *American Sociological Review,* 1941, *6,* 904-907.

MacIver, R. M. "Review of P.A. Sorokin, *The Reconstruction of Humanity.*" *The New York Times Book Review,* April 18, 1948. 21-22.

Nagel, E. "Review of R.M. MacIver, *Social Causation.*" *The Journal of Philosophy,* 1942, *39,* 552-556.

Park, R. E. "Review of R.M. MacIver, *Community.*" *American Journal of Sociology,* 1918, *23,* 542-544.

Russell, B. *The autobiography of Bertrand Russell.* London: George Allen and Unwin, Ltd. 1967-69. 3 vols.

Sorokin, P.A. *Contemporary sociological theories.* New York: Harper & Brothers, 1928.

Sorokin, P.A. *Social and cultural dynamics.* New York: American Book Company, 1937. 4 vols.

Sorokin, P.A. "Review of R.M. MacIver, *Social Causation.*" *Harvard Law Review,* 1943, *56,* 1023-1027.

Tarde, G. *Underground man.* London: Duckworth, 1905.

6

PITIRIM A. SOROKIN
Master Sociologist and Prophet

Robin M. Williams, Jr.

The participants in this symposium have been given to understand by its organizers that they hope to avoid having any of these presentations—as they might have politely put it—"degenerate into anecdotal reminiscences." This stricture could severely hamper my efforts to describe for you how sociological knowledge and tradition was transmitted *to* me *from* Sorokin. For much of his influence was highly personal, diffuse, and often paradoxical in the Weberian sense of *Paradoxie der Folgen;* he served as an exemplar both of professional and personal virtues and of styles of professional work that many of his students rejected. Whether in emulation or rejection, those of my generation who experienced his teaching at first-hand often found their own identity and their values and styles clarified and extended by the experience. So, in keeping with the advice I have received, I shall not tell *anecdotes*. But it will be essential to give a few *examples* of Sorokin, the Teacher and Model, in action.

During my first few weeks in Cambridge, the new graduate students in residence for the summer were invited for an evening at the Sorokins' home in Winchester. The hospitality was informal and charming. As we sat on the veranda in the twilight, our genial host made repeated rounds urging us to refresh ourselves with what appeared to be cold grapejuice which he poured with a flourish from a large and seemingly bottomless pitcher. Full awareness of the quality of the beverage came when I found myself belting out the chorus of a folksong, without recalling at all how I had begun singing in the first place. I then asked, "Professor Sorokin, could you please tell us

93

what is in this drink?'' Sorokin replied, ''Of course I cannot tell you; obviously that is a military secret.'' Later that same evening, one religiously oriented member of the group asked Pitirim what religious instruction his sons, Peter and Sergei, were receiving. Sorokin put his arm paternally around the shoulders of the questioner and replied: ''Do not worry, my friend. I myself was brought up by the most pious of Russian peasant families—and Look at Me now! You shall see—my children receive no religious instruction: therefore, they will grow up to be saints.''

Of such episodes are lasting, vivid, complex impressions formed. By the end of one evening in Sorokin's home, I had learned that all prior stereotypes of the famous sociologist had to be reevaluated. The teaching had already begun.

THE TIMES AND THE INTELLECTUAL CLIMATE: HARVARD IN THE LATE 1930s

My personal acquaintance with Sorokin began in the summer of 1938. As it turned out, however, I was to spend just twelve months in residence, subsequently writing a dissertation on evenings and weekends while on the staff of the University of Kentucky, and officially receiving the doctorate only in 1943. That one year, nevertheless, was intensive enough to make up for its brevity.

The Harvard scene on the eve of World War II was one of intense intellectual ferment in the social and behavioral sciences and closely related fields. In psychology, there was Gordon Allport, Henry A. Murray, E. G. Boring, Jerome Bruner. I had a minor with John D. Black in agricultural economics in the Littauer School, a minor with Gordon Allport in psychology of personality, an informal ''minor'' with E. P. Hutchinson in statistics. I had memorable courses with Sorokin, Talcott Parsons, Robert K. Merton, and Carle C. Zimmerman, and was tutored in German by Hans Gerth—who interlarded the language lessons with extraordinary minilectures on Weber, European politics, and intellectual history. Later I became acquainted with the anthropologist, Clyde Kluckhohn, the sociologist, Florence Kluckhohn, and the literary historian, Bernard de Voto. In Black's courses in economics, I encountered a young instructor whose name was Kenneth Galbraith. In the Department of Sociology, Edward Devereux and Nicholas Demerath were acting as tutors and I learned a great deal from them and the other ''senior'' graduate students, including Logan Wilson. And, in some ways, I learned most of all from the frequent and intense discussions with persons in my own cohort of graduate students; in these discussions Sorokin's latest pronouncements were often examined.

My first impressions of Sorokin's work had been formed while I was a graduate student in rural sociology, with C. Horace Hamilton at North Carolina State College and with Rupert Vance, Guy Johnson, and Howard Odum at the University of North Carolina at Chapel Hill. My earlier training had been primarily in agricultural economics and my research experience had been strongly empirical. I was continually exposed to courses in statistics and to the use of statistical methods in research. Hamilton was enthusiastically engaged in studies of farm tenancy, rural relief programs of the New Deal, and studies of rural-urban migration. My first publication was as junior author with Hamilton of a research note using multiple correlation to infer causes of variations in rates of tenancy in rural North Carolina. A vivid memory is of Hamilton casually telling me I needed to "learn calculus" in order to start work—the following week—on calculation of stationary populations.

With this sink-or-swim background in quantitative methods and field research, I had been pleased and impressed with Sorokin's ingenious interpretations of large bodies of diverse data in *Social Mobility*. A rereading of that work brought to the center of attention the wide scope of his conceptual scheme and his grasp of historical variations in stratification, in rates and types of mobility, in the sources of these variations and their consequences for other aspects of social systems. With this dawning appreciation of "theory," I turned to *Contemporary Sociological Theories*. My first reading was in 1933–34, and I still have that copy of the book. The margins are filled with comments, which seem in roughly equal proportions to voice approval or agreement and disapproval or (often angry) rejection; the latter notations were the more vehement, e.g., "Nonsense," "Bosh," "a smart-alec remark," "let's keep *your* preferences out of this," and others even less respectful.

But I did have considerable respect for the solid merits of both these major works. It later became apparent that *Social Mobility* (1927) had a great influence upon American sociology almost immediately. By the mid-1930s it had become a much-criticized but indispensable point of departure. Its conceptual apparatus, historical richness, and wide range of data—and its scathing critiques—made it part of the required reading of graduate students. The then-dean of empirical American Sociology, F. Stuart Chapin, edited the Social Science series in which *Social Mobility* was published. In his "Introduction," Chapin said, "In this book is assembled for the first time in accessible form a vast amount of factual evidence and quantitative data. . . the book. . .represents the first thoroughgoing attempt to describe social mobility in terms of social stratification and social distance" (1927, vii). Sorokin himself emphasized the empirical and quantitative aspects of the work.

Speculative sociology is passing over. An objective, factual, behavioristic, and quantitative sociology is successfully superceding it. This explains why I have tried to avoid basing my statements on the data of "speech reactions" only; why in the book there is not much of speculative psychologizing and philosophizing; why wherever it has been possible to obtain reliable quantitative data, I have preferred to use them instead of purely qualitative description. (*Social Mobility,* 1927, pp. ix-x)

And again, observe this vehement rejection of evaluative sociology, also from the preface to *Social Mobility*.

Another "plague" of sociological theories has been their permeation with "preaching or evaluating judgements" of what is good and what is bad, what is "useful" and what is "harmful." Sociological literature is inundated with "preaching works," 90 per cent of which are nothing but mere speculation, often quite ignorant, given in the name of science. As the primary task of any science is to face the facts as they really exist; and as such "preaching" only compromises the science itself, it must be avoided by all who care for and understand what science means. This explains why the book, with the exception of a very few casual remarks, is free from such "preaching." Trying to face the facts I naturally do not care at all whether my statement are found to be "reactionary" or "radical", "optimistic" or "pessimistic." (Sorokin, 1927, p. x)

In the later works, from World War II on, his polemical statements against quantitative data and research methods were frequent and colorful, e.g., "'test-centered' psychology and psychiatry are largely responsible for the affliction of sociology with testomania" (Sorokin, 1966 p. 66). But in his early works he both used and advocated quantitative data and "behavioristic" methods. Thus part of the transmission of sociological tradition from the generation of the 1920s and 1930s to the generation of the 1940s and 1950s was to pass on a critical rejection of "merely" speculative and subjective sociology.

But of course there was another Sorokin—indeed, several others. One of them was strongly evaluative, socially engaged, and committed to a special kind of interpretative-historical approach. In the late 1930s, Sorokin's (often pessimistic and sardonic but passionate) involvement in ideological questions was at one with much of the political mood and the intellectual style of the times.

In 1938, the United States was only slowly and fitfully recovering from the savage impact of the Great Depression. To many young students it was at best an open question as to whether anything short of revolution could bring about whatever changes might be required to produce a Good Society. Anyone who was at all seriously concerned with ideas at that time simply was obliged to read Marx, to think about the "Russian Experiment," to consider the emergence of Fascism and Nazism in Europe. It was a time of intense social tensions, acrimonious controversies, widespread anti-intellectualism, rampart racism and growing anti-Semitism in many parts of the society. In Boston cinemas, the newreels frequently elicited noisy responses and not infrequently, led to fist-fights as well. The German-American Bund was highly active. Brawls between Harvard students and Nazi sympathizers could interrupt a Saturday evening song, conversation, and beer at a popular downtown tavern. Day by day, the prospect of war in Europe became clearer, closer, and more ominous.

German emigré scholars were salient in the Harvard environment. I had the unforgettable experience of being tutored for my doctoral examination on a reading knowledge of German by Hans Gerth. Between paragraphs of *Wirtschaft und Gesellschaft* I learned a great deal about the rise and the character of Nazism.

The students who argued about Sorokin's ideas in 1937–38 had little prospects of "careers" in sociology. But so far as I can recall none of us ever worried about the "social relevance" of the subject.

THE MAN AND HIS LIFE

Sorokin's long, turbulent and active life had the qualities of which legends are made. Here is one sketch:

> Pitirim Alexandrovich Sorokin was born in humble circumstances in the rural north of Russia in 1889. A prodigious zeal for work, combined with enormous erudition, had led him to write more than thirty volumes, many of which—for example, *Social and Cultural Dynamics* (1937–1941), *Social Mobility,* (1927)..., and *Contemporary Sociological Theories* (1928)—have become classics. (Tiryakian, 1968, p. 61)

And there is Don Martindale's more recent comment:

> Whatever else is said of Pitirim Sorokin, he is the last of the pioneering sociologists, who promoted an historically based, global program of social theory and social reconstruction similar in many essentials to that of Comte. His personal odyssey was to carry him from the status of an itinerant workman on the Russian frontier to a professorship at Harvard and presidency of the International and American Sociological Association. (Martindale, 1977, p. 353)

Much of Sorokin's early life has become part of the folklore of the sociological profession. He studied at the University of St. Petersburg and the Psycho-Neurological Institute where Pavlov was emphasizing the necessity and virtue of observing overt behavior and the explanatory power of the idea of conditioned reflexes; this was a deep but far from permanent influence on Sorokin's thinking. Very early he was active in the noncommunist left, then in the Revolution; he was a member of the Constituent Assembly, editor of a newspaper (*Volia naroda*), and secretary to Prime Minister Kerensky. Having survived being three times imprisoned by the Czarist regime, he was then three times imprisoned by the Bolsheviks. On the last occasion, he was sentenced to death, and escaped execution only by the intervention of Lenin. His first-hand observations of the horrors of large-scale famine had a deep and lasting impact (Sorokin, 1977). By the time he had made his way to the United States, he was profoundly disillusioned with simplistic ideas of progress as well as with totalitarian solutions to social ills.

Sorokin authored, by various counts, some 40 books and approximately 400 essays and articles, during his four careers: the early Russian period through 1920; the crisis years, 1920–23; the University of Minnesota period, 1924–30; and the long period after that at Harvard. There were 40 or more translations of his works into most of the major literary languages of the world. His first publications date from 1910; the Russian-language works continue up to 1923. Beginning in 1924 with *Leaves from a Russian Diary,* he launched a second career in America. Observe the notable early productivity in the United States:

1925 — *Sociology of Revolution,* and two innovative minor classics in his articles on millionaires and rulers.
1927 — *Social Mobility*
1928 — *Contemporary Sociological Theories*
1929 — *Principles of Rural-Urban Sociology* with Carle C. Zimmerman
1930 — *A Systematic Source Book in Rural Sociology* (3 volumes)

When I went to Harvard in 1938, I had read most of these works. But I had not anticipated what awaited me in the first three volumes of *Social and Cultural Dynamics* (1937), which were then on my "must" list of readings to be done at an early date. Nor did I forsee that during my one-year stay in Cambridge, the prolific Sorokin would find time to publish *Time Budgets of Human Behavior.* By then already reeling from the impact of multiple reading lists that promised to require 48-hour days, I could only savor the irony implied in the title of the empirical monograph.

Many commentators have shared Truzzi's conclusions:

> His works encompassed the entire range of sociological endeavor, including ... such diverse areas as macrosociological and cultural theory, small-group experimentation, social stratification, rural sociology, the philosophy of history, and the sociology of alturistic love. There are very few areas in sociology upon which he did not leave a lasting imprint. An immensely productive scholar, Sorokin was also a man of political action and a major critic of contemporary social trends. (Truzzi, 1971, p. 3)

He wrote empirical articles and monographs, synoptic historical and cultural interpretations, critical summaries and evaluations, systematic conceptual treatises, political statements, ideological polemics, and professional critiques. The performance was enormously varied in content; it was often infuriating to many sociologists; it was dazzling in scope, detail, and perspectives; it simply could not be regarded with indifference.

The first three volumes of *Social and Cultural Dynamics* were published in 1937 and were reviewed in the *American Sociological Review* in December by an art historian (M. R. Rogers), a historian (John Herman Randall, Jr.), and a sociologist (Hans Speier). My copy of the *ASR* shows pencil and ink underlinings indicating the interest with which I read the reviews at the time; both the agreements and disagreements of the reviewers with Sorokin's views were noted, especially with reference to main empirical findings or conclusions.

In the same issue of the *Review,* the lead article was Robert Bierstedt's "The Logico-Meaningful Method of P. A. Sorokin"—with an inevitable "Rejoinder" by Sorokin. Both authors were brilliant and witty controversialists and both saber and stiletto were enthusiastically employed. The performance was exhilarating, even if the issues were never squarely joined. It was clear to a beginning graduate student in North Carolina, watching the fray from afar, that sociology was a field in which a willingness to engage in direct intellectual combat was a prerequisite for full participation. Thus informed and alerted I had set forth for Harvard in June of 1938.

SOROKIN AS TEACHER

Part of the present task of describing how Sorokin transmitted his conceptions and evaluations of the sociological enterprise to the next student generation already has been done by Arthur K. Davis (1963). As Tiryakian has noted, whatever else could be said about it, Sorokin's teaching was rarely bland or dull:

> All of us who have been fortunate enough to have been a student in a course taught by Pitirim Sorokin have undoubtedly been caught in the excitement he generated in us about our discipline. Listening to him—whether in enthusiastic admiration or in violent disagreement—the student (at least speaking from personal experience) always felt the call to do great things and never to rest on his laurels: is this not the hallmark of the true teacher, this ability to generate this restless tension within his students? (Tiryakian, 1963, p. xii)

But Davis says that the majority of his graduate-school generation "did not learn much from Sorokin, and . . . because of this fact North American sociology is the poorer" (Davis, 1963, p. 2). What was it that was not learned, or at least not learned well enough or widely enough? Davis answers:

> . . . an emphasis upon social change as the primary frame of reference; the corollary that change is inherent or immanent in social systems; the premise that social conflict and social problems are basically organic aspects of a society rather than external accidents; the revolutionary nature of our time; and the

necessity of taking a universal view of social life and social thought, both ancient and modern, rather than a perspective limited to modern Western societies. (Davis, 1963, p. 2)

This is a discerning and useful listing. From my point of view, several additions to it would help to complete the inventory of orientations which Sorokin left in the awareness of some of his students and many of his readers. To a generation imbued to a substantial extent with humanitarian liberalism and with hopes for the gradual alleviation of social ills through rationally-conceived programs, he insisted not only upon the frequency and ferocity of collective conflicts but also upon the radical separation of the "effective" from the "good" in social systems. He never tired of pointing out the long periods of successful domination and privilege enjoyed by many autocratic, ruthless, cruel and rigid ruling formations, saying in effect, you may deplore it, I may deplore it, but here are the brute facts. He was relentless in his attacks upon any and all social panaceas—except later, perhaps, altruistic love—and upon the reassuring belief that each war, revolution, or other major calamity is an abnormal interruption of a more orderly and reasonable world. He hammered away at all unilinear doctrines of development or change. He incessantly pronounced judgments upon the importance of the triviality of the topics studied by other sociologists. Shorn of his peculiarly personal rhetoric, these were arguments *for* objective diagnosis, *for* full awareness of complexity, *for* historical context, and *for* cross-cultural perspectives.

All of the points thus far mentioned have a central focus in Sorokin as gadfly, iconoclast, scoffer at conventional wisdom, enthusiastic advocate of unpopular views—the Peck's Bad Boy and Devil's Advocate of American sociology for four decades. Although he did change his views, sometimes in line with changes in the social and intellectual climate of the time, it probably is broadly true that ". . . he remained relatively unmoved by passing political tempests, just as he has been generally unaffected by most of the short-term enthusiasms in social science" (Davis, 1963, p. 6).

He was a merciless and often intemperate critic. It was as if, having reduced a city to rubble, one must pound the fragments to dust—and then sow the site with salt. Thus he characterizes an article by a distinguished colleague as ". . . a peculiar mixture of elementary trivialities with defective speculations concerning the 'universals' or prerequisites for human sociocultural progress" (Sorokin, 1966, p. 606). He was likely to react to claims of "new" theories or "recent discoveries" by attributing to their proponents a "Columbus Complex"—the belief that previously-known phenomena are now being recognized for the first time. One year in Sorokin's classes was enough to make me permanently somewhat cautious about claiming that any fact, statement, concept, or theory is "the first" of its kind. Sorokin was given to reminding his audiences of statements made by Plato, Socrates, Aristotle, Confucius, Lao-tse, Polybius, Aquinas, Grotius, Machiavelli, Hobbes, Locke, Rousseau, and so on indefinitely. For students who would eventually have to undergo questioning by him enroute to the doctorate, to be this forewarned was to attempt to become forearmed.

He argued vigorously against the critics of his own work:

> My sensate, ideational, and idealistic supersystems are not mere 'ideal-typical generalizations,' or schema[ta] but unquestionable realities or facts solidly demonstrated by a vast body of logical, empirical, and quantitative evidence so vast and so complete as to make the fact of the integration of some cultures into these supersystems undeniable (Sorokin, 1966, p. 285).

Sorokin continually used his own "principle of limits" as a critical device. Let anyone assert a unilinear trend or an unbounded generalization or an exclusive conceptual dichotomy and Sorokin was prompt to assert that no trend continues indefinitely in the same direction, that all concrete generalizations have limits, that one always must suspect that further distinctions are needed in the dichotomies such as sacred–secular, *Gemeinschaft–Gesellschaft,* or mechanical–organic.

With Sorokin, any student had to confront numerous divergencies, incompatibilities and incongruities in the teacher's writings. There was the Pavlovian behaviorism of *Hunger, Leaves from a Russian Diary* and *The Sociology of Revolution;* in these works "mere speech-reactions" were dismissed with scorn in favor of objective accounts of overt behavior.[1] There was the highly abstract edifice of concepts of his *System of Sociology.* There was the outpouring of the empirical-synthesizing works of the Minnesota period. And there were the sweeping generalizations and value-laden interpretations, especially of the later works.

From Sorokin I learned in depth how passionately evaluative one could be in rejecting value-judgements. His teaching almost literally forced his students to disagree with him on many points—if not openly in the class or seminar, then certainly in later discussions with fellow students. There was an informal group of seminar participants during my year in Cambridge which constituted a kind of Society for Mutual Indignation and Intellectual Self-Defense. Sometimes after two hours of Pitirim's nonstop dicta, we adjourned across the street to a restaurant where the real discussion took place. place. In these sessions, we criticized, rejected, modified and elaborated the ideas, concepts and evaluations of the teacher. Particularly gratifying, of course, was the discovery of apt refutations which we could have made in the seminar, if only we could have thought of them at the time.

---

[1]Even then, however, "psychological *experiences* are not excluded from the field of study" (Sorokin, 1977, pp. xxxviii-xxxix).

Sorokin often gave one invaluable practice in dealing with the unexpected and the outrageous; he could have outdone anything lately reported by ethnomethodologists as demonstrations of how to upset conventional understandings and other "constructed realities." Once, more than a decade after my graduate days, I was with Richard William of the National Institute of Mental Health (also a Harvard Ph.D) on an official visit to a research program in the Boston area. Leaving the Harvard Club after a business lunch, the two of us encountered Pitirim, emerging from a swirl of snow as we opened the door. Without the least hesitation he roared, "Well! Williams, and then Williams again! How are you?" We shook hands. He continued, "And *what* are *you* doing *here*?" Somewhat abashed at the challenge, with its tone of impending disapproval of whatever we might have been doing, we mumbled something about reviewing a research program. "Research!" intoned Sorokin in mock-disbelief, "and whose money are you so wasting now?" We later thought of many witty replies, but none of them occurred to us on the spot.

To listen to Sorokin's classroom lectures was to be bombarded with a torrent of fact, references, concepts, generalizations, hypotheses, alleged laws, value judgments, criticisms and historical anecdotes. The erudition, although not always specific (or even accurate in the imputations of various views to others), was likely to suggest that if one wished to criticize or refute the master's assertions, it would be well to read some of the major sources he cited. The frequent condemnations of other social scientists for provincialism, "ignorance," "simplistic thinking," "one-sided interpretations," and the like implied the need to become sufficiently well-informed to hold one's own in the academic arena. I think that under this treatment at least some of the aspiring sociological neophytes came to realize for the first time that the search for truth might not be only a cool, detached process of investigation but also a matter of vigorous confrontations and complex intellectual combat.

The kind of teaching to which I refer was intense, uninhibited in tone, and intensely personal; it had an aura of total commitment; everything was at least a little larger than life. Over time, one necessarily came to detect not only large shifts in emphasis and tone, but also apparent inconsistencies and contradictions. Within a single hour one heard the objective scientist and the fervent moralist, the sensitive humanist and the vituperative critic, the systematic analyst and the intuitive prophet. What one saw was not only a mind at work, but also a personality and character being expressed and a life being developed. When Sorokin lectured on changes in Western art, his presentations were not finely-polished cameos but vast disorderly paintings or sculptures in process—the room often seemed filled with flying paint and chips of marble. So far as my own observations go, it seems that our group of nascent sociologists, regardless of their positive or negative attitudes toward the person or the content of the presentations, quickly came to define Sorokin as a phenomenon *sui generis* that simply had to be accepted as part of the nature of things, like a mountain, a seascape, an earthquake or a volcano.

THE LEGACY

What was the legacy of this sociologist to sociology and to intellectual history? Let me start with the microcosm: what did Williams as student take away from Sorokin as teacher?

A hasty inspection of a few of my own works, stimulated by the writing of this paper, shows that I have made highly *selective* and *specific* use of Sorokin's formulations. In *American Society* (3rd edition, 1970) there are citations to his works for the concepts of "vehicle" (means for externalizing and communicating meanings), cultural integration, law-norms (imperative, two-sided, fully specified), institution, stratification, social class, social mobility, power and morality, education, ideational and sensate cultures, social and cultural systems. Under the "Suggested Readings" at the end of Chapters II and XV are two annotated references that warrant quotations:

For Chapter II: Sorokin, Pitirim A. *Society, Culture, and Personality*

The best single source for gaining a view of the main outlines of Sorokin's vast body of writings. Do not be put off by the terminology or the opinionated style, but look for the sophisticated conceptions of norms and institutions. The concept of 'law-norms' goes to the heart of the matter.

For Chapter XV: Sorokin, Pitirim A. *Social and Cultural Dynamics. 4 vols. New York: American Book Company, 1937-1941.*

Monumental, erudite, and opinionated overview of historical fluctuations in art, science, ethics, law, social relationships and collectivities, war, and revolution. Develops cyclical theory of history—ideational, idealistic, and sensate phases. Sees our culture as late sensate.

You may sense from these fragments that I found a substantial number of Sorokin's concepts and generalizations to be useful and important. What I did not accept were (1) his overarching framework or paradigm, (2) his sweeping diagnoses of contemporary society, (3) his strongly evaluative mode of discourse. The latter seemed to me to be stimulating and interesting—and authentic for Sorokin—but not suitable for the empirical, inductive, tentative, research-based codifications and syntheses that I thought most likely to lead us toward a more valid and scientific sociology.

In a 1964 review of the *Festschrift* for Sorokin edited by Tiryakian (1963), I essentially stated the thesis of the present discussion.

> Perhaps the individualized nature of the separate contributions to this volume is a sign of one prominent fact concerning Sorokin: he is respected, and often admired, by many sociologists who are not disciples and who disagree with him on major issues. The present work will not reflect his thought, but it does hint at the power of his stimulating ideas and wide-ranging sociological interests. (William, 1964, p. 125)

Sorokin's strong influence upon some of the major contributors to rural sociology in the United States is clear, e.g., upon C. A. Anderson, O. D. Duncan, Charles P. Loomis, T. Lynn Smith, Conrad Taeuber, and Carle C. Zimmerman (Tiryakian, 1968, p. 63). Through these persons and their students, he was a major force in the development of historical, comparative and systematic emphases. These same emphases were evident in the generation of Ph.D's who had his tutelage at Harvard in the 1930s; although they emphatically were not "disciples," the "generations" of John W. Riley, Jr., Kingsley Davis, Logan Wilson, Arthur K. Davis, knew Sorokin's work in detail. By the end of World War II, he no longer attracted many graduate students, and his attention turned elsewhere. Yet his works have continued to be rediscovered (cf. Tiryakian, 1968; Truzzi, 1971, pp. 3–15, 233–234).

As many as twenty years after the publication of Volumes I-III of *Social and Cultural Dynamics,* his place of prominence as a "theorist" in American sociology can be seen by the frequent references to his works. For example there are 68 page citations in *Modern Sociological Theory in Continuity and Change* (edited by Howard Becker and Alvin Boskoff)—roughly on a par with the number of citations to Parsons, to Znaniecki, and to Weber. In the *American Sociological Review,* articles or comments by Sorokin appeared in Volumes 1, 2, 3, 4, 10—and not again until Volume 30, when the *ASR* published his Presidential Address, delivered when he was 76 years of age. Reviews of his books, more nearly obligatory, appeared in Volumes 1, 2, 6, 8, 10, 13, 14, 16, 21, 25, 29, and 32. For more than forty years, he was a salient and often towering feature of the American sociological scene. He essentially founded several subfields of major importance. He was an inveterate taxonomist, who left numerous provocative sets of distinctions and typologies. He was a central figure in making "theory" important in the United States. He stimulated a great deal of counter-theorizing by the sheer volume and vigor of his own work.

Rarely did Sorokin leave his readers or hearers in doubt as to either his evaluations or his existential propostions. He flatly asserted causal regularities; for example:

> The explosion of war or famine or any other great emergency invariably leads to an expansion of governmental regimentation in all societies of a certain kind; and the termination of war, famine, or other emergency regularly leads to a quantitative and qualitative decrease in governmental regimentation. This is an example of two sociocultural phenomena bound into a causal unity by a direct causal tie. (Sorokin, 1966, pp. 18-19)

Or take this formulation:

> Any great culture, instead of being a mere dumping place of a multitude of diverse cultural phenomena, existing side by side and unrelated to one another, represents a unity or individuality whose parts are permeated by the same fundamental principle and articulate the same basic value. (Sorokin, 1941, p. 17)

Equally decisive and sweeping were his many well-known diagnoses of modern civilization.

> . . . the present crisis of our culture and society consists exactly in the disintegration of the dominant sensate system of modern Euro-American culture. . . .the crisis is not a maladjustment of this or that single compartment, but rather the disintegration of the overwhelmingly greater part of these sectors, integrated in and around the sensate form. (Sorokin, 1941, p. 21)

The crises of the twentieth century thus are manifestations of a revolutionary shift in an entire cultural system—". . .when one fundamental form of culture and society—sensate—is declining and a different form is emerging" (Sorokin, 1941, p. 22). This change is not, says Sorokin, "the death of Western culture"—all such biological analogies he dismisses as fallacious—for much of the total congeries will survive, and new and creative forms will be created. But the period of transition will be chaotic, tragic, bloody, cruel, and destructive of many values.

In the later years many within the profession paid little attention to the substance of his work and responded primarily to the style or manner. In 1967, for example, in a review of *Sociological Theories of Today,* John Finley Scott observed:

> Much of this book deserves more serious attention than it is likely to receive. Sorokin gets read today less for content than for style. His broadsides of bombast and perjoration are an antiquarian's delight, and he fires them at all whose views are not his own. Here a scholar's scourge is come: and the text runs red with blood (*American Sociological Review,* 1967, p. 683).

His intellectual style was not at base analytical; rather it was encyclopedic, synthesizing, classifying, intuitive, pattern-finding—and adversative. The great Cornell historian, Carl Becker, took up the old German definition of a professor as "a man [read, person] who thinks otherwise." Sorokin was in that sense the prototypical professor. He thought otherwise against the Czarist regime, against the Leninist regime, against the thousands of eminent scholars of the past with whom he disagreed. He thought otherwise about material prosperity, progress, optimism, social planning, world peace, socialism, communism, fascism, democracy; to the great consternation of many of his fellow sociologists, he thought otherwise about sociology. Indeed his gift for invective—gleefully publicized by the mass media—sometimes seemed at its height when he assailed the fads and foibles of his own, his native discipline.

Sorokin exemplified energy and commitment. He believed strongly in the value and importance of sociology. As he thundered against the fads and foibles, he nevertheless held the conviction that good sociology offered the way to a profound grasp of the basic realities of human life and the basic processes of social systems. Even if his books were filled with "coming crises," they were crises of Western civilization, or of "our age,"—not merely "crises" of sociology—and he remained completely convinced of the worth and lasting historical significance of sociological study and understanding.

Strongly present throughout Sorokin's many works, and frequently exhibited in his teaching, was the search for "integral," "multidimensional" conceptualizations or theories. The search for synthesis fed the search for encyclopedic knowledge; the vast assemblages of facts fed the search for pattern, integration, closure. These characteristics are salient in the earliest books (*System of Sociology, Hunger, Sociology of Revolution*) and continue to the last writings. The 1965 Presidential Address, indeed, closed on a note of reconciliation of "singularistic" and "systemic" sociology:

> In their sound parts the singularistic-atomistic theories of social, cultural, and personal congeries are reconcilable and complement the sound body of the systemic theories, for each class of these theories gives a real knowledge of singularistic and systemic forms of the total superorganic reality. . .
>
> Similar considerations apply to almost all the other differences among seemingly discordant theories. . . Almost all of them contain part of the truth. . . . and these sound parts can be, and will be increasingly, integrated into scientifically more adequate theories in the future sociology.
>
> . . . sociology will choose the road of creative growth and will eventually enter its new period of great syntheses. (1965, *30*, pp. 842-843)

Thus did the great controversialist, in his last official act as President, make his prophecy that there would be a future arrival in a better land, after the long sojourn in the sensate desert. Whatever the merits of the prophecy, we do know at least that Pitirim Alexandrovich Sorokin spent a long and intense life trying to make it come to pass.

REFERENCES

Bierstedt, R. "The Logico-Meaningful Method of P.A. Sorokin." *American Sociological Review,* 1937, *2*, 813–823.

Davis, A.K. "Lessons from Sorokin." In E.A. Tiryakian (ed.), *Sociological theory, values, and sociocultural change: Essays in honor of Pitirim A. Sorokin.* New York: The Free Press of Glencoe, 1963, 1-7.

Martindale, D. Book review. *Contemporary Sociology,* 1977, *6*, 353.

Scott, J.F. Book review. *American Sociological Review,* 1967, *32,* 683–684.

Sorokin, P.A. *Social mobility.* New York: Harper & Brothers, 1927.

Sorokin, P.A. "Rejoinder." American Sociological Review, 1937, *2,* 823–825.

Sorokin, P.A. *Social and cultural dynamics.* Four volumes. New York: American Book Company, 1937–1941.

Sorokin, P.A. *The crisis of our age.* New York: E.P. Dutton & Co., Inc., 1941.

Sorokin, P.A. "Sociology of Yesterday, Today and Tomorrow." *American Sociological Review,* 1965, *30,* 833–843.

Sorokin, P.A. *Sociological theories of today.* New York: Harper & Row, 1966.

Sorokin, P.A. *Hunger as a factor in human affairs,* E.P. Sorokin, Trans., T.L. Smith, (ed.) Gainesville, Fla.: The University Presses of Florida, 1977.

Tiryakian, E.A., (ed.) *Sociological theory, values, and sociocultural change: Essays in honor of Pitirim A. Sorokin.* New York: The Free Press of Glencoe, 1963.

Truzzi, M., (ed.) *Sociology: The classic statements.* New York: Random House, 1971.

Williams, R.M., Jr. Book review. *American Sociological Review,* 1964, *29,* 124–125.

Williams, R.M., Jr. *American society: A sociological interpretation.* New York: Alfred A. Knopf, 1970.

7

E. FRANKLIN FRAZIER
Race, Education, and Community

G. Franklin Edwards

I first came to know Edward Franklin Frazier in the mid-1930s when as a sophomore at Fisk University I enrolled in his course in "Introductory Sociology." The basic text was Park and Burgess, *An Introduction to the Science of Sociology* (1921), a volume little known to students today. Its organization consisted of long chapters of introductory statements by the authors which were followed by a series of excerpts from basic writings designed to illustrate the ideas being made. The Frazier style was to give the student the shock treatment to command his attention, for he wanted the student to understand that the objective of sociology was to provide a realistic analysis of the world about him. The lectures and discussions were rich in humor that helped provide insights into the subject matter. Frazier's handling of illustrative excerpts from many sources almost always resulted in one's reading the entire work from which they were taken. The basic approach was to teach "big ideas" which, once grasped, would help the student educate himself. I was privileged to take another of his courses, "The Family," before his departure for Howard University.

I was reunited with Frazier in 1941 when I joined the staff of the Department of Sociology at Howard, as an instructor. Over the course of the following two decades I came to know him as a mentor and as a warm friend, to share in his successes and frustrations. I and others were beneficiaries of his guidance that helped us to finish our formal studies and fulfill the qualifications for tenure.

The inclusion of Frazier among the eminent sociologists discussed in this volume must take account of the fact that his work setting differed importantly from those of the others under review. At no time during his tenure at Fisk and Howard was Frazier identified with a graduate program leading to the doctoral degree in which there were substantial numbers of colleagues and graduate students engaged in high-level research and the attendant interaction and exchange which characterize such programs. At Fisk University, where he became a research professor in 1939 and remained until he left for Howard five years later, a few selected departments offered the Master of Arts or Master of Science degree. Frazier, himself, taught few courses, usually no more than one a semester, and for the rest, engaged in research on the Negro family, this being an extension and enlargement of the work he had completed at the University of Chicago for the doctorate. He came to Howard as a faculty member several years after the Graduate School of Arts and Sciences was organized there. By the mid-thirties, nearly all of the departments, including sociology, were authorized to offer the Master's degree. Doctoral programs in the arts and sciences were not approved until the 1950s, and then on a selective basis, beginning first in the natural and biological sciences, and, much later, in the social sciences. The doctoral program in sociology was not authorized until 1974, twelve years after Frazier's death.

For most of Frazier's early years at Howard, until approximately the end of World War II, the major concern of the administration was to strengthen existing academic programs in the arts and sciences to assure their being validated by accrediting associations. Toward that end, the graduate program was continued on a modest scale, with attention being given principally to the recruitment of increasing numbers of highly competent faculty members to strengthen and enlarge the graduate faculty in general and to improve the quality of work in particular departments. During much of this period, the entire program of the University operated within an annual budget of about one million dollars. A disproportionate share of this sum was given to the professional schools of medicine and dentistry which, though costly to operate, the administration considered a fundamental part of its mission to train professional personnel for service to the Negro community.

This context makes it clear that in the case of Franklin Frazier and sociology at Howard, our purview must be broadened to consider more than his relationship to graduate students, of whom there were few, and his social science colleagues as they were influenced by and, in turn, influenced

Frazier's sociological views. It becomes necessary to consider as well Frazier's influence upon undergraduate students and upon the broader sociological community.

FAMILY CONTEXT AND SOCIOLOGICAL TRAINING

An account of Frazier's social origins and his academic and early professional experiences—what I regard as the most influential sources of his intellectual and sociological perspectives—is needed to understand the interface between Frazier's aspirations and viewpoints and the possibilities of the situation in which he found himself at Howard.

Franklin Frazier was born in Baltimore, Maryland, in 1894, the eldest of five children of James H. and Mary Clark Frazier. His father, who had moved from the Eastern Shore of Maryland to Baltimore, had no formal schooling but taught himself to read. In Baltimore he found employment as a bank messenger. Most of James Frazier's reading was centered on articles and books dealing with racial problems, this during a time of acute conflict in race relations. His position as bank messenger provided easy access to metropolitan dailies, particularly those of Baltimore and Atlanta. He read these materials not only for himself but after work hours he would read selected passages to his children and require them to discuss the substance of the readings with him. From the notebooks kept by this highly race-conscious father, it is clear that the topics of discussion included the achievement of Negroes and their leaders and instances of discrimination against Negroes and acts of violence visited upon them.

In addition to James Frazier's efforts to have his children gain a proper understanding of the racial situation as it affected Negroes, he would write letters to the editors of newspapers, on occasion with evident delight, to express viewpoints opposed to the newspapers' editorials. When the editor of an Atlanta newspaper railed against the alleged increase in sexual assaults of white women by Negro men, the elder Frazier wrote to ask whether the alleged increases were the result of heightened aggressiveness by Negro males or increased rates of seduction on the part of white females. His letter, which, strange to tell, the newspaper published, was signed: "White Lady." Frazier apparently took some pride in his self-determined activities for the clippings and letters were kept in notebooks, on the covers of which were inscribed: "From James H. Frazier to His Children."

It is quite clear that this profoundly socially aware father, who died when Franklin was eleven years old, was passionately concerned that his children have an understanding of the racial situation and that they be deeply motivated to secure an education. This, rather than money or real property, was the only heritage he could leave them. Following James Frazier's death, Franklin's mother, a shy woman, did all she could to support the family ideals. She worked as a domestic servant so that the children could continue in school. Two of Franklin's brothers became professional men—one a lawyer, the other a physician—and his sister became a wife and mother.

Frazier was regarded as an extremely bright student by his teachers, so that upon completion of his high school studies he was given the school's scholarship for study at Howard University. Several of his teachers were themselves graduates of Howard. His great aptitude for learning, his intellectual curiosity and his academic discipline were soon recognized as well by his college teachers and fellow students. His student peers nicknamed him "Plato."

At Howard he took the classical program and was influenced by well-trained, dedicated teachers, many of them representing a first generation of Negro college teachers. His curriculum included courses in both classical and modern languages, literature, mathematics and natural sciences, and some social science. From the social sciences, he selected courses in political science and history, although courses in sociology were available, having been introduced by Kelly Miller, an important teacher and administrator, as early as 1903. His interests in extracurricular activities included dramatic arts, debating, the political science club and, signifcantly enough, the Intercollegiate Socialist Society. He managed to engage in extensive curricular and extracurricular activities while doing menial work outside the University to supplement his scholarship funds. His robust physical energies and enthusiasm for study saw Frazier through the college course in the required four years and he was graduated *cum laude* in 1916.

After three years of work as an instructor in three high schools in southern and border communities, Frazier received a scholarship to Clark University where he studied sociology for a year and received the Master of Arts degree in 1920. His mentor there was Professor Frank Hankins whom he credited with having introduced him to the rich possibilities inherent in sociology for providing an objective analysis of social problems. It was Frazier's view that the year spent with Hankins at Clark marked the beginning of his work as a sociolgist. He continued to acknowledge this indebtedness to Hankins although he made it plain that he did not always agree with Hankins's views on race problems. Frazier's Master's thesis was entitled "New Currents of Thought Among the Colored People of America."

After a year of study under a Russell Sage Research Fellowship at the New York School of Social Work where he conducted a study of Negro longshoremen, Frazier went to Denmark as a fellow of the American-Scandinavian Foundation where he studied the Cooperative Movement. In

1922, he began his first teaching experience at the college level as Professor of Social Science at Morehouse College in Atlanta. Soon after his arrival there, he helped organize the Atlanta School of Social Work in response to community demand for an institution to train Negro social workers. He later added the duties of Director of the School to his work as Professor of Social Science.

In 1927, Frazier was forced to leave Atlanta as a result of white community reaction to his article on "The Pathology of Race Prejudice" which appeared that year in the June issue of *Forum*. His life was threatened and he had to be spirited out of Atlanta by friends. Later that fall, he began study under a fellowship grant at the University of Chicago and during the following two years served as a research fellow while working for the doctorate. He soon came under the influence of Professors Park, Burgess, Ogburn, Faris and Mead and, of prime importance, became associated with a lively group of young teachers and fellow students—Louis Wirth, Herbert Blumer, Everett Hughes, Edgar Thompson among them. His sociological views crystallized during the period of study at Chicago and even at that early stage of his lifework, there were elements of intellectual independence in those views. His doctoral dissertation on the Negro family in Chicago, published by the University of Chicago Press in 1932, made creative use of the ecological and case-study methods.

Frazier's demonstrated ability as a sociological researcher led to the Department at Chicago sponsoring his more comprehensive study of the Negro family under a subvention from the Social Science Research Council. He once told me that Professor Park informed him that he could remain at Chicago to do his work or he could make Fisk University his base of operation by joining its Division of Social Sciences, then headed by Charles S. Johnson, another student of Park. Frazier left Chicago for Fisk to be nearer the sources of his data in the South, where the Negro population was still concentrated. He remained at Fisk until 1934 when he became the Head of the Department of Sociology at Howard.

THE THEORETICAL AND RESEARCH ORIENTATION

Frazier was sanguine in his belief that at Howard he could join forces with both the established and the younger, promising scholars at that University to develop a significant program in the social sciences centered on the study of the Negro. He did not believe, however, that the Department of Sociology could, or should, become an important graduate center for sociological study. In his opinion, the University's resources, both material and human, were too limited to provide for the standard of excellence in graduate education at the doctoral level which he thought imperative. It could, however, provide sound training in sociology for undergraduates and a program at the Master's level for a selected number of students, some of whom would be encouraged to pursue the doctorate at universities with established departments. This expressed his conviction that graduate education, or any education for that matter which was provided to Negroes, should not be second-rate, a thesis he had eleaborated just a year before he began work at Howard in an article on "Graduate Education in Negro Colleges and Universities":

> Graduate education in Negro schools will further the educational segregation of the races and encourage a double standard of scholarship . . . . It cannot be denied that if graduate education in Negro schools were to become the means by which the majority of Negro students got advanced training, this development would lead to the creation of barriers on higher levels of intellectual culture. The intellectual culture which the Negro has made so far has depended upon his sucess in breaking down the isolation which his color has forced upon him. The opportunity to attend the best universities and colleges in the country has been the chief means by which the favored few have escaped from the intellectual thought of the masses. The best Negro colleges and universities are presided over by faculties composed of men who have the widest contacts. The most backward colleges are those administrated by teachers who have only partially escaped from the isolation of the masses. Therefore, any proposal to set up barriers on the very level where the Negro has been permitted to share in the intellectual heritage of the world should certainly be regarded with suspicion and invite opposition . . . .

Although he resisted a full-scale effort to develop graduate study, Frazier did envisage the prospect of a profitable cooperation with his new colleagues who were already at work on investigations of aspects of Negro life. Alain Locke, the first Negro Rhodes scholar, for example, was a senior professor at the University and served as chairman of the Department of Philosophy. He had edited *The New Negro* in 1925, a volume generally considered to be the single most important expression of the Negro Renaissance Movement of the 1920s. This was the volume to which Frazier contributed his first significant essay on the Negro middle class under the title: "Durham: Capital of the Black Middle Class." Locke was continuing his interest in the study of Negro life through editing and publishing a series of "Bronze Booklets" in the Humanities on Negro art, drama, music and fiction, and on such subjects as "A World View of Race," "Economic Reconstruction," and "The Negro in the Caribbean" in the social sciences. Most of these booklets were written by members of the Howard faculty.

In addition to Locke, Frazier's new colleagues included the economist Abram Harris, who in 1931 had published (with Sterling Spero) the celebrated volume entitled *The Black Worker: The Negro and the Labor Movement.* In the mid-thirties, Harris was bringing to completion a study of

Negro banking institutions, later published as *The Negro as Capitalist* (1936). Charles Wesley, the Harvard-trained historian, had written, even earlier, a volume entitled *Negro Labor in the United States* (1927).

By the late 1930s and early 1940s, the Howard circle had been enlarged to include Eric Williams, an Oxford-trained political scientist and now the Prime Minister of Trinidad-Tobago. He had published *The Negro in the Caribbean* (1942) and was later to publish *Capitalism and Slavery* (1944). In history, Rayford Logan was at work on trust territories and the diplomatic relationship between the United States and Haiti, and William Leo Hansberry was pursuing his studies of ancient African kingdoms. In sociology, Frazier was joined by W.O. Brown who had worked on race relations in South Africa and had developed an interest in Puerto Rico. Frazier himself had completed the field investigations for his larger family study which was published as *The Negro Family in the United States* (1939).

A Division of the Social Sciences was established as a part of the formal organization of the University and provided the vehicle for collaboration among the several departments of social science. The major functions of the Division were to offer an introductory survey course in the social sciences and to oversee an integrated divisional degree program at the Master's level. The Division began to sponsor annual conferences on topics in the social sciences which resulted in publications under such titles as *The Economic Future of the Caribbean; The Negro in the Americas; Trust and Non-Self-Governing Territories; The Integration of Negroes into American Society;* and the like. Several of these publications were edited by Frazier.

In addition to serving these formal, manifest functions, the Division brought together department heads such as Frazier, Harris, Locke and the political scientist, Ralph Bunche, to develop proposals designed to make Howard a center for the study of Negro life. Washington, Baltimore, and Richmond were to be the laboratories. At a time when large-scale funding was not yet available, these proposals were presented to the University administration in the hope that it would help get necessary research funds. But again the structural context was in the way. The administration was preoccupied with accreditation by regional rating bodies as its prime concern and it failed to grasp the significance of the proposals placed before it for developing the social sciences at Howard. The actual outcome fell far short of the plans and dreams of this small group of scholars.

Along with the organizational incapacity for launching such a program within the University were external, constraining forces. First were the Depression years which confronted Howard with serious financial problems as it did many other educational institutions. Nevertheless, the Myrdal study of the American Negro was launched in the 1930s and commanded the attention of the foundations and the social science community. Franklin Frazier and Ralph Bunche made prime contributions to the Myrdal volumes, perhaps at the temporary expense of advancing the Howard program. The onset of World War II led to a talent drain: Bunche left the University to work, first, under the Joint Chiefs of Staff and the Office of Strategic Services, then, as the first Negro to head a division in the State Department, and, by 1947, proved so effective as principal secretary of the United Nations Palestine Commission, as to receive the Nobel Peace Prize in 1950. Plainly, the nation's and the world's gain was Howard's loss. So, too, W.O. Brown, Frazier's colleague in sociology, left the Department in 1942 to work on the African desk at the State Department and did not return when the war ended. The talent drain continued in nongovernmental domains. The brilliant Abram Harris became disenchanted with studies of Negro life and began to devote more attention to institutional economics and to theoretical issues in the economics of social reform. In 1946, he left Howard to join the faculty of the University of Chicago where he remained until his death in 1964. Hylan Lewis, who had moved from economics to sociology and for whom Frazier and Harris had a deep affection, left the University to complete his doctoral studies and never returned to the Department.

I have dwelt at some length upon this critical period in the social sciences at Howard because it had a special meaning for Franklin Frazier as well as for the Department of Sociology. Undaunted by the failure to institute a major program of Negro studies and the disassembling of the considerable talent in the University which at one time offered such high promise, Frazier remained steadfast in the conviction that the scientific investigation of Negro life was the proper study of a department of sociology and of the social sciences in Negro institutions. Such studies should be carried forward within a framework of the broader society. He regarded as unfortunate the hiatus in the study of Negro life by Negro scholars at predominatly Negro institutions which existed since the DuBois studies at Atlanta University in the early 1900s. He saw his *Negro Family in the United States* as the first major study of the subject since the volume published by DuBois in 1908.

The study of the Negro community, Frazier held, would provide Negro colleges and universities with an institutional identity in much the same manner as the University of North Carolina was then becoming an important center for the study of the southern region through a focus on problems and prospects of that geographical and cultural area. Equally important for him was the concept that Negroes had a special advantage as "Insiders" to become engaged in such studies. His viewpoint on this matter was not parochial, as some blacks later came to formulate the "Insider" position, but accorded more with the formulation of Robert Merton on the rewards that come from the independent, sometimes competing views of "Insiders" and "Outsiders" with contributions to knowledge resulting from the interaction of divergent views. Frazier recognized the ideological distortions that might inhere in both positions, and held that true "social reality," one of his favorite terms, would emerge from the analysis furnished by the differing perspectives.

Frazier did not envisage a research focus on Negro life as unduly narrow. He would often point out that the presence of the Negro American had affected every period in the history of the United States and was the source of many of its major problems and successes. For him, to study the Negro community and its institutions was to study the American community and its institutions. He would insist upon a standard program in sociology for the training of students. In a letter to the Dean of the College shortly after he had assumed responsibility for the Department, he wrote:

> The work of the Department has continued to show advancement and improvement over that indicated four years ago. The courses in the Department are described as providing the student with a well-organized program covering the major fields in sociology. The work in the statistical laboratory has been particularly helpful in enabling students to make greater use of statistics in their studies. Several studies have been undertaken. . . . The Head of the Department has been the director of the Middle States Division of the Study of Minority Status on the Personality of the Negro for the American Youth Commission. The Department has continued to function effectively in community welfare and the conduct of community studies. (*Annual Report,* College of Liberal Arts, 1937–38)

An examination of the sociology curriculum finds that in 1934 Frazier introduced a course entitled "The Negro in America" which he regarded as important for the orientation of minority-group students—and for majority-group students as well. He taught the course every year, usually every semester. When he was not in residence, it was taught by another member of the staff. The scholarly significance of the course eventually reached far beyond the confines of Howard University. The course outline and notes provided the basis for Frazier's *The Negro in the United States* (1949), widely considered to be the most comprehensive one-volume treatment of American Negro-white relations. Its twenty-eight chapters are divided into five parts: "The Negro Under the Slave Regime," "Racial Conflict and New Forms of Accommodation," "The Negro Community and Its Institutions," "Intellectual Life and Leadership," and "Problems of Adjustment." The book presents Frazier's views on the subject of Negro-white relations from the first forced introduction of Negroes in the seventeenth century to an appraisal of the possibilities of the integration of Negroes into the society. Its framework shows an appreciation of the historical dimensions of the problem for, as Louis Wirth pointed out in his "Introduction," the book focussed on the analysis of social processes rather than social policies. The book also reflects Frazier's fundamental conception derived from his Chicago training—a conception not always endorsed by others—that the demographic and ecological bases provided a substructure which shapes in important ways institutions, associations, and other aspects of a people's social life. Sociological study is primarily concerned with the social aspects of a people's behavior and the process by which they come into existence and change. In this connection, we note that the section of Frazier's book which treats what are ordinarily categorized as social problems (Health and Survival, Unemployment and Poverty, Family Disorganization, Crime and Delinquency, etc.) is entitled "Problems of Adjustment," not "Social Problems."

Finally, this major book reflects all of the areas in which Frazier conducted his researches and to which he greatly contributed: The Negro Family, Free Negroes, Ecological Structure of the Negro Community, Social Stratification in the Negro Community, and Race Relations generally. This one book provides greater insights than any of Frazier's more specialized works into his sociological orientation and perspectives.

There was a basic consistency in Frazier's ideas about the proper subject-matter and method of sociological study. He rejected what he regarded as the atomistic conception which holds that society is based upon the similiarity of individual responses and attitudes. Inasmuch as social behavior involves meanings, the subjective aspect of human behavior cannot be ignored. It is vital to an understanding of consensus and social control which enable men to act collectively. As a result of collective living, institutions and other structured forms of associations emerge and these, in turn, determine the behavior of individuals. Opposed to the atomistic view, Frazier consistently adopted an organic conception.

As early as the late 1930s when he participated in the American Youth Commission studies of minority status and the personality of Negro youth—contributing the book *Negro Youth at the Crossways* (1940)—Frazier insisted that these studies should not be conducted in terms of conventional attitudinal research or by the emerging techniques of the survey. He maintained that a more meaningful approach to the problems addressed by the Commission would focus on the social world to which Negro youth were responding, together with their conceptions and interpretations of that world. Thus the volume for which he had responsibility, and which focussed on Negro youth in the border cities of Washington, D.C. and Louisville, Kentucky, was largely based on interviews with Negro youth and their parents, stratified according to social class, structured around certain themes which examined the influence of the basic institutions of the family, church, school, and neighborhood associations upon their lives. The study also examined their responses to questions dealing with employment prospects and to various ideologies and social movements.

The reliance upon the analysis of personal and other types of documents, as exemplified in his early family studies, provided Frazier with an understanding of social reality. For him, this approach was the best method for obtaining insight that made for understanding of human behavior. Whatever its limitations when applied to large bodies of complex data, it was the approach with which Frazier felt most comfortable. This does not mean that he failed to appreciate the significance of quantitative techniques, especially the more complex statistical approaches which were developing with advances in sampling theory and the analysis of variance, and the more sophisticated research technology of the 1940s. He regarded training in these statistical techniques as essential parts of the curriculum. The techniques to be employed in a particular study, however, should be related to the problems under investigation. For his particular work, he relied more heavily upon such approaches as a thematic analysis of literature and other documents for the insights they furnish into perceptions of issues and social change within the Negro community than upon the more quantitative data which could have been available to him. Sterling A. Brown, the distinguished Negro poet and Professor of American literature at Howard, noting Frazier's use of literary documents, referred to Frazier as his favorite "literary sociologist."

From 1951 to 1953, Frazier served in Paris as Director of the Division of Applied Social Science of UNESCO. One of his major responsibilities there was to oversee the Tensions and Social Change Project, designed to examine the interactions between people of different racial and cultural backgrounds and to assess the effects of such relationships upon the larger community. UNESCO had a concern focussed upon the changes posed by developing nations, both with regard to internal changes resulting in the crystallization of nationalistic sentiments and the establishment of relationships between these new nations with other established nations. The customary first step was an examination of existing knowledge bearing on the subject and inviting proposals for the commissioning of further studies. These exercises highlighted for Frazier the differences between his conceptualization of the problems and situations under examination and those employed by many other scholars. He came to the conclusion that previous scholarly discussion and action regarding the Tensions and Social Change Project had given evidence of a disproportionate influence of traditional psychology (A psychologist had previously been the Director of the Applied Social Science Division.) Frazier's concern about sharp differences between his views and those of many other social scientists led him to accept the invitation to give a series of lectures at the University of London in May, 1953. This provided him with a forum in which he could set forth his frame of reference for the study of social tensions and social change. A condensed version of these lectures was published under the title "Theoretical Structure of Sociology and

Sociological Research'' in the December, 1953, issue of The *British Journal of Sociology.*

Unlike the others permanently separated from Howard in the brain drain resulting from public service and recruitment by "white" universities, Frazier returned to Howard in the fall of 1953. He talked much about his UNESCO experiences and his continuing hope that the Department of Sociology would make a major theoretical contribution by presenting a framework for the study of race and cultural relations. This preoccupation, along with the opportunity provided by a Ford Foundation grant to set up an interdisciplinary program in African Studies in 1954, led to his beginning work on a manuscript which was published in 1957 under the title *Race and Culture Contacts in the Modern World.* Frazier regarded its conceptual framework as sociological, even though it relies on the contributions of such disciplines as human geography, anthropology, economics, and political science. The titles of the various parts of the volume suggest its theoretical orientation: "The Ecological Organization," "The Economic Organization," "The Political Organization," and "The Social Organization." Everett Hughes has noted that Frazier's framework is mainly borrowed from Robert E. Park. But he goes on to say that Park never took the time to systematize his ideas on this subject. Although much of the basic view is Park's, Hughes states, the book is Frazier's, a disciple who had gone the master one better. All those who know the two men will readily agree with Hughes's judgment, but it is also clear that Frazier's formulation places much more emphasis on political and, to some extent, economic factors in race and culture relations than did Park's.

The theoretical orientation set forth in the 1957 book was the final expression of a long development beginning with his early decision to become a sociologist during his days with Hankins at Clark and greatly influenced by his studies at Chicago. The orientation was also formulated in "Race Contacts and the Social Structure," his Presidential Address to the American Sociological Society (1948) and in some of his other writings. Since the Department of Sociology at Howard was primarily devoted to teaching rather than sustained empirical research, he could not easily put his formulation to empirical test. A rare opportunity was afforded by the study of "Segregation in Washington" sponsored by the National Committee on Segregation in the Nation's Capital. The Committee was composed of 92 distinguished Americans, representing almost every important area of American life—education, religion, law, communications, philanthrophy, government, social welfare, and public service. Frazier was a member of both the National Committee and the Research Committee of eight, five of them prominent sociologists with records of research in race relations.

The study, based in the quarters maintained by the Howard Department of Sociology, was conducted in 1946 and 1947. It undertook to examine every aspect of segregation of the races in Washington—patterns of community living and employment as well as the major institutional arrangements, including, in a most important way, the role of government. It was the Committee's purpose to bring the findings of its study of the problem, which it considered a national disgrace, to the attention of the American public in the hope that changes could be effected during the socially fluid times of the post-war period. Frazier, who had been an undergraduate student at Howard during the Woodrow Wilson years when the pattern of segregation in Washington became fixed, played a major role in shaping the research.

The study documented the history and institutionalization of segregation, and made an important contribution to our knowledge of the part played by organizational processes and bureaucratic structures in the development and maintenance of segregation. Comparison of a wartime agency having a large proportion of professional workers, such as the Office of Price Administration, with an old-line agency having a larger proportion of less skilled workers and well-established racial norms, such as the Bureau of the Census, suggested that observed racial patterns and attitudes were more closely related to the structured norms within an agency than to individual dispositions of its staff. A major determinant of the norms in an agency proved to be the role played by the agency head in interpreting personnel policies. The use of his discretionary powers and the manner in which he conducted himself became important because lesser functionaires and workers in general tended to conduct their behavior in accord with their perceptions of the behavior of top leadership.

Such findings may seem rather commonplace against the background of today's knowledge, but we must remember that serious research upon which such findings were based began only during the World War II years. The study sponsored by the National Committee on Segregation in the Nation's Capital afforded Frazier an opportunity to test his conception of the role of government in effecting racial changes. It was this type of study which Frazier thought the Howard Department of Sociology should be undertaking, but both manpower and funding were lacking.

In the quoted passage from Frazier's *Annual Report* to the Dean of the College, he stated "that the Department has continued to function effectively in the conduct of community welfare and community studies." He was referring to some of his own work and to his conception of the role of community participation in the training of students. Just as in Atlanta where he assisted in organizing the Atlanta School of Social Work in response to a felt community need for trained Negro social workers, he organized a program in social work at Howard shortly after he took up his duties there in sociology. The program was begun in response to community requests for the development of a training facility for Negro social workers. The program was accredited as a degree-granting curriculum in the early 1940s when the Howard University School of Social Work came into existence. Once the crucial accreditation was achieved, Frazier withdrew from systematic identification with the work of the School.

At the same time he had become involved with the program in social work, Frazier became a member of the local committee of the United Community Services instituted to work with the Bureau of the Census in the establishment of census tracts for the District. Not least among his local activities in this period, he became an organizing member of the District Sociological Society.

THE FRAZIER STYLE AND THE "HOWARD CIRCLE"

It was not always clear what Frazier considered the inevitable course that the Howard Department of Sociology might take if research programs he thought desirable were carried out. Although it is a matter of record that he thought it undesirable in his early years at Howard to develop an academic program leading to the doctorate in sociology, had his research program been instituted it would have inevitably attracted a number of highly trained sociologists and other social scientists to Howard. Social research on the scale he envisaged would also have required a good number of promising graduate students. While funding may have been a problem at first, the founding of the National Science Foundation in 1950 and the growing programs of social science support by the National Institute of Mental Health and other federal agencies after World War II suggest that funding would have become available had Frazier been willing to supply the leadership in applying for grants. The emergence of new private foundations, most particularly the huge Ford Foundation, and the readiness of older foundations to increase their support of social science research suggest that ample research funding would have been available to a sociologist of Franklin Frazier's accomplishments and standing.

But the fact is, as the record of his scholarly career shows, Frazier was most effective as a solitary researcher. His long list of publications shows that he co-authored only a single article and co-edited only a single monograph. While he contributed articles and chapters to a substantial number of publications edited by others, and doubtless made important suggestions for the development of such works, the limits of his responsibilities were usually well-defined and his role individualistic. He intensely disliked managerial and administrative duties and was disposed to execute them as quickly as he could. When the Department of Sociology began to expand after World War II, the day-to-day operations were turned over to a younger colleague, Harry J. Walker. Although the African Studies Program was not started until 1954, Frazier relinquished primary responsibility for the development of the program to another colleague, the anthropologist Mark Hanna Watkins, well in advance of his retirement in 1959, while continuing to teach his popular course on "The Impact of Western Civilization upon Africa" and to offer a seminar on Africa.

Nothing is more revealing of Frazier's dislike for administration than his distaste for the process of recruiting personnel and for the internal bargaining and competition for staff which typically occur among related departments in educational institutions. The absence of a vigorous recruitment policy in sociology kept the size of the staff small and led to the appointment of some staff members who could not do their job adequately. These colleagues presented real problems. But through it all, Frazier maintained good collegial relationships, if not warm fellowship, with most members of the Department.

For all of his seeming gregariousness, there was about Franklin Frazier a great reserve and sense of privacy—almost of loneliness. He once told me that he considered it one of his shortcomings that he had few confidants. In the long history of our association, he was not disposed to talk about his personal or familial history or even about many of the difficult situations he encountered in the South which would have discouraged less tough-minded persons. Withal, he was always a witty and, with full respect for others, a lively conversationalist, whose classroom teaching was studded with humorous illustrations of the fundamental points he would make. In his class on "The Family," for example, after talking at length about the family as a pivotal institution in all societies, he delighted in regaling young students about the romantic impulse which influences the family in the Western World. This led to a discussion of the family, after the fashion so familiar at the University of Chicago, as a "unity of interacting personalities." In the midst of his discussion he would assert that family members, especially the spouses, were well aware of this sense of oneness. He would then march to the blackboard with chalk in hand and, taking the role of Mrs. X addressing her spouse, he would state: "Honey, we are as one, and I can prove it." Whereupon he would write on the blackboard $1 + 0 = 1$ and, he would announce: "and I am the *one*." This established the unity. The not-so-subtle point was made and not likely to be forgotten.

Students enjoyed Frazier's courses and found them rewarding. Even with the lively sense of realism which characterized his pedagogical style, and his apparent warmth, few students came to know him as a person for, as I have said, he was deeply reserved and reticent about himself. Among the few who came to know him well were some students from other disciplines who were taking one of his favorite courses, either the "Negro in America" or the "Impact of Western Civilization upon Africa." Some of them remained in touch with Frazier as they completed their work at Howard and went on to distinguished careers in History, Medicine or other disciplines. In the case of the few students in the Department of Sociology who came to know him well, Frazier would spend a great deal of time talking with them and, in a most effective way, teaching them. He took their concerns seriously and, together with deliberately helping to shape their career goals, he often used his influence to help them get the training needed to enter upon their careers. A sensitive appreciation of Frazier as a teacher and as a man is given in the following passages by a former graduate student who took the Master's degree with him, and then went on to the doctorate at another institution:

> I knew Professor Frazier as a student and as an assistant. This may have given me an opportunity to know him somewhat better than the student who took only one course from him. In explaining why his students liked him so much one cannot speak in traditional Mr. Chips terms. We do not revere Professor Frazier because he was a doddering, outspoken, kindly gentleman who led up to learning with a gentle hand. Professor Frazier was an irascible man, and a brilliant and demanding teacher. He growled and roared. All questions were not answered in polite dulcet tones. One time I asked him: "Why *are* you so irascible?" He did not deny that he was, and answered: "Why, if I had been born white like you I would have a perfectly lovely disposition."

> But he was not always irascible. On one especially busy day a student came into his office with a racial theory that would have enraged Professor Frazier had it come from a professional scholar. But because he was a student, Professor Frazier spent two hours discussing the subject with him and in effect teaching him. He was as calm and softspoken as I have ever heard him.

> Professor Frazier was convinced that "ignorance is the worst thing that is. It is worse than poverty!" The purpose of a university is to do just one thing, to dispel ignorance. A university is not supposed to be "building moral character," it ought to make students skeptical and critical, which is what, he thought, being an intellectual meant. He exhorted us not to "be good," but to "be good for something."

> He gave the best of himself and literally the last of himself, to the students of "The Negro in the United States." He died getting ready to come to that class. The students loved Professor Frazier because he told the truth and for his warmth, his wonderful personality, his scholarly work, his brilliance, wit, compassion, and his courage in fighting for the excellent things that life holds out to

people. But the heart of the attraction was his respect and profound understanding of what a teacher was and could be. It simply came down to this: he valued the student.

There is an abundance of evidence that Frazier's reserve did not permit him to appreciate fully the esteem in which he was held by students. He was already critically ill when the Student Council, an undergraduate body, proposed a lecture series in his honor for which it sought his consent and cooperation. The series was held in the Spring of 1962, with Everett Hughes delivering three lectures on "Social Institutions." The Council's program contained the following tribute:

> For more than twenty-five years you have served as Professor and Head of the Department of Sociology at Howard University. During those years of relentless and unselfish pursuit of truth, you wrought authoritative, highly esteemed works on the Negro in the United States.

> In addition to serving society as a scholar, you have labored as a teacher, inspiring generations of students who were privileged to begin their study of society under your guidance. The Student Council of the College of Liberal Arts gratefully acknowledges the debt owed to you by sociology generally, and by Howard Unversity specifically.

Frazier's interaction with his colleagues in the social sciences was selective. He did not share experiences with a wide range of faculty members but did enjoy a small group of associates in the social sciences who called themselves "The Thinkers and Drinkers." The group of about eight members met in the homes of its members on a periodic and rotating basis, usually on a week-end evening. The gatherings were altogether informal; there was nothing like a set agenda. The group discussed a wide range of subjects, much of it focussed on the nature of changing social conditions in the United States and the world at large. Race relations, of course, received much attention, as did life at Howard University. Heated debates were frequent, easily sustained by this cohesive small group.

Frazier was often at his best in this type of setting. His broad knowledge and adversarial skill made him a dominant figure in the group which contained such knowledgeable colleagues of the first class as the distinguished litterateur Sterling Brown and, at one period, John Hope Franklin, the historian who went on to become John Manley Distinguished Service Professor at the Unversity of Chicago and President of the American Historical Association. Despite the consensus which inheres in such a self-selected group, there were differences of viewpoints, largely growing out of differences in personal history and training. As I have said, the strong-minded members of the group felt comfortable with one another and did not hesitate to express those differences.

These sessions provided much mutual knowledge to the members of the group. In Frazier's case, it became evident to the others that his fondness and admiration for Park were based not only upon wide areas of agreement regarding human and race relations, but upon broad areas of disagreement as well over such formulations as Park's theory of the race relations cycle and his early notion of racial temperament. Both Park and Frazier welcomed frank exchanges, and Park would visit Frazier in order to have conversations with him on controversial matters. It was the mutual respect of these men, rather than a relationship of dominance and subordination, as some Frazier critics would have us believe, which served as the fundamental linkage between the two.

One learned also from "The Thinkers and Drinkers" about the bases of Frazier's deep respect for W.E.B. DuBois and Paul Robeson. Both of these men were eminent scholars and achievers with whom Frazer as an intellectual himself could readily identify. But his admiration was based as much on his perceiving them as tough-minded personalities who dared to defy the racial system which oppressed them.

The admiration of Frazier for the behavior of DuBois and Robeson was in sharp contrast to his contempt for Negroes who permitted themselves to be voluntarily segregated. When Negroes, excluded from March of Dimes balls held in downtown hotels in the District of Columbia, took part in a ball held in an uptown arena from which the circus had only recently departed, Frazier found their behavior demeaning and totally devoid of self-respect. When some of those attending the segregated ball later entered a public protest because of conditions at the arena, particularly the stench left by the circus animals, Frazier wrote a letter to the newspaper in which the protest appeared. He reminded the protesters that they had no valid cause for complaint since they had sanctioned the self-segregation by attending the ball held in the "Cabin" when they could not participate in the ball held in the "Big House."

"The Thinkers and Drinkers" represented as intimate an association as Frazier had at the University and in the Washington community. The respect the members had for Frazier finds expression in a statement by one of its members:

> As a student and colleague Frazier brought great distinction to our university. When he was elected as honorary member of our chapter of Phi Beta Kappa his address was on the topic, "The Scholar's Responsibilites and His Failures." He talked honestly on this subject as of course we expected, he could not do otherwise. He hewed to the line; he let the chips fall where they would. He wanted to be objective; he was never a racial chauvinist, never a professional race man; but his concern for his people was strong and abiding and his race pride was real.

One of his major concerns was the duty of the intellectual to lead in the struggle for human betterment. As strange as it may sound, there was a reformer in Frazier, the sociologist. Combined with his scholarly approach was a strong satirical bent. In his early years, the influence of men like Bernard Shaw, Thorstein Veblen, H. L. Mencken and Sinclair Lewis was powerful. In his most controversial book, *Black Bourgeoisie,* Frazier exerted the satirist's license. But the essential reality, he always insisted, was grounded upon careful observation and thinking.

To some, Frazier was noted for brusqueness, even for acerbity. I believe that this aspect is far from the complete man and, taken alone, is misleading. It is true that he did not suffer fools gladly. In the give and take of intellectual battle he might deliver sharp blows, but he expected them in return and could take them. Some, blessed with his friendship, knew that Frazier could be a *bon vivant,* that he loved company, good people, good food, and he even sought the truths and oracles that inhered in the grape and the grain. But after the conviviality he could settle down to the task at hand, supported by his great resources of body and will as well as of mind.

As one might expect, the autonomous, intellectual Frazier had a healthy disrespect for the promises of administrators of Negro educational institutions. He regarded them as authoritarian, and possessed of competitive attitudes toward their faculty members. He had had an unhappy experience in Atlanta in 1927, having received no support at all from the administration when he had to leave Morehouse College after publication of "The Pathology of Race Prejudice." Those in authority went so far as to try to discourage him from continuing as an academician. He regarded the general climate of Negro educational institutions as anti-intellectual, this being reinforced by their presidents and boards of trustees.

Frazier's jaundiced view of the organizational and intellectual climate of Negro institutions crystallized as a result of varied educational experiences. He began work as a teacher at Tuskegee Institute the year after the death of Booker T. Washington; at Tuskegee, vocational education was dominant. His early life paralleled the emergence of segregated public higher education following the passage of the second Morrill Act in 1890. These early Negro land-grant colleges were led by a group of educators who, in Frazier's views, were essentially plenipotentiaries serving as the sole mediators between white legislatures and the colleges for which they had responsibilty. Frazier was highly critical also of the role of private foundations which he thought sponsored double standards in education. He came to the opinion that segregated education was particularly harmful to the Negro's cause because it placed primary reponsibility for values in the hands of a few, not always the right persons, and sanctioned a double set of values. He refused to accept this schizoid division of standards and consequently gave strong support to desegregation in education.

Academics in American society are often not accorded high prestige. Negro academics and intellectuals are often accorded an even lower rank than academics generally. The conditions under which they work are often stressful. As an academic and intellectual, Frazier experienced unusual stresses, but, to my knowledge, he never considered another type of career. He was a particulary tough-minded individual whose metier was the academic profession. His tough-mindedness and perserverance expressed for his associates what the intellectual life demanded in terms of discipline and style of work. A Frazier admirer, a younger colleague of another period, refers to him as a gladiator—a true warrior—who battled relentlessly for an opportunity to develop the ideas he believed in and for an opportunity to improve his craft. The barriers he faced included the threat of physical violence in southern communities and the narrow intolerances and orthodoxies within the academy which cast him in the image of an improper Negro.

Frazier's tough-mindedness was also expressed in his reaction to ingroup criticisms of his *Black Bourgeoisie.* Critics of his evaluation of behavior found in the new Negro middle class, with its rapid upward mobility and its disposition to place greater emphasis on "status" rather than "substance," failed to understand that his primary concern was to point to this behavior as one consequence of the escalation characterizing Negro life. For those who regarded his analysis as brutal or inhuman, he would quote from a review in a Catholic journal: "A sad truth is better than a merry lie."

Although Frazier was unhappy over his failure to develop the type of organization he regarded as necessary for improving the corpus of our knowledge of Negro life and for the training of sociologists, he experienced some small satisfaction in being able to define the nature of the Negro problem in this country and, as teacher and researcher, to contribute to its understanding. At no time did he regard himself as a primary agent of social change.

Little has been said here about Frazier's community experiences other than in relation to his work as a teacher and to the shaping of his professional beliefs and career. But it must now be said that Frazier believed deeply in the values of the professional associations to which he belonged and which, often enough, did him honor. Not least, he valued the work of the Eastern Sociological Society and the fellowship it afforded. The Society, in its turn, expressed its regard for E. Franklin Frazier, as scholar and colleague, by electing him President for two terms and bestowing upon him its first MacIver Award.

REFERENCES

Frazier, E. F. *The Negro family in Chicago.* Chicago: The University of Chicago Press, 1932.

Frazier, E. F. *The Negro family in the United States.* Chicago: The University of Chicago Press, 1939.

Frazier, E. F. *The Negro in the United States.* New York: Macmillan Company, 1949, rev. ed., 1957.

Frazier, E. F. *Race and cultural contacts in the modern world.* New York: A.A. Knopf, 1957.

Frazier, E. F. *Bourgeoisie noire.* Plon: Paris, 1955. American education published as *Black bourgeoisie.* New York: Macmillan Company, 1957.

Frazier, E. F. *Negro youth at the crossways.* Washington: American Council on Education, 1940.

Frazier, E. F. *The economic future of the Caribbean: Seventh annual conference of the division of the social sciences.* E. Williams and E. F. Frazier (eds.). Washington: The Howard University Press, 1944.

Frazier, E. F. Durham: Capital of the Black Middle Class. In *The new Negro.* A. Locke (ed.). New York: A. and C. Boni Co., 1925, 333-340.

Frazier, E. F. "The Pathology of Race Prejudice." *Forum,* 1927, *70,* 856-862.

Frazier, E. F. "Graduate Education in Negro Colleges and Universities." *The Journal of Negro Education,* 1933, *2,* 329–341.

Frazier, E. F. "Race Contacts and the Social Structure." *The American Sociological Review,* 1949, *14,* 1-11.

Segregation in Washington: A Report of the National Committee on Segregation in the Nation's Capital. (Chicago: 1948)

8

SAMUEL A. STOUFFER
Social Research as a Calling

Jackson Toby

In the first days of August 1960, Sam Stouffer was in New York, planning an international study of the obstacles to reducing fertility rates, sponsored by the Population Council. He felt that this was another opportunity for social research to show what it could do: in this case to contribute to the solution of one of the world's most serious problems. On August 24th he died of cancer. The disease was so far advanced by the time it was diagnosed that no treatment was possible. He was hard at work until the week before his death.

Earlier that same year, Stouffer assembled a selection of his papers for publication, not realizing they were to be his final statement to the profession. He chose an appropriate title, *Social Research to Test Ideas,* and he carefully selected a favorite Shakespearian quotation to open the book that would draw attention to the value of skepticism:

> Glendower: I can call spirits from the vasty deep.
>
> Hotspur: Why, so can I, or so can any man; But will they come when you do call for them?
>
> —King Henry IV, first part, Act III, Scene 1.

Social Research to Test Ideas was an appropriate title because Stouffer was not interested in research to learn about trivia; he always insisted that the payoff of data collection was the opportunity to understand what was going on. That is to say, he was interested in theory. Here is how he put it in his Preface:

> The press of a button, drunkenly or soberly, can destroy life on earth. But, if

131

vouchsafed continuity, the human spirit has, thanks in part to modern science and technology, seemingly illimitable possibilities for understanding and mastery.

For the better understanding of man's relations to man, we have had for centuries the records of history and the insights of philosophers and poets. For only a few decades have we attempted also to study society with the theoretical and empirical tools of science and the results are small and tentative, when compared with the accumulated wisdom of the ages.

Too much has been promised, too fast, by some social scientists, especially by those unchastened by the arduous, meticulous, and often unrewarding labor of empirical testing of ideas. Overexuberance generates a predictable reaction, which is probably wholesome even when the reaction extends to sharp attacks on the basic strategy of studying man with the tools of science.

The most effective response to critical essays will not be more and better critical essays. Rather, it will be demonstration, by patient example, of what social science can do. (Stouffer, 1962, p. xiii)

Sam Stouffer's prose style reflects a little of his commitment to and enthusiasm for social science. His personal style, however, was less imposing—he was slightly below average height, wore steel-rimmed glasses, and sported a vestigial moustache. When he wasn't smiling, there was nearly always a cigarette dangling from his lips. It provided chronic suspense because Stouffer did not use ash trays. Students and colleagues would watch the ash grow longer and longer as he talked excitedly about a research problem until at last it fell. If he noticed the ash on his dark suit, he would brush at it ineffectually, enough to produce a light smudge. At the beginning of the day, when Stouffer strode into his office and flung off his coat and battered hat, he looked quite dapper; by nightfall his suit would be covered with smudges from the volcanic ash rained down upon it.

I often wondered whether the elegant Ruth Stouffer chided her husband for sloppiness. I guessed that, after more than twenty years of marriage, she did not. As far as I knew, she raised no objections either to the long hours that he put in at his office, or, more usually, in the "machine room"—the "machine" being an IBM counter–sorter. Stouffer frequently grew so absorbed as he ran cards through the sorter and calculated percentages on his slide rule that he would fail to start home for dinner on time. When he realized how late it had gotten, he would hastily dash to his office, throw on his hat and coat, and rush grimly down the wide stairs of Emerson Hall, stairs that had been trodden in previous generations by William James. On occasions, ten minutes after his frantic departure, Ruth Stouffer would appear at the door of the machine room and ask, disconsolately, "Is Mr. Stouffer here?" He had forgotten that they had arranged to meet at the office and go together to some engagement. I felt vaguely guilty as I confirmed what she must have already suspected.

In a curious way Sam's sloppiness and tardiness enhanced his attractiveness. They obviously sprang from an enthusiasm for social research that enabled him to blot out distractions. This blotting out of mundane distractions had its disadvantages, too. To be a passenger in a car he was driving while concentrating on a research problem was perilous. For example, during a trip between Emerson Hall and his home we discussed relationships in some role-conflict data tabulated that afternoon. This was thirty years ago; neither of us was wearing seat belts. Sam would refer to the tables as he drove the familiar route, sometimes studying the data for several seconds as we sped along. He would look up just in time to see the car in front of him or a traffic light and would jam on the brakes. We made it from Cambridge to Belmont. But Sam was wholly unaware of the dangers we had escaped.

Robin Williams (1979) had similar experiences with Stouffer, which he interprets as follows:

> Sam was a person of amazing energy. My image of him is one of ceaseless motion and intense mobilization. When he walked, his pace was what to most people would have been running. He chainsmoked—dropping ashes heedlessly. His mind seemed always to be racing beyond what could be said or done in any given period of time. . . . He was wholly committed to the task. If one thing didn't work, he would try another and another and another. It follows that he was ingenious and inventive. He was an entrepreneur of legendary alertness and adaptability—always under the flag of social science.

STOUFFER AT HARVARD

Sam Stouffer spent the last fourteen years of his life (1946–1960) as Professor of Sociology and Director of the Laboratory of Social Relations at Harvard. I knew him fairly well between 1946 and 1951, first as one of a group of graduate students in his seminars, then as his teaching assistant in statistics, his research assistant, and finally as a junior colleague on a research project dealing with conflicting social norms. He was more than a teacher to me; he was a role model. I imitated him as best I could in small matters as well as large; I found myself putting my feet up on my desk as he did when having a relaxed conversation. I am tempted, therefore, to portray him as a charismatic figure who exercised a distinct influence on Harvard graduate students at that period of time. In retrospect, however, I think Sam's influence on students, though great, was inextricably bound with the influence of his friend and colleague, Talcott Parsons. Stouffer as Director of the Laboratory of Social Relations and Parsons as Chairman of the Department of Social Relations formed a leadership team. And, although there were outstanding individuals on the faculty—Gordon Allport, Clyde and Florence Kluckhohn, Henry Murray, Jerome Bruner, Alex Inkeles, George Homans, Frederick Mosteller, Richard Solomon, Leland DeVinney,

Henry Riecken, Brewster Smith—it was the joint influence of Stouffer and Parsons on colleagues as well as students that gave the Social Relations Department its distinctive character.

How did it happen that the ebullient Sam Stouffer, skilled at organizing huge empirical research projects, should hit it off so well with a sociological theorist whose style of work required only a quiet room and a typewriter? Stouffer and Parsons had known each other only casually before Stouffer was invited to join the Harvard faculty. (The decision to make this offer was by an *ad hoc* committee that included prominent sociologists who were *not* members of the Harvard faculty.) Few persons could have anticipated in 1946 that Stouffer and Parsons would become close personal friends and would develop a theoretical-empirical orientation that was able to unify an exciting multidisciplinary department for more than a decade. In my opinion, a major ingredient of their joint stewardship of the Department of Social Relations was a common commitment to social science, a faith that both theory and empirical investigation were necessary for scientific progress and a willingness to work incredibly hard to bring this progress into being. Stouffer and Parsons were not merely sociologists by profession; they felt *called* to be sociologists in the religious sense (emphasized by Weber) of feeling called to work in the secular world. This common conception of the sociological enterprise enabled them to bridge temperamental and stylistic differences. They respected each other enormously.

Mutual respect helps to explain why, when Parsons completed the manuscript of *The Social System,* he asked Stouffer to read it before sending it off to the publisher. Despite his busy schedule, Sam read the manuscript through. He considered *The Social System* a major accomplishment, but he hoped that it would receive some months of editorial polishing. Sam had edited his father's newspaper in Sac City, Iowa, from 1923 to 1926, and before that he had taken a Master's degree in English at Harvard. He always took a keen interest in maximizing clarity of expression. He was sorry that Talcott was too impatient to get his thinking before the profession to postpone publication.

Stouffer's impact on Harvard went beyond the Department of Social Relations. President Conant and Provost Paul Buck consulted him frequently about appointments and policy decisions. For example, when Francis Keppel was appointed Dean of the School of Education in 1948, Stouffer had been at Harvard for only two years. Nevertheless, he had been influential enough for Keppel (1979) to write ". . . I have always suspected that Sam had something to do with my appointment as Dean in 1948." Somehow, Stouffer's small-town Iowa background did not prevent him from gaining powerful admirers in sophisticated Cambridge.

At the memorial service for Stouffer on October 25, 1960, Paul Buck re-called the close relationship between James Conant and Stouffer in the fol-lowing anecdote:

> On election night 1948, Conant and I heard the returns together. When the result became known, Conant (who incidentally was a warm admirer of Sam) turned to me and said, "When you see Sam tomorrow tell him not to be dis-couraged. We too in Chemistry have explosions in our laboratory. They are most embarrassing but they don't end Chemistry."

Of all the people who suffered that night, Thomas Dewey, who lost the election to Harry Truman, George Gallup, who suffered publicly on na-tional television as the returns made a shambles of his confident prediction of a Dewey victory, and others like Elmo Roper, who were almost as embar-rassed, it was Stouffer's possible discomfiture from his identification with social research that evoked Conant's expression of sympathy. And Sam had not made *any* election predictions!

STOUFFER AS TEACHER

Sam Stouffer communicated in his teaching the same enthusiasm for research to test ideas that he expressed in his busy round of daily activities. Students responded. Undergraduate and graduate students alike found him interesting, stimulating, even exciting. He worked hard at teaching as he did at everything. Before going to class, he would sit nervously in his office for twenty minutes to a half hour writing and rewriting the outline of his re-marks. When he delivered the lecture, it flowed smoothly, effortlessly, and it would probably have surprised his listeners to know that he had prepared for that lecture as though he had never given a lecture before. Once, when he seemed particularly overwrought over an undergraduate class he was to meet in about five minutes, I expressed puzzlement that such an experienced (and successful) teacher was so concerned about an upcoming class. "Look," he said, "there are two hundred students in that class. If I give a poor lecture, I will have wasted two hundred hours of people's time. That's a responsibil-ity." I hadn't thought of it that way before, although I did from then on. He prepared new lectures, not because he couldn't locate his old lecture notes, but because he felt that he owed it to his listeners to provide his freshest and best thoughts on the topic at hand.

Stouffer's good friend and colleague from the University of Chicago, Philip Hauser, remembers Stouffer's teaching as follows:

> As a lecturer, Sam was one of the most stimulating and disheveled professors that ever existed. His substantive work at the blackboard was always first-rate

but the perpetual cigarette in his mouth made it difficult often to distinguish between what part of his jacket and vest were the dripping ashes and what part was the chalk dust. Both were evident and profuse. (Hauser, 1979)

Good as Stouffer was as a lecturer, his best teaching took place in seminars, particularly the seminars he conducted with Talcott Parsons. The 1948–49 seminar on social mobility was co-directed by Stouffer, Parsons, and Florence Kluckhohn, and illustrated Stouffer's approach to graduate teaching. Sam wanted to give graduate students the opportunity to see senior professors at work, thinking about a problem, analyzing data, making mistakes, arguing among themselves. He spoke of "conducting my education in public." And so the three faculty members, along with the fifteen to twenty graduate students enrolled in the seminar, launched an empirical study of intergenerational mobility in the Boston metropolitan area as reflected in the educational plans of students in ten public high schools. Questionnaires were constructed and administered; selected students and their parents were interviewed intensively; data were coded, punched on IBM cards, and tabulated. Theoretical papers were written—by Talcott Parsons as well as student members of the seminar—trying to describe the social processes that were occurring. Presentations of data analyses were made—some by Stouffer and others by his colleagues and students—testing the fruitfulness of these theoretical models.

Few publications resulted directly from the Harvard mobility project and, to the best of my recollection, only a couple of Ph.D. dissertations. However, the continuing seminar on social mobility gave succeeding cohorts of Harvard graduate students inside views of their professors at work. Students who saw themselves as "theorists" conducted live interviews and "got their hands dirty" (in Sam's words) from moving a couple of thousand punch cards through the counter–sorter. I have in my mind's eye the image of Talcott himself interviewing a suburban schoolboy—and failing to achieve the richness of Florence Kluckhohn's interview protocol; she used no tape recorder but seemed to have total recall. Even if Talcott did not actually conduct interviews—my memory may be playing tricks—he certainly treated empirical data with the greatest attention and respect. Students could not fail to get the message. Theory and research are both necessary for sociological contributions.

Correlatively, students whose initial orientation was empirical learned in the seminar to appreciate the value of theory. During one session Sam would present the painstaking analysis of how primary- and junior-high school marks provided clues "as to when those who are not college oriented fell off the ladder" (Stouffer, 1962 p. 230). The next week Talcott would arrive bearing copies of a 63-page dittoed memorandum with some such title as "Theoretical Problems in the Study of Social Mobility." Sam would listen attentively, puffing on the inevitable cigarette, feet up on the seminar table, as Talcott developed his analysis. Talcott's presentation would be directed toward the data; he sought to provide plausible theoretical explanations for what Sam was finding as well as to generate further predictions. For example, Stouffer noted a suggestion in the data that boys whose mothers had more education than their fathers were especially likely to aspire to higher education. He and Talcott had discussed this finding during a weekend at the Parsons' New Hampshire farm over one or more glasses of apple wine. Talcott's memorandum for the seminar the following week set forth what he called "the apple-wine hypothesis," namely, that women disappointed in their husbands' accomplishments were especially apt to redirect their frustrations over this by encouraging educational and occupational accomplishment on the part of their sons.

Stouffer taught many things in that seminar that went beyond the topic of social mobility. He suggested by his example that research findings do not leap out of the data if the researcher is brilliant enough, that they emerge at the end of a long process that includes much drudgery.[1] Furthermore, he showed a willingness to assume a good part of that drudgery himself. Although he had research assistants—I was myself his research assistant for a time—he treated them as colleagues and worked alongside them. He did not sit in his office waiting for machine runs to be brought to him. Perhaps he found it embarrassing to order assistants to do this and get that. He sought to avoid even the possibility of exploitation in his relationship with graduate students. (He shared credit generously when it came time to publish the results of research.) But there was another reason he did his own tabulations of data: his impatient temperament. In his eagerness to see results quickly, he frequently didn't want to wait for someone else to find out within a few hours what the data showed when he could find out RIGHT AWAY. According to M. Brewster Smith, who worked with Sam in the Research Branch of the War Department in World War II and then became one of Stouffer's colleagues in the newly formed Department of Social Relations at Harvard, the advent of computers led to his nonhierarchical style of research becoming less feasible.

> His personal style of research fitted the stage of precomputer technology, when the investigator, running his sets of data cards through the counter–sorter himself, could quickly adapt his tactics of analysis to the emerging results. Stouffer's career ended just as the requirements of modern electronic computers were tending to impose a greater separation between the investigator and his data. (Smith, 1968 p. 278)

[1]Merton (1957, pp. 103-108) introduced the term "serendipity"—coined by Horace Walpole in 1754—into social science as a way of referring to an adventitious aspect of research findings.

Howard Schuman, a distinguished University of Michigan researcher, disagrees.

> Although the early development of the computer separated social scientists from their data, use of interactive programs on terminals has returned us to where we were in the 1950s but with enormously increased powers to recode and calculate. Stouffer would have been quite at home in today's terminal room! (Schuman, 1979).

Stouffer might well have led the way in adapting computer technology not only to a democratic style of leadership but to the subordination of computers to the intellectual requirements of the research problem.

Certainly, Stouffer's ingenuity should not be underestimated. When Stouffer was President of the American Sociological Society in 1952–1953,[2] and concerned that young sociologists did not find it easy to get to the annual meetings of the Society, he arranged that the annual program consist *entirely* of contributed papers. His purpose in doing so was not dissatisfaction with previous programs. It was to enable more sociologists, especially younger sociologists not likely to be *invited* to participate in the program, to give a paper and thereby to increase their likelihood of having travel expenses to the meeting paid by their employers. From then on, contributed papers were always included at annual meetings. In addition, the total number of papers increased enormously, thereby broadening participation further.

STOUFFER THE APPLIED SOCIOLOGIST

Because Sam Stouffer had enormous faith in the potential importance of sociology, in its ultimate capacity to help transform the world, he was glad to put sociological ideas and research techniques to work in practical applications. But he was under no illusions that either our theories or our methods were very useful *yet*. He was on the side of those who tried to improve and to fine-tune measurement techniques so that theories could be tested more adequately.

> Just as research in medicine has depended on the invention of instruments like the thermometer and microscope, so the new social research depends and will increasingly depend on what some people deprecatingly call gadgets. A questionnaire or an attitude test is such a gadget (Stouffer, 1962, p. 7).

---

[2]Stouffer's name was originally Andrew Samuel Stouffer. His parents did not foresee that his initials, A.S.S., might lead to ridicule. The same unfortunate initials, A.S.S., characterized the American Sociological Society. Sam Stouffer campaigned (eventually with success) for the change to "American Sociological Association."

However, he did not think that society could be expected to share his vision of the potentialities of sociology; sociologists could not reasonably expect to be given two hundred years of financial support while developing their theories and methods, on the assumption that *then* the profession would be ready to make big contributions. He had other reasons for being interested in applied sociology, but in my opinion his main reason was his feeling that sociology had to pay its way currently.

> . . . I do not think it is either necessary, desirable, or indeed possible for us to take an extreme position of withdrawal from practical application. There are three reasons. One, we are citizens as well as social scientists, and we have an inescapable obligation to society in our citizenship role. Second, financial support of long-term research will not be forthcoming unless what might be called the engineering applications of that research can be shown to have manipulable consequences. Third, efforts to deal with practical problems can sometimes, though not always, help sensitize basic research to the location of strategic variables. (Stouffer, 1962, p. 4)

Stouffer put his ideas and his skills to practical use on all levels. Within Harvard, he served on strategic committees, advised the President and other high officials, and designed surveys when information was needed from faculty or graduate students. In the larger society, he was also in demand. A constant stream of long-distance telephone calls interrupted his flow of work. The Bureau of the Census. The Social Science Research Council. The Russell Sage Foundation. Chairmen of Sociology Departments at other universities. The sociology editor at John Wiley & Sons. One of the reasons he worked in the machine room instead of his office was that there he could usually escape the telephone. Sometimes his trusted secretary, Shirley Atkinson, would wordlessly poke her nose into the machine room when a particularly urgent call was coming in; he would understand; rather grimly , he would then stalk across the hall and into his office. When he picked up the phone, he responded with warmth to the caller, as though the call could not have come at a better time. He would concentrate on the problem being propounded to him for as long as necessary. Then he would return to the machine room, leaving the pile of unanswered letters on his desk. Mrs. Atkinson would plead with him to answer his mail, but she was rarely successful. Once in a while she would get him to dictate a few pressing letters. He explained to me that, if he answered his mail, he would never get to his research.

Sometimes he would explain the problem on which he was being consulted if I happened to be in his office when a call came in. His flexibility sometimes surprised me. For example, a high official of the Greyhound Bus Company was considering hiring Elmo Roper to conduct a poll of users and potential users of long-distance buses. Roper's fee was $50,000. Question:

"Was this a judicious expenditure of Company money?" Stouffer's answer: "Elmo Roper is one of the best people in the polling business; he can do a poll as well as anyone. But he's also a damn smart guy. You might consider hiring him to travel on your buses from New York to California and back again and write a report for you on what he observes. He'll charge you $50,000 anyway; his time is valuable. But you might get even more useful information for your money than you would from a poll." I never learned whether the Greyhound Bus Company took Sam's advice. But the advice itself was not what I expected one of the leading practitioners of quantitative social research to give. Stouffer adapted his response to the requirements of the problem, as he perceived them; he was not a doctrinaire statistician.

In 1948, Harry Truman won the presidency, defeating Thomas E. Dewey and third-party candidate Henry Wallace after nearly all the polling organizations had predicted a Dewey victory by a wide margin. And, as recalled above this was not only a public-relations disaster for George Gallup and Elmo Roper; it seemed to threaten the credibility of quantitative social research more generally. The Social Science Research Council responded by calling upon some outstanding academic social scientists to reanalyze the pre-election polls and explain what went wrong. Although Stouffer's time was fully committed to a variety of projects, including preparing the two volumes of *The American Soldier* (1949) for publication, when the SSRC asked him to help, he took it as his professional obligation to help clarify the situation. He and Duncan MacRae, Jr., contributed a chapter to the monograph published by the SSRC in 1949; they examined evidence, overlooked or ignored by the professional pollsters, of a last-minute swing to Truman. They recommended greater caution about predicting Election Day behavior from polls taken during the course of the campaign.

When I was a student of Stouffer in the late 1940s, a consequential book by Gunnar Myrdal (1944) was still being read and discussed in the Harvard community as elsewhere throughout the country. I remember a large public forum devoted to *An American Dilemma.* It was billed as "Myrdal's Dilemma: Is It Real?" The theme of much criticism of the book was that its assessment of the prospects for racial equality in the United States was overly optimistic. Recall Myrdal's thesis: that the egalitarian implications of the American Creed and the blatant racial inequality institutionalized in the system of white supremacy were on a collision course. Something had to give, and Myrdal predicted that it would be the doctrine of white supremacy. Myrdal proved to be right; his optimism was fully justified by the civil-rights revolution. What was not generally known at Harvard in the late 1940s and is still less well known today were the organizational and substantive roles Sam Stouffer played in this important project. Organizationally, Stouffer worked under Myrdal's direction helping to coordinate the efforts of a large number of scholars working on the preparation of research papers. When Myrdal returned to Sweden after the outbreak of World War II, Stouffer inherited the full organizational responsibility for the project—until Myrdal was able to return. Without him, there might have been no publication of *An American Dilemma*. Substantively, Sam contributed a working paper on Negro migration. Myrdal incorporated Stouffer's research in one chapter of the final manuscript, but there was a fundamental difference of interpretation between Myrdal's chapter and Stouffer's working paper. Stouffer considered the trends of black migration from the rural South to the large cities, especially the Northern cities of large industrial states with many electoral votes, to be of major causal significance; Myrdal emphasized the pressure of cultural inconsistency. Both thought that the position of the Negro in American society would improve dramatically, but they arrived at this conclusion from somewhat different lines of reasoning. Who was right? Even in retrospect, the answer is unclear. But the post-World-War-II influx of black population into the industrial states of the North and West certainly provided political leverage for the civil-rights movement. After it was shown that the margin of John F. Kennedy's victory over Richard Nixon in 1960 was provided by black voters in large Northern cities, it became much easier for the federal government to support the civil-rights movement.

In 1941, after finishing his work with Myrdal, Sam Stouffer moved to Washington to direct the survey-research activities of the War Department. He organized several hundred questionnaire surveys of soldiers in most areas in which American troops were stationed. Stouffer surely did not direct research in the Army in order to provide illustrative material for his classes after the war, although that was one byproduct. The halls of Emerson Hall overflowed with cabinets containing drawers of punch cards from these various surveys while Sam worked on *The American Soldier,* a distillation of what was learned from this vast research. And Stouffer shared with fascinated students what he was learning from attempting to present his military research to a social-science readership.

He also shared with us the political background of his military research, background that did not appear explicitly in *The American Soldier* or in the subsequent two volumes of the four-volume series of *Studies in Social Psychology in World War II*. We learned that, despite the strong support of his boss in the Information and Education Division, General Frederick Osborn, who knew Franklin Roosevelt personally and had other social connections useful for bureaucratic leverage, the Research Branch enjoyed a chronically precarious status within the Army. Old-line senior officers were shocked to learn that these academic types wanted to ask troops their opinions of their officers' leadership abilities. So-called morale surveys might put ideas into heads that never considered the possibility that orders could be questioned. Stouffer had to prove the value of social research to these skeptics. The battle to convince skeptics was fought over and over again during Sam's years in Washington. One of his victories gives the flavor of the problem. An early survey showed that conscripts hated spit-and-polish basic training. In addition, physical-conditioning experts raised doubts about the *effectiveness* of traditional approaches, including close-order drill. Stouffer and his colleagues obtained permission to conduct an experiment. They designed a new program of conditioning based on the methods of college coaches. The new program was compared with the traditional approach; comparative morale studies of soldiers undergoing the different types of training were made as well as before-after tests of strength and endurance. The experiment demonstrated that the new approach put men in *better* physical condition *faster* than the old and also reduced griping about basic training. The report of the experiment was read by senior officers at the War Department, perhaps by General George Marshall himself. It had two consequences. It resulted in a change in the methods used by the Army to improve the stamina of recruits, and it convinced some generals that social research was useful.

At the same time that Stouffer was preparing *The American Soldier* for publication, he was also working on a codification of methodological studies, especially studies of attitude scaling, that would eventually be published as *Measurement and Prediction* (1950), the last of the four volumes comprising *Studies in Social Psychology in World War II.* In the course of this codification, Louis Guttman and Paul Lazarsfeld came and went through the corridors of Emerson Hall. They and other specialists in measurement problems, including Frederick Mosteller, who was only peripherally involved in *The American Soldier,* cultivated at graduate seminars an appreciation of the possibilities and the difficulties of rigorous ordering of shades of opinion. We talked about Guttman scales and Lazarsfeld's latent structures, paired comparisons and scales of intensity. Sam was pushing one of his pet ideas: through the improvement of methodological tools, sociologists would enhance their ability to test hypotheses. Stouffer never lost this interest in improving methods of social measurement. Along with a group of younger colleagues, he published an article (Stouffer *et al,* 1952) demonstrating an ingenious technique for increasing the concentration of the underlying dimension in a Guttman-type scale. The published article was purely methodological, but the illustrative data were obtained in the course of investigating sensitivity to social sanctions on the part of Air Force officers—under a contract with the Human Resources Research Institute of the Air Force. He continued to believe that applied research was often an opportunity for sociologists to develop stronger research tools.

One reason Stouffer did so much data processing himself was that he wanted to see the results as soon as they emerged from the counter-sorter.[3] But he was not impatient when it came to presenting his findings. He would search for exactly the right words to convey his theoretical ideas. Doubtless, he discarded dozens of verbal tags before settling on the terms, "relative deprivation," and "intervening opportunities."

As diligently as Sam worked to express his research findings in clear, precise English, he strove equally hard to find the best way of presenting *quantitative* data in tables and charts. Take, for example, the well-known chart from *The American Soldier* in which he highlighted the anomalous responses of a probability sample of enlisted men to the question, "Do you think a soldier with ability has a good chance for promotion in the army?" (See Figure 1.)

Stouffer's objective was a fairly complete multivariate analysis of the responses to the question; at the same time he did not want to overwhelm the reader with complexity. He toiled for hours until he achieved a readily understandable presentation of data that ran counter to common sense. He was pleased with what he accomplished. He showed branch of service (Military Police versus Air Corps) in a straightforward way on the horizontal axis of the chart. He dichotomized rank on the veritical axis (noncoms versus privates and pfc's). He then dichotomized the resulting four categories by educational achievement (grade school and some high school versus high school graduates and beyond). None of this was especially ingenious, although considerable thought must have gone into the reduction of rank and educational attainment to dichotomies. In his presentation of the dependent variable, however, Stouffer conveyed a great deal of information in a deceptively simple format. He arranged the eight bars so that, although the percentage in each of four categories was revealed in full, a dark horizontal line *dichotomized* each bar. Furthermore, the bars were arranged in steps in proportion to the percent saying "A very good chance." The result was to show quite clearly what he wanted to show, namely, that soldiers in the Air Corps had *less* favorable attitudes toward promotion opportunities than soldiers in the Military Police and that better educated soldiers had *less* favorable attitudes than poorly educated soldiers even though better-educated soldiers and soldiers in the Air Corps were *more* likely to be promoted. (Since the samples were probability samples of the populations from

[3]Robin Williams (1979) put it this way: "He liked to operate the IBM counter-sorter, eagerly watching the cards drop into slots to see whether his current hypothesis would survive the empirical test."

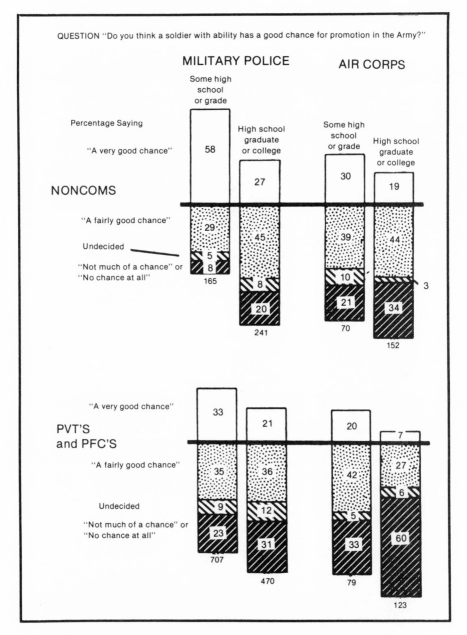

Figure 1. Opinions about promotion opportunity—comparisons by education and rank between Military Police and Air Corps (white enlisted men in the Army one to two years, continental United States). Military police data from special survey of a representative cross section of MP's, S-107, March, 1944. Air Corps data are a segment from representative cross section of all white EM in United States, S-95, January, 1944.

which they were drawn and since Stouffer included the number of cases on which the percentages in each bar were based, the reader could infer from the data that soldiers in the Air Corps were *objectively* more likely to be noncoms, than the better-educated soldiers were *objectively* more likely than poorly educated soldiers to be noncoms.) That the better-educated soldiers were dissatisfied with promotion opportunities did not in itself suggest the concept of relative deprivation. Stouffer could have explained their dissatisfaction by Durkheimian reasoning: *expectations* as well as *objective* personal circumstances give rise to satisfaction or dissatisfaction. But the finding that soldiers in the Air Corps were more dissatisfied than soldiers in the Military Police suggested a further consideration; it suggested that the social context should be examined in order to understand the level of expectations. He developed the concept of relative deprivation initially to account for anomalous results by branch of service and then, by extension, to contextual effects in other subject areas. I myself find "relative deprivation" useful in thinking about crossnational crime rates (Toby, 1979).

STOUFFER THE PATRIOT

Sam Stouffer died before the Vietnam War heated up to the point that young Americans began burning draft cards, wearing the flag on the seats of their jeans, and suggesting in other ways suspicion of their country, if not outright hostility. But even in the 1940s and 1950s, Sam's unabashed love for the United States seemed excessive compared with the "cooler" sentiments of colleagues and students. He told me, for example, after a visit to a base of the Strategic Air Command in connection with a research project, that the young pilots, navigators, and bombadiers that he met made him feel proud to be an American. Born as he was in the small town Sac City in Iowa (in the first year of the twentieth century, Sam must have been routinely exposed during his early years to the assumption that the United States was the greatest country in the world, the favorite of God, and that it contained wonderful and moral people. Furthermore, he went to Morningside College in Sioux City, where that assumption was unlikely to be challenged. And even after attending Harvard (as a graduate student in English from 1921 to 1923), he returned to his home town where he edited the Sac City *Sun* from 1923 to 1926. I can imagine him covering 4th-of-July celebrations organized by the American Legion post and responding enthusiastically to the speeches and the parades. One of the last pieces of writing Sam did was a preface to the textbook I co-authored with Harry Bredemeier. *Social Problems in America: Costs and Casualties in an Acquisitive Society* might well have seemed to Sam too critical of American life. As consulting editor for

John Wiley & Sons, he could have recommended putting greater emphasis on positive features, but he did not suggest changing a comma. He did include a paragraph in his Preface that might be interpreted as a mild rebuttal:

> The authors love America and American institutions. But as social scientists they know that in any society there are tensions, generated often by the very ideals which are most basic and most honored in that society. America is, of course, not an exception. And the authors pull no punches in showing in detail wherein this is so. The rewards for sucess are high—higher than perhaps anywhere in human history. Bu, correspondingly, the *relative* deprivation of failure is necessarily also high, even though *absolute* deprivation may be lower in America than in societies most of whose members can have only minimal aspirations. (Bredemeier & Toby, 1960, p. vii)

Sam's personal history predisposed him to be a patriot but not an unthinking one. He was committed to certain values—civil liberty, intellectual freedom, education, individual opportunity—and he perceived the United States as favorable to those values. Such values help to explain why he accepted the invitation of the Fund for the Republic, the brain-child of iconoclast Robert Hutchins, to conduct a survey of public attitudes toward civil liberty at the height of the McCarthy era (1953–1954). It may not seem today to have been a particularly dangerous undertaking. But at the time, Senate and House committees were vying with one another to run suspect Communists out of public life. Careers were being ruined, most of them in government but some in academia as well. The Fund for the Republic, whose then President was Clifford P. Case, was widely considered left-wing and possibly subversive. Stouffer conducted the survey and published his findings in *Communism, Conformity, and Civil Liberties* (1955). He did not escape unscathed. In connection with consultation work for what had become the Department of Defense, he had had a security clearance; the Department attempted to revoke it. Anonymous but "reliable" informants had questioned his loyalty. Stouffer fought the revocation. To this day his son, John, treasures the transcript of the hearing, which resulted in his complete vindication.

A fascinating aspect of *Communism, Conformity, and Civil Liberties* is the light it throws on Stouffer's brand of Americanism. Although born and raised in a small town, Sam clearly identifies the big city as the seed-bed of tolerance. Part of the reason for the greater tolerance of city people is the opportunity city life provides for contact with diverse people and ideas. Another reason is indirect; city life is associated with educational opportunities, and Stouffer tended to regard education as conducive to progress.

> ... schooling *puts a person in touch with people whose ideas and values are different from one's own.* And this tends to carry on, after formal schooling is finished, through reading and personal contacts. Now, we can plausibly argue that this is a necessary, though not the only, condition for tolerance of a free

market place for ideas. To be tolerant, one has to learn further not only that people with different ideas are not necessarily bad people but also that it is vital to America to preserve this free market place, even if some of the ideas traded there are repugnant or even dangerous for the country. The first step in learning this may be merely to encounter the strange and the different. The educated man does this and tends not to flinch too much at what he sees or hears.

Similarly . . . the citizen of a metropolitan community is more likely to rub shoulders with a variety of people whose values are different from his own and even repugnant to him than is the man or woman in a village. The city man has to learn to live and let live in his heterogeneous community to an extent not necessary for the village. (Stouffer, 1955, p. 127)

In view of his strong patriotic feelings, Stouffer was fortunate to be in charge of the Research Branch during World War II. Indeed, it is not too much to say that the surveys that he commissioned contributed their part to achieving victory over Germany and Japan, even when they did *not* test ideas or help to develop research tools. One of the last surveys to guide an administrative decision was one of immense practical importance. The War Department wanted to avoid a chaotic demobilization following military victory, such as had occurred after World War I. The Research Branch proposed a point system based on systematically surveyed opinions of soldiers about the weight that should be given to various factors in setting priorities for discharge.

But there were strong pressures from some important generals to change the system after V-J Day, especially to reduce or eliminate points for combat credit, in order to retain as long as possible the best trained men and give priority in discharge to those with less experience. From one military-efficiency point of view, this demand was not unreasonable. But what about morale implications? (Stouffer, 1962, p. 185)

General Marshall decided to accept the recommendation of the Research Branch. The point system was institutionalized as the guide for demobilization, and demobilization proceeded uneventfully.

Stouffer's work for the War Department was deeply satisfying. He had an opportunity to help his country and at the same time to demonstrate that social research was useful. He fostered the development of new tools of social and attitude measurement. And he must have known that he would eventually codify the substantive findings in social scientific publications. Yet there was one aspect of his War Department service that, as a patriot and as the clear leader of a fairly large military unit, must have disappointed him. He was never given a commission as a brigadier general. Francis Keppel (1979), who worked closely with Sam in the Research Branch, comments as follows:

I first met Sam when he was brought to the War Department by Frederick H. Osborn (later Major General Osborn) to advise on what became in time the

Research Branch of the Information and Education Division. The very idea of setting up a group to sound out the opinion of soldiers on anything—much less on what they thought of their commanders—was astonishing. It scarcely fitted into the old Army's notion of discipline and command relationships. But General George Marshall, the Chief of Staff, was not an ordinary man, and he supported Frederick Osborn's plan. As you may recall, Osborn made himself into a social scientist through his work in genetics and population, and he selected Stouffer as the best man to be the chief professional. What Sam brought to it, in addition to his scholarly qualifications, were three qualities: transparent honesty and patriotism, bubbling enthusiasm, and a good eye for talent. The group he helped to assemble, as I remember it, would have made a first-rate faculty anywhere, anytime.

There was no question in anyone's mind that Sam was the leader—but he was not ideally fitted to be the Commanding Officer in the military sense. As his colleagues one by one changed from civilian clothes to uniforms, he wanted more and more to wear one himself. There was a time when he had reason to hope that this would come about. But in the end General Osborn decided that the freedom of civilian status—which let Sam see anyone from messenger to General without difficulties of status—was the best arrangement. There was also a haunting worry that Sam's jacket would be covered with cigarette ashes much of the time. And anyway Sam did not operate through channels naturally.

STOUFFER THE HUMAN BEING

I can still see Sam in my mind's eye, moving rapidly from place to place, partly, I suppose, because of his reservoirs of energy, but also because of a zest for the task at hand. Much of the time the task at hand was social research to test ideas. His commitment to sociology was passionate. He gave the data a fair chance to disconfirm his hypotheses because he couldn't imagine doing otherwise. But he had a relentless desire to know how the particular hypothesis he was testing at the moment made out.

I can also see the warm smile that played around Sam's lips when he chatted with a student or colleague. Although no one was busier, no one seemed more accessible. How much clock-time he spent with his family I do not know. But in whatever time he shared with his children, he must have communicated the same warmth that total strangers glimpsed. His son writes, "My perception of my father is that of a very warm and loving human being" (John Stouffer, 1979). And Ann Stouffer Bisconti (1979) reports the joint recollections of herself and her sister, Jane Stouffer Williams:

> The characteristics of my father, as a person, that were most outstanding to me were his humanity, his strict adherence to his values, and his rather outlandish sense of humor. He never forgot—or could forget—his roots. As you probably

know, he was the older son of a devout Methodist couple who lived in a small town in Iowa. His father owned and edited the local newspaper, the *Sac Sun.* Early studies of the Bible, especially the Old Testament, and the classics stimulated his imagination and developed his lifelong love for geography, history, and literature.

After graduating from Morningside College in Sioux City with a major in classics, my father took his master's in English at Harvard. The experience was an eye-opener. As he used to tell us, he spent nearly all his time the first year in Widener Library reading the unexpurgated versions of Boccaccio's *Decameron* and other similarly racy volumes to which he had no access in Iowa.

During this period, he maintained constant contact with his parents. He sent all his English papers to his father for him to critique, and those that remain bear the witty and clear-thinking commentary of this man who so obviously influenced the intellectual development of the son. The enclosed exercise in writing editorial paragraphs is of particular interest, I think, because it illustrates not only this correspondence between father and son but also the blossoming statistical orientation of the young English major.[4]

Even after he became engrossed in the mission of making sociology a science, my father carried with him a boundless appetite for knowledge about the world around and a fascination for history and literature. You may recall that, in his lectures, he illustrated his points with references ranging from Shakespeare to Sherlock Holmes to Iowa corn fields to baseball. I remember because I was a student in the last course he ever taught.

He had an overwhelming need to communicate to his family his tremendous enthusiasm. My sister, brother, and I remember the fervor with which he read poetry aloud to the whole family. He also enjoyed reading spine-chilling short stories with a voice that evoked a most sinister mood. When I was a child, he rarely missed my bedtime story; a favorite was Hillyer's *A Child's History of the World.* I also remember a good many Saturdays spent in the machine room at Harvard's Laboratory of Social Relations where we both watched in awe as the little cards fell into boxes in the sorter.

Wherever we traveled, my father knew more than the guides; he seemed to have a story for every street corner in Europe. It was a standing joke that my father took his family from Chicago to the summer place in Vermont by way of California. The detours often were somewhat unusual; always they were a learning experience.

After a car trip to New York, we were taken to Grand Central Station to see the red carpet laid out for the Twentieth Century Limited. On a trip to Mexico, we

---

[4]Stouffer wrote for his English course as follows: "Who said the profession of poetry writing is unpopular to-day? The Reader's Guide of Periodical Literature lists 2,575 poems which actually were printed in current magazines from January to November of last year. And at the end of the list one is told to 'see also Children's Verses.' This is an average of 232 poems a month or 7 4/5 a day. Every three hours, somewhere in the English-speaking world, a poet's eye ceases its 'fine frenzy rolling' and another product of love's labor is ready for butchery in the abattoir of the critics."

stopped over in Houston to see how far the airport had been built from this rapidly expanding city; we also stopped in Atlanta to see the drinking fountains labelled "for whites only."

My father was intensely patriotic and had a great love of the American heritage. As a youth, he was responsible for saving the oldest log cabin in Sac County; the cabin is still preserved in a local park. He would go miles out of his way to cross over a covered bridge or to pass through a quaint New England town. It would be impossible to describe the anguish he suffered when under personal attack during the McCarthy era.

He set high goals for himself and his family, never accepting second best. In some ways, this may have been a weakness as well as a strength. After losing in the finals of a college tennis championship he put down his racquet and never played again (Bisconti, 1979).

Even his attempt to prevent the introduction of a television set into the Stouffer household was recognized as well intentioned. He did not forbid it exactly. In 1951, when the technology of color television was still on the horizon, he told me gleefully that he was assuring his children that the Stouffers would have the first *color* television set on the block. I learned from his son that he finally gave in. According to John Stouffer's letter (1979):

What finally broke down his resistance was his insatiable interest in what was going on in the world around him.

Ann Stouffer Bisconti (1979) remembers the place of the television set in the Stouffer household as follows:

I can see my father now in our large panelled library, with one eye on the evening news and one hand holding a martini, while the other eye and the other hand are working away at the rumbling Monroe and casually recording columns of numbers on long sheets of paper rolling over onto the floor.

If there is a heaven and if Sam Stouffer is in it, perhaps the Monroe calculator is still rumbling and the long sheets of paper are still rolling onto the floor.

REFERENCES

Bisconti, A. S. Personal letter dated March 7, 1979.

Bredemeier, H. C. & Toby, J. *Social problems in America: Costs and casualties in an acquisitive society.* New York: Wiley, 1960.

Buck, P. An appreciation. Text of unpublished remarks delivered at the memorial service for Samuel A. Stouffer, October 25, 1960.

Hauser, P. M. Personal letter dated March 19, 1979.

Keppel, F. Personal letter dated March 1, 1979.

Merton, R. K. *Social theory and social structure.* New York: Free Press, 1957, rev. ed.

Myrdal, G. *An American dilemma: The Negro problem and modern democracy.* New York: Harper & Brothers, 1944.

Schuman, H. Personal letter dated June 19, 1979.

Smith, M. B. "Samuel Andrew Stouffer." *International Encyclopedia of the Social Sciences,* 1968, *15,* 277–280.

Stouffer, J. E. Personal letter dated February 15, 1979.

Stouffer, S. A. *Communism, conformity, and civil liberties: A cross-section of the nation speaks its mind.* Garden City, N.Y.: Doubleday, 1955.

Stouffer, S. A. *Social research to test ideas: Selected writings of Samuel A. Stouffer.* New York: Free Press, 1962.

Stouffer, S. A., et al. *The American soldier.* Two volumes. Princeton, N.J.: Princeton University Press, 1949.

Stouffer, S. A., et al. *Measurement and prediction.* Princeton, N.J.: Princeton University Press, 1950

Stouffer, S. A., et al. "A Technique for Improving Cumulative Scales." *Public Opinion Quarterly,* 1952, *16,* 273–291.

Toby, J. "Delinquency in Cross-Cultural Perspective." In L. T. Empey, *Juvenile justice: The progressive legacy and current reforms.* Charlottesville, Va.: University Press of Virginia, 1979, 105–149.

Williams, R. M., Jr. Personal letter dated February 16, 1979.

9

PAUL F. LAZARSFELD
The Substance and Style of His Work[1]

James S. Coleman

It is important, when we dwell upon the lives and times of those who have preceded us in the discipline, to be clear about the purpose for doing so. For there are many possible reasons, and most of them do not stand up very well under inspection. For example, one frequent reason for former colleagues and students to do so is to engage in nostalgia, evoking old memories about "the good old days," and the times that were spent with the departed friend. Another is to pay homage belatedly to one's mentor or colleague, out of a conscience occupied by a feeling of guilt that one had not done so when he was alive. Still a third, engaged in mostly by disciples whose own position will be enhanced if the stature of their master is increased, is to expand his status and that of the activity he (and they) represent. A fourth, engaged in by opponents, is to analyze the spell under which a powerful predecessor has placed the discipline, in hope of exorcising it.

Unless one is aware of the various potential reasons for such an enterprise, the product may be infused with and contaminated by them, and thus be of little value to the discipline. There is, however, one compelling reason for attending to the recent past, and in particular to the lives of men who have been important to the discipline. By capturing something of the problems that gave direction to their careers, we can understand better how the discipline came to be where it is now, and where its momentum—given to it

[1]This paper owes much to David Sills, who was kind enough to show me a draft of his biography of Lazarsfeld (Sills, 1979). I have used this biography both to correct errors of fact and to enrich the entire paper.

by those giants of the preceding generation—is taking it now. And by capturing something of the *way* they worked, the way they made their influence felt, we learn more about how we got from where things were before to where they are now. The value of this to the discipline is that it can gain a self-consciousness, a self-consciousness about where it has been and where it is going. Such a self-consciousness has never been definitively demonstrated to aid the development of a discipline, but it seems probable that it does so, just as it is probable that a rich knowledge of social and political history is valuable to heads of state. Such a self-consciousness about the discipline's past can aid, for example, in the strategic selection of problems on which to work, and it can give hints about the way a problem may be fruitfully addressed. There is, of course, another basic reason that our discipline in particular gives us for looking carefully at the intellectual histories of those who have helped make the discipline what it is today. For this contributes to the sociology of knowledge, that is to our understanding of how scientific and scholarly disciplines grow.

This distinction between two classes of reasons for examining the lives of sociologists who have brought us where we are today—those that are irrelevant to the growth of the discipline, and those that can aid that growth—provides a criterion for testing facts about a person's life. For example, from this point of view, it is more important to know that when Max Weber took over the editorship of a journal (*Archiv für Sozialwissenschaft und Sozialpolitik*), which before him had been directed by socialist editors, he had a particular orientation toward two different roles that he expected social scientists to play as contributors to the journal, than it is to know that he suffered from lengthy periods of extreme depression.[2] Such a criterion does not, of course, make irrelevant all details of personal life, but it acts as a filter for determining which details are relevant to the enterprise.

All this is preface and frame of reference for what I shall say about Paul Lazarsfeld. I will be selective, and the criterion for my selectivity will be that suggested above—just what it tells us that can be helpful for the discipline, *not* what it tells us about Paul Lazarsfeld the person. For those of you who, like me, would also enjoy reminiscing about those days, I beg your indulgence.

[2]Weber distinguished the role of social scientists in the *analysis* of the functioning of society, and their role as *persons* in society, making prescriptive statements about what ought to be. He recognized that social scientists could legitimately write in both these capacities, and he wanted both kinds of contributions to the *Archiv*, but he wanted the contributors to clearly distinguish in which capacity they were writing—and even before that, to be clear themselves about the capacity in which they were writing. See Max Weber (1949, p.60). The controversy about the possibility of a "value-free" sociology, which has been hotly debated in recent years, is illuminated by this distinction. I have discussed this at greater length elsewhere (see Coleman, 1979).

THE LAZARSFELD SUCCESSES

It is perhaps best to begin from the present and work backwards: Just what did Paul Lazarsfeld do that is now important to the discipline of sociology, and to those that border on it? Accounts will differ, but as I see it, Paul's enduring contributions, which must serve as the starting point in seeing the direction he has taken us, are the ones I now list in an arbitrary order:

(1) He was of major importance in transforming public opinion polling methods into survey analysis, that is, into the analytical use of sample surveys to draw inferences about causal relations that affect the actions of individuals. It is difficult to imagine sociology without these methods (which have been extensively developed in recent years through the extra power that computers provide), but before Lazarsfeld and a few others carried out this transformation, this methodological tool central to empirical research in sociology was nonexistent. Here the impact of Lazarsfeld resides as much in the examples he provides in papers which make substantive contributions to audience research, voting behavior, and other areas as in formal methological papers. However, one methodological paper was of particular importance. This is a paper with Patricia Kendall (1950) that attempted to codify the new directions that he had been taking, showing analytical methods for identifying spurious relations and intervening variables. This work has been carried considerably further and integrated into the main body of statistical analyses, first by Herbert Simon and H.M Blalock, and subsequently by others.[3]

(2) He pioneered in the use of survey panel methods, that is, the further transformation of public opinion polling beyond cross-sectional surveys into panels involving two or more interviews of the same sample (or "panel"). The introduction of panels allowed Lazarsfeld to pose a central question, which is even now not satisfactorily answered: How can panel data be used to draw inferences about the effects of various attitudes and actions on one another? The problems that Lazarsfeld posed, both in panel analysis generally and in his well-known "16-fold table" problem (which asks about the "mutual effects"—as Lazarsfeld termed it—of two attributes on each other), are among the most enduring in sociological methodology. The problems have spawned literally hundreds of publications, ranging from those in which the term "cross-lagged correlations" appears somewhere in the title (Pelz & Andrews, 1964 and Campbell, 1961), to Leo Goodman's use of loglinear models to address the causal problems posed by panel data (Good-

---

[3]Simon, whose seminal paper on causal ordering with continuous variables paralleled Lazarsfeld's on categorical variables, addresses this problem again in the volume in honor of Lazarsfeld (Simon, 1979).

man 1979). A considerable part of my own methodological work has been directed to this class of problems posed by Lazarsfeld. (Coleman, 1964, 1968).

(3) One of the principal initiators of audience research and mass communications research generally, Lazarsfeld was a major force in shaping the fledgling market-research industry. And because he was one of the few persons in an academic center to carry out audience and market research (and because being at Columbia he was in New York), he populated this infant industry with persons who had worked under him at the Columbia Bureau of Applied Social Research—some who obtained their Ph.D.'s, others who never did. I should remark in passing that there are many in sociology who ignore or disdain work in market research. They do so at the peril of missing new ideas. Ever since the Lazarsfeld–Stanton program analyzer and the panel-analysis problem which he found in market research, the field of market research has been the source of both prototypical problems and innovations of technique. In the '30s and '40s, market research was comparable to policy research today. Business then, and government now, brought problems that helped invigorate the discipline. Market research has since largely left the academy, with a loss to both the academy and market research; and it seems probable that policy research will do so as well, spawning as before a new industry, but at a loss to both the social sciences and policy research.[4]

(4) First with the 1940 "Sandusky Study," to use Lazarsfeld's shop-talk title, (*The People's Choice*, 1948), and then with the 1948 "Elmira Study" (*Voting*, 1954), Lazarsfeld initiated the methods that have come to dominate the empirical analysis of voting behavior, both in sociology and political science. For those who today as a matter of course carry out studies of the determinants of voting behavior, it may seem natural and normal that such work be pervasive in political sociology. But until Lazarsfeld's voting studies, such an assumption could hardly be made. Work in political behavior was based on analyses of election outcomes, and of different results in different voting districts. It was Lazarsfeld who opened up this area of behavior to sample surveys.

---

[4]The last statement is made in view of the large number of research organizations that have sprung up outside the university in the past ten years. There are many reasons for the growth of such organizations (for some see Coleman, 1973) but their existence outside the constraints of a professional association and academic journal publication means that they lack the self-disciplining qualities that the academic discipline imposes on the work that does take place within the academy.

(5) Lazarsfeld was one of the "founders" of modern mathematical sociology. Although there have been attempts to apply mathematics to sociology since its inception, only in the 1950s did there come to be extensive growth and development, leading this mode of work to become an established part of the discipline. Lazarsfeld was of major importance to this development in a variety of ways: through his own work on latent structure analysis, through his teaching, through a lecture series at Columbia that resulted in *Mathematical Thinking in the Social Sciences* (1953), through the Behavioral Models Project at the Columbia Bureau of Applied Social Research (in which Duncan Luce, Howard Raiffa, Theodore Anderson, Gerald Thompson, Lee Wiggins, and others took sustained part), and in still other ways. At that time, there were several attempts to use mathematics seriously for the study of social behavior. One was by Stuart Dodd, at the University of Washington. Another was by Nicholas Rashevsky, a biophysicist at the University of Chicago. There were others. But of all those then struggling to make headway, it is Lazarsfeld's contribution more than any other that has grown and become an intrinsic part of sociological investigation. A major reason, I suspect, is that Lazarsfeld's empirical concerns were as strong as his methodological or formal concerns. His interest was in solving substantive problems, and his use of mathematics was continually guided by this interest. He was sometimes swayed, by the presence of the mathematicians and statisticians in the environment he created around him, to let the mathematics of a problem overwhelm the substance. Yet this never went very far, because he was always most interested in understanding what made persons act as they did.

(6) By bringing into being the Columbia University Bureau of Applied Social Research (and before that, similar organizations in Vienna and at the University of Newark), Lazarsfeld created the prototype of the university-based organization for large-scale social research, a prototype that has been the model for many other research centers, both in the United States and abroad. The university social research organization for large-scale social research has evolved since Lazarsfeld brought it into existence, and it is unclear what directions future evolution will bring. But the notion of a university social research organization carrying out projects financed by foundations, business firms, labor unions and government was an early idea of Lazarsfeld's, and it has grown and been transmuted into the university organizations for policy research, carrying out projects largely financed by government.

(7) Through his work in audience research, market research, and voting, Lazarsfeld began to bring about an understanding of the way mass com-

munications, social relationships, and attitudes *interact* to shape action. From this work developed such important ideas as those of "opinion leaders," "the two-step flow of communication," and "contextual effects," as well as such methodological innovations as snowball sampling and dense cluster sampling. A principal insight gained into the way mass media affect action is that much of the effect is an indirect one, mediated by opinion leaders who use the media especially for that purpose. Some of this general conception of the relation between mass communications and personal interaction appears in his book with Elihu Katz, *Personal Influence* (1955), some appears in *The People's Choice* and *Voting*. It is characteristic of the mode through which Lazarsfeld's ideas had an impact that the conception is reflected just as fully in publications that do not bear his name: the "drug study" published in papers and a book by others (Coleman, Katz & Menzel, 1966) and the "typographical union study" also published by others (Lipset et al; 1956). Work at the Bureau was permeated by these ideas and interaction was sufficiently intense that they diffused throughout it.[5]

(8) Along with a few others, Lazarsfeld was a major force in moving the Ford Foundation to establish the Center for Advanced Study in the Behavioral Sciences in 1954, and even more central in leading it to establish the Institut für Höhere Studien in Vienna in 1963. His interest in both cases was to have an institute for *advanced training* in research, through it was only the Vienna Institute that took this form.[6]

(9) Because the present state of a discipline depends on the particular people who have had a dominating influence on the discipline in its recent past, it is important also to point out that the combination of Lazarsfeld and Merton at Columbia probably constituted the dominant force in sociology for a period of about 15 years in the 1950s and '60s. This means that their work had an impact far beyond that which can be traced by publications or other directly attributable accomplishments. The nature of this impact was toward systematic empirical analysis, informed more by social-psychological theory and "middle-range" sociological theory than by grand sociological theory. The problems studied were more micro- than macro-sociology, although throughout that work the locus was in natural settings rather than laboratories.

These nine kinds of impact on the discipline by Paul Lazarsfeld are the data with which we must begin. How and why did he get from his starting

---

[5]Lazarsfeld's ideas on snowball sampling led to a seminar I gave at Chicago in 1956, and a subsequent paper on the topic by Leo Goodman. This is one of the very large number of indirect influences of Lazarsfeld's "program of problems."

[6]For a further discussion, see Glock, 1979 and Barton, in press.

point—a socialist mathematics student in Vienna in 1925—to these spheres of intellectual impact? Where was he going? Where was he trying to take social science? In what ways did he try to do it?

Before going on to these questions, we must consider the things that Paul Lazarsfeld wanted to accomplish but where his efforts were less than successful. Looking at what he wanted to do but failed to do can help give us a sense of the intellectual direction of his life.[7]

THE LAZARSFELD FAILURES

(1) Lazarsfeld was never very successful in a major enterprise on the borderline of theory and methodology, and closely akin to philosophy of science: the explication of how we come to form *concepts* in social science, and the relation of empirical *indicators* to theoretical concepts. He made a number of attempts at this, both on his own part and by focussing the work of others on it. In the summer of 1954, for example, he held an extended seminar or workshop, including people from Columbia, and a variety of others (Leon Festinger, Harold Kelley, John Thibaut, Gustav Bergmann) whose ideas interested him, the workshop being designed to clarify "Concepts and Indices in the Social Sciences." But despite much effort on his part and that of others, and despite the publication of several papers on these matters (such as work with Herbert Menzel that continued for some time after this seminar), nothing emerged that has had a lasting impact on the discipline. There were publications, but they did not affect the directions of the discipline.

(2) Despite the fact that Lazarsfeld, more than anyone else, can be described as the "founder" of modern mathematical sociology, the momentum he generated could only with some charity be said to be in a *sociological* (as distinct from a psychological) direction. Partly because of his own interest in the empirical analysis of action (as he liked to call it), and partly because the problems were more mathematically tractable, much of the mathematical sociology he himself did or stimulated others to do was psychological rather than sociological in character. His latent structure analysis, as a basic example, is an attempt to infer underlying psychological states from observed individual responses. The mathematical work he did or stimulated on the modelling of attitude change is another example of models designed to deal with psychological processes rather than sociological ones. It is in a way puzzling that a major substantive-cum-methodological direction he initiated was that of "contextual effects," "structural effects,"

---

[7]Lazarsfeld himself was fond of discussing his "successes" and "failures." Just as he was always ready to say that he "did not understand," he was always willing to say he had failed at certain things he had tried to do or at problems he had tried to solve.

"personal influence," and the "two-step flow of communication," but that none of the sociological aspects of this work found its way into his mathematical sociology. There is little *structural* work in the mathematical sociology he initiated, and little examination or development of the mathematics needed to relate the level of individuals as actors to that of collectivities as actors—what economists call the problem of aggregation, though the decisive point is that it takes more than mere "aggregation" to make the leap between these levels.

Lazarsfeld recognized this less-than-fully sociological character of the mathematical work he initiated. It was he who led me and others to take an interest in Herbert Simon's contemporary work on aggregation, and on other approaches in economics to deal with aggregation. In the introduction to one of his later books (1972, p. xvi), he says, "I obviously cannot change the past, but in some recent work I am seriously trying to build some kind of bridge between it and . . . the promised land of a precise and yet nonatomistic sociology."

(3) Paul Lazarsfeld always wanted to develop an institute or program for advanced training in research in the social sciences, a kind of professional school. The chief ideas of that aspiration can be seen in a paper, published as Chapter 18 of his *Qualitative Analysis* (1972), which he and Robert Merton wrote in 1950; but there were many more detailed memoranda, projects, plans, and continuing expressions of hope. As I have implied, the closest approximation to success in this effort was the Institut für Höhere Studien in Vienna; but this was more nearly a substitute for the lack of research training of Austrian social scientists in their Ph. D. programs than an advanced professional school. Paul's vision (and to a degree Merton's too) as expressed in this joint paper was for systematic training in methods for what he called "Social Bookkeeping" and in "social research bearing on specific problems of policy and social action" (1972, p. 365). We would now call this training for policy research, and the absence of such systematic training is considerably more apparent now than it was a generation ago when he had these ideas.

One point about this proposal is especially interesting. It is perhaps as close as Paul got to expressing an interest in macrosociology. The methods, to be sure, would be largely those of surveys, but unlike the kind of survey analysis he himself did, which was the analysis of individuals' actions, this research, "social bookkeeping," would be designed to characterize the society, or certain parts of it, at one or more points in time. But the upshot of it all was that no such graduate or postdoctoral or professional program of education in social research ever came into existence.

These are for me the three spheres—concepts and indices, an explicitly *sociological* mathematical sociology, and a professional school for social research—in which Paul Lazarsfeld wanted to accomplish certain things but failed to do so. If he were here, he would add to the list, because he saw his business as quite unfinished, but this must serve for present purposes.

WHAT WAS LAZARSFELD TRYING TO DO?

Paul Lazarsfeld began his professional career in the psychological laboratory of Charlotte and Karl Bühler at the University of Vienna, in 1925, with a Ph.D. in mathematics. His first publication of any note was in 1933, *Die Arbeitslosen von Marienthal,* a study of an unemployed community, with Marie Jahoda and Hans Zeisel. This research is useful for what it tells us about Lazarsfeld's early orientation, both in methods and in substance. What is most striking about the methods used in this study is their diversity and range, and particularly the mixture of qualitative interviews which obtained not only the respondents' current condition, but also life histories, with quantitative data. The study included time budgets and money budgets, menus of households, measures of changes in subscriptions to a politically-oriented newpaper, *Arbeiterzeitung,* and an entertainment-oriented newspaper, *Kleine Blatt,* (showing the lesser reduction in subscription to the latter, thus confirming the inference of loss of interest in politics), loss of membership in different kinds of organizations (leading to a similar inference), demographic information about the village, the health of children whose fathers were working and those whose fathers were not. The research team even measured the speed of walking of men (whose lives had been totally transformed by unemployment) and women (whose daily schedule, as they show elsewhere, was not greatly different from before). They showed that over half of the 33 men they observed walked at less than two miles per hour, while less than a quarter of women did. They observed, at the noontime peak of pedestrian traffic in Marienthal, 68 men and 32 women walking the 300-meter stretch of the village's main street, and they counted the number of stops these pedestrians made. Fifty-seven percent of the men made three or more stops; only nine percent of the women did.

This range of methods shows a combination of types of data and analysis that reappeared again and again in his work. In the concluding paragraph to his introduction to *Qualitative Analysis,* written late in his career, he noted:

> I have always believed in the interdependence of quantitative and qualitative work; [8]but I was also aware that whatever talent I had was weighted on the quantitative side. Therefore, in the choice of my associates, I continually

---

[8]This combination of qualitative observation and quantitative analysis in Lazarsfeld's work is expressed in the title of the recent volume written in honor of Lazarsfeld, *Qualitative and Quantitative Social Research* (Merton, Coleman & Rossi, eds., 1979).

looked for balance. My relations with the Horkheimer group, my joining forces with David Riesman and the late Ludwig Wagner, and my long and gratifying collaboration with Robert Merton, are examples as well as symbols.

Another characteristic of the methods used in Marienthal is that they exemplified the transformation of qualitative observations into quantitative measures. Lazarsfeld was always looking for a way to do this. Many observers on the main street of Marienthal in 1931 would gain a sense of slowness of life, the "weariness" of the community, as the authors termed it. But not many would discover how to translate these impressions into quantitative measures, such as the speed of walking, or the number of stops made. And even fewer would have recognized the necessity for some kind of baseline for comparison, in this case provided by the women whose daily lives had not changed as much.

There is another aspect of methods used in this study that was evident throughout Lazarsfeld's career. Some time after I came to Columbia in the early 1950s, Lazarsfeld showed me a sheaf of extended quotations from various qualitative studies, mostly community studies, many from the Chicago school of Robert E. Park—like *Black Metropolis* or *The Gold Coast and The Slum*—and some from an anthropological tradition. These quotations were examples of what Paul called "global indicators"—indicators of some concept or property of the community or the neighborhood, much like the examples cited above from Marienthal. They had been gathered by members of a seminar that he and Patricia Kendall had held, and he wanted somehow to systematize them, to create a transmissible method out of what had been an art.

Lazarsfeld had a continuing interest in such global indicators—indicators of a concept that characterized a collective or social group, and could not be derived from individuals by aggregation. He describes this interest in one of the essays ("Notes on the History of Concept Formation") that appeared in his *Qualitative Analysis*. It was this interest that led him to induce colleagues and students to examine work they would never otherwise have seen. For example, with this sheaf of global indicators, he directed me also to read such diverse authors as Wilhelm Dilthey (on the characterization of a cultural system), Harold Guetzkow (on properties of a group), Meyer Schapiro (on the use of art to characterize the "style" of a period).

But the descriptions I have given of Lazarsfeld's interests, both in the Marienthal study and in his continuing interest in "global indicators," are misleading. For these do not express the principal problems that occupied him. They do not typify the questions by which he was possessed.

Perhaps, however, one cannot make sense of the multiplicity of ideas and problems that occupied his attention, and extract a common direction toward which he worked.[9] Perhaps it would be more accurate to say that what characterized him most was energy and drive—the capacity to impress a much wider range of concerns on the discipline than would someone with less drive.

But despite the diversity, despite the range, there are central concerns, one above all. This is what Lazarsfeld called the empirical analysis of action. As I will suggest, it is largely because he so fully moved the discipline as a whole to this as a central task that we find it hard to identify it as his legacy. If we all had six fingers on each hand, we would simply regard this as in the nature of things, and would not recognize that it arose through a mutation in a common forebear. I suggest that Lazarsfeld is that common forebear for a kind of work that now pervades the discipline.

THE EMPIRICAL STUDY OF ACTION

Lazarsfeld's concern with the analysis of *action* may have derived from the focus of the Bühlers in their laboratory in Vienna. But whatever its source, it manifested itself from the beginning in both his quantitative work and his qualitative work. What he called "reason analysis" and his attempt to dissect expressed motives, as exhibited in his classic paper, "The Art of Asking Why" (1972 [1934], p. 183) were attempts to get at this by analytical use of the actor's own explanation of his action. His selection of market research, or "buying decisions," as a research focus exhibited this intention. His political sociology, or the study of "voting decisions," exhibited it as well. His mathematical work, in the study of attitudes, and in the development of latent structure analysis, is an attempt to model what goes on inside the individual to make him act as he does. But above all, the directions in which he took survey research were precisely these: to use survey data to analyze individual action in a social context. Panel analysis was an extension of this. It could have gone otherwise in the hands of someone else: survey methods could have been used to characterize groups, organizations, communities, institutions. We should not forget that in the immediately preceding and even contemporary research in American sociology—such as the Lynds' *Middletown,* the large number of community and neighborhood studies that came from Robert E. Park's students, Lloyd Warner's and August Hollingshead's studies of social stratification in American communities—in all this research, the community or some other social unit was

---

[9]Marie Jahoda addresses exactly this question in her paper "PFL: Hedgehog or Fox?" in Merton, Coleman & Rossi, eds., (1979).

the object of interest. Not so in Paul Lazarsfeld's work, after *Marienthal*. Even when a community was the setting, as in the Sandusky *(The People's Choice)* and Elmira *(Voting)* studies of voting, or in the Decatur study *(Personal Influence)*, the analysis was not of a community, but of individual decision-making in a social context. This direction of work Paul Lazarsfeld so impressed upon the discipline of sociology that we all do it now, not just those in a "Lazarsfeld tradition" or a "Columbia tradition." For example, what is path analysis (to refer to a technique which largely grew up elsewhere)? It is a powerful method used by sociologists primarily for quantitatively pursuing the direction in which Paul Lazarsfeld started the discipline: the empirical analysis of action. It is, I think, this shift of sociological direction that has led to the criticism of what Europeans once called "American sociology" and C. Wright Mills labelled "abstracted empiricism."[10]

As these critics point out, this direction of work precludes others; but what they fail to see is that it *is* a substantive direction, not merely a methodological convenience; and as the continuing strength and vitality of that direction attests, it is an important one. In Paul's own work, it probably arose through his immigration to America and the sudden exposure to a society with mass media: where closed communities, once like Marienthal, had been pried open by the mass media, resulting in a vast amorphous society in which products seemed to be sold, attitudes seemed to be formed, and individual actions seemed to be shaped, no longer by *interpersonal* communication, but by communication from the mass media to atomistic individuals. As I indicated earlier, perhaps the most enduring substantive contribution of Lazarsfeld to sociology was to show that the process is not so simple, that interpersonal communication *does* play an important part, that there are opinion leaders and followers, that there is a two-step flow of communication.

In such a society, where the old structures were no longer so binding, encompassing, and powerful, the focus of interest *must* be on individual action. It cannot any longer be the community, treated as an inviolate unit, as a single actor. This does not mean, of course, that social structure is no longer important, but that it cannot be treated as fixed, and sociological analysis cannot be confined to fixed social units, but must include both individuals and social structure. There are various ways of doing this, and I will not argue that those taken by Lazarsfeld are the best, or even debate whether they are adequate to the task. But I will argue that this substantive direction, the analysis of individual action in a social context, is a mutation in the discipline which occurred more through Paul Lazarsfeld's work than the work of any other.

[10]See C. Wright Mills, in *Qualitative Analysis* (Lazarsfeld, 1972).

The mutation in the discipline followed a similar change in society itself, a change from closed communities like Marienthal to the individualistic society that we know today, characterized by social and geographic mobility. The studies of social stratification in communities of New England and Illinois carried out by Warner and Hollingshead were truly sociological, studies in which the community was the unit of analysis. But what made them anachronistic shortly after their publication was the radical change that American society went through beginning before World War II, and accelerating after it, and which European society went through some years later. Stratification systems of communities lost their compelling quality, both because greatly increased role-segmentation of life allowed escape from an oppressive environment, and because, in the West at least, emigration from the community became such an easy and attractive alternative. The society changed from one in which the relevant units of analysis were geographic communities to one in which they were no longer so. It may be that the reason neither the American critics of Lazarsfeld's "abstracted empiricism" nor the European critics of Lazarsfeld's "American sociology" could recognize this change in society and reflect it in their work is that neither experienced the abrupt change of setting that Lazarsfeld did. In 1931 he was observing the closed community of Marienthal, a community with many links to its feudal origins; in 1933, he was in New York, the center of the mass communications industry that more than ever before, was helping to transform life throughout America. The critics may not have liked Lazarsfeld's way of studying this more amorphous social structure; but it was certainly more appropriate than their methods that assumed the fixity of structures that were dissolving—and they had no alternatives to offer.[11]

There is much more I could say about the substantive aspects of Lazarsfeld's work, or about the methodological innovations he pioneered. I cannot, however, do so in limited space and will turn instead to the other major topic of my analysis of Paul Lazarsfeld: his style of work. For Lazarsfeld, this is central to an understanding of his influence, and perhaps it may add to our knowledge about how such influences in a discipline occur in general.

---

[11]It is true that Lazarsfeld's focus on individual action failed to capture much about social structure. The strain toward dissolution of rigid social structures based on geographic community did not mean that social structure was absent—yet the survey methods had great difficulty in showing the functioning of this social structure. Many at Columbia felt some unease at the individualistic character of analysis made on the basis of survey research. In 1955, after completing graduate work and while still at Columbia, I designed research that reflected my own unease. This was a study of communities of adolescents, whom I felt were still enough bound to their environments to make the "adolescent community" a relevant unit to study. Although I did not carry out that research at Columbia, I did so later at Chicago (Coleman, 1961).

I begin with a personal incident I mentioned earlier: the sheaf of "global indicators" culled from community studies that Lazarsfeld set me to work on. In this case, as in many others, here was a problem that Paul's fertile mind had isolated and begun to examine. But characteristically, he did not keep the problem to himself, nor did he give it up. He gave me this sheaf of "global indicators," together with a menu of readings about "group properties," materials that he himself had read, but did not have the time to integrate and to confront with the empirical material. In this case as in so many others, Paul saw the person he put on this as an extension of himself. When the work I did failed to agree with his ideas, he argued with me at length over it. He could not be persuaded that the way I had done it was right. He did not want to see it published in the way I had conceived it, and I would not change. So he went ahead and with Herbert Menzel developed these ideas further in a paper that was subsequently published, while I, some years later published my long paper separately (Lazarsfeld & Menzel, 1961; Coleman, 1970).

The example I have given above could be duplicated with minor variations by many of Lazarsfeld's students. When I arrived at Columbia the "Decatur study" was one, on which C. Wright Mills, as well as others, had been tried and found wanting. Katz was set to work on it and it ended successfully, as the book *Personal Influence* referred to earlier. I reproduce here another example written by Patricia Kendall from her experience with what she calls "The Curtis–Farber Study."

In the late '30s or very early '40s, PFL had the idea (I don't know its origins) of studying whether women were more likely to be entertained or uplifted by the various women's magazines then in existence. He therefore set up a small-scale study, with Alberta Curtis in charge.

Interviewers were apparently told that they were to inquire about the 'gratifications' which women got from their preferred magazines. But, insufficiently instructed about the dimensions of gratifications that were relevant, they accepted a motley array of answers. Thus, some women were pleased by the price of their preferred magazine, others by the quality of the illustrations, still others by the special sections of the magazine they liked best. Very few answered in terms of entertainment or educational benefit. (It was very much like the problem of asking "why" questions.)

Alberta apparently struggled valiantly to make sense of the incompatible—uncombinable—categories. After a time, however, she gave up. Not so PFL. He was convinced that something could be made of the study, and persuaded Maurice Farber to work on it. I don't know what tack he took, or how long he labored. (Long enough to get his name attached to the study.) But he too left the study as he found it.

When it came time, about 1943 or 1944, for me to write my Master's essay, PFL said, "I've got just the thing for you." I worked at it, wracked by frustration, for six months or so. I also felt unworthy. If Professor Lazarsfeld said that the study could be analyzed meaningfully, then it could. The fact that I could not see how was a sign of my deficiency.

At the conclusion of the six-months period, PFL tactfully assigned me to something else. Although nothing further was heard of the Curtis–Farber study, I am quite sure than PFL was occasionally tempted to assign it to an exceptionally bright student in the hope that s/he could finally settle the matter.

This case illustrates a central aspect of Paul's style of work. He was fully occuped with ideas, yet he himself had the time to investigate only a subset of them. So he was engaged in a continual search for *people*—people who, as extensions of himself, could take the problem and carry it further. Yet he continued *himself* to be occupied with the problem, with strong and definite ideas about *how* the problem should be solved. This led to unlikely combinations, some of which aborted, while others, perhaps equally unlikely at the outset, flourished. When he set C. Wright Mills to work on the problem of personal influence in Decatur, Illinois, this did not last long. Or when he began to work with the pollster Lou Harris on a study of college faculty, this aborted. (Lazarsfeld completed the study with Wagner Thielens as *The Academic Mind* (1958).) His work with Martin Lipset on a review of political behavior was more productive, but rather short-lived. But no one would have predicted that he and Ernest Nagel could have managed such a successful series of seminars in mathematical sociology, or that David Riesman and he could have managed—even at arm's distance—to come as close together as they did in the study of college faculties.[12] And who could have guessed, *a priori,* that the association with Merton could have flowered and grown and become so important?

This was his personal style—he could not stand to have a bright person, whether colleague or student, whom he respected, in the vicinity and yet not working on problems *he* saw as important. He used his own time, flattery, and attention; he used money; he used summers in Hanover, New Hamp-

---

[12]Riesman gives a detailed account of this in his *Ethical and Practical Dilemmas of Fieldwork in an Academic Setting: A Personal Memoir* in Merton, Coleman & Rossi, eds., (1979).

shire; he used projects at the Bureau; he used all the inducements at his command to bring this about. Some of those around him hated this and thrived on it. They felt trapped, yet once out of Paul's reach, were bereft and adrift. But the impact on the discipline was a strong one, and the medium was a strange one. It did not fit the dichotomy of teaching (a medium which for Merton was enormously powerful but was not so for Lazarsfeld), or publication (a medium which of course was important for Lazarsfeld), but was something strange and different. It was a medium of *personal influence,* to borrow the title of his book with Elihu Katz (whom he set to work on the Decatur study after Mills's defection and that of a succession of others), influence in posing the problem, influence in shaping the way the problem was addressed, and influence in even the details of the final outcome.[13]

To appreciate the uniqueness of Lazarsfeld's style and to see the power it can have, it is sufficient to note that the *opposite* of this style is far more frequent: the desire to be the one to solve a problem, regardless of what the problem is. A person with this style is concerned to exhibit his intelligence on whatever problem might be posed, but is at a loss to pose a problem himself. It is a person with this kind of style who can most fully work with someone like Lazarsfeld. And it is the high frequency of persons with this style that made Lazarsfeld such a magnetic force. He needed them to solve his problems; they needed him to pose the problem.[14]

It is interesting to search in Paul's writings for some clue to the strategies he used, some description of how he himself operated. The closest I have come to finding such a statement is in a speech he gave at the opening of the Institute of Behavioral Science at the University of Colorado in 1962

[13]I reproduce a comment by R.K. Merton in the margins of an earlier draft of this paper to indicate that my perception of Lazarsfeld's style of work is shared by the man who worked most closely with him: ". . . this was in order to get ideas developed. Paul was obsessed by the conviction that the ideas and problems must be worked out—somehow, by someone, preferably by himself but if not, by someone brought to see the importance of the problem, or failing that, by someone who could be persuaded to work on the problem. But, at all costs, the ideas, the problems must be worked out."

[14]I have often thought, in speculating about Lazarsfeld's personal style, that the difference in styles I have described above must be due to the kind of reward system experienced as a child. A system in which most rewards came as praise from adults for carrying out tasks they set must lead (according to this speculation) to the adult style which is eager to solve problems but needs external direction to generate them. A system in which rewards came less from adults than from the successful completion of a task (as in games like baseball or chess where the outcome is determined by the play itself) must lead, again according to the speculation, to an adult style that is more nearly autonomous in generating problems, and thirsts less to be recognized for solving them. The former reward system (which is not only characteristic of socialization by some parents, but is also prevalent in schools) is of course one which more often leads to adult-oriented, including intellectual, activities, which may account for the high frequency of this style in academic settings.

(one of many university research institutes modelled after Paul's Bureau at Columbia.) He said there, in describing the role of the Institute Director (Lazarsfeld, 1964, pp. 18-19):

> The Institute Director knows the skills and interests prevailing among the faculty members, and he brings men and money into contact; this is not badly described as the role of *idea broker*. Often he will have to work hard to get funds for a more unusual research idea suggested to him; at other times a possible grant looks so attractive that he will try to discover among some of his faculty colleagues what he would diplomatically call a latent interest.

This may not be the closest Paul Lazarsfeld got to describing his strategies, but it's the closest I have found.

Another illustration of the same kind of process: in the spring of 1952, my first year at Columbia, Paul Lazarsfeld's attention fixed on me for the first time. (I had come to Columbia because of someone whose work I had read in evening school—someone named Lazarsfeld, or Lasswell, I wasn't sure which—and after arriving, I had been in a methods course of his, which was relatively uneventful.) But then he accosted me. The problem was that there was a biophysicist from Chicago, Nicholas Rashevsky, whom he had invited to give a lecture in a series on mathematical sociology the year before, and now, for the book Lazarsfeld was attempting to put together from the lectures series, Rashevsky had written up his lectures in ways that Paul saw as totally unintelligible. Paul had set Allan Birnbaum, a Ph.D. student in statistics, to work on writing an intelligible parallel to exposit Rashevsky, but didn't like what Birnbaum had done (just as later, he didn't like what I did on global indicators). Could I try something, over the summer? We talked, he outlined what he wanted, and for the first time ever in the educational system, I felt that someone had given me a responsible task to do. We met twice during the summer—one a typical Lazarsfeld breakfast meeting in a hotel where he briefly alighted on a trip back from Europe—and finally I gave him the product he wanted at the end of the summer. Lazarsfeld's project was now complete—Rashevsky was exposited, and he could send the book to the publisher. The incident is characteristic in one way especially: he did *not* simply *accept* the paper of this distinguished mathematical biophysicist. It was unintelligible to him, and he wanted each of the papers in that book (which became *Mathematical Thinking in the Social Sciences*) to teach *him* something. Until it did so, he was not willing to publish Rashevsky's lectures.

Indeed, in many respects one could characterize part of what was going on at Columbia at the time—certainly in mathematical sociology and to a considerable extent in Paul's other areas of interest—as a collection of people gathered by Paul around himself, for the purpose of teaching him. His appetite for learning—and thus for people—was insatiable. He brought the economist William Baumol from Princeton to a seminar to teach him how differential equations could be adapted to study dynamics of qualitative attributes—and then remained unsatisfied. He brought the philosopher, Gustav Bergmann, from the midwest to Hanover, New Hampshire to teach him about intervening variables, and then so pestered Bergmann with insistent questions that ended with Bergmann, a round little man, rolling on the floor, flailing with arms and legs in helpless frustration. He brought Harold Kelly, John Thibaut and Leon Festinger to Hanover to teach him about how Lewinian and other social psychologies constructed concepts. He brought William Vickrey from the other side of campus, to learn how economists treated the concept of utility. He listened intently to any one of his students, Lee Wiggins, or Allen Barton, or Elihu Katz, or Hanan Selvin or (most often) William McPhee, whenever he thought he could learn from them. He invaded the Statistics Department, and got Theodore Anderson to teach him about Markov chains and Howard Raiffa to teach him about statistical decision theory. He brought Duncan Luce to work on mathematical problems he couldn't solve, he brought Merrill Flood from Rand, and, irreverent to Flood's previous distinguished work, immediately found Flood uninteresting.

One never got the sense, at this time at Columbia, that Lazarsfeld had any interest in *publishing,* but only in *learning,* only in *solving the problems* that so fully occupied him. In this sense it became a pure atmosphere, with the attention of each of those in Lazarsfeld's orbit directed to problems, unconcerned about the outside sociological world, concerned only with convincing Lazarsfeld that he or she had solved one of the problems that Paul had set. For each of us after we left (and I speak now only of those who did, for some found it exceedingly difficult to break away from this attractive force, and some were institutionally affixed to Columbia)—for those of us who left, we found what seemed at first a strange and far less exciting world outside. We found no one in the new environment who *cared* as Lazarsfeld did. If there was a sociological community out there, we found it a distant and impersonal one. No one seemed as interested in solving problems, and certainly no one was interested in the problems that anyone *else* might solve.

Yet with all this, many of those around Paul Lazarsfeld felt extreme frustration, frustration because at times the problems themselves appeared spurious, or unimportant. And frustration because Paul was not satisfied to see his protégés and colleagues solve problems that others outside felt were important, but was only satisfied when a problem *he* saw as important was solved, and solved in a way that made sense to *him.*

Perhaps the best imagery to characterize Paul's style of work, and his relation to those around him, is that of a wealthy Don Juan, who uses his possessions and wealth to draw beautiful women into his orbit. For Paul, his wealth consisted in the problems and his vision of what lay on the other side once they were solved, and in place of beautiful women were colleagues and students. Indeed, as this analogy suggests, it is not clear in retrospect whether the people were used to solve the problems, or the problems were used to attract the people. Whichever it was, the end result was a highly charged atmosphere, with extreme forces, both attracting and repelling, holding a large number of persons in orbit around him.

To maintain this configuration was costly to Lazarsfeld. He could not maintain a posture, as many professors are tempted to do (and as many succumb to doing) of knowing more than he did. To engage the efforts of others on a problem, he had to declare his own defeat. But this he was willing to do. For him, getting the problem solved was most important; the fact that another might be the one to do so was a sacrifice he was willing to make.

This unassuming aspect of Lazarsfeld combined with another quality to make him a perfect complement to substantive sociologists. For Lazarsfeld, despite his work in Marienthal, had a difficult time understanding sociological theory. In some of his writings (the best sampling can be found in his *Qualitative Analysis*, published in 1972), he exhibits his long-standing concern to understand *action*, and his rich sense of the history of the theory of action. But substance that was more sociological came slowly to him.

The success of his seminars with Merton was the peculiar complementarity, not only of the theorist and the empirical researcher but of two personality types. Merton *knew* what Weber and others had written, say, about bureaucracy, he knew the theory. Lazarsfeld most explicity *did not know*, and asked, Why? And, How do you know that? (or, How did Max Weber know that?), and, How do you *use* this theory? In part, Lazarsfeld asked these questions because he simply did not understand the substance. And in part, he asked them because his desire for an answer outweighed any concern he might have had about being regarded as sociologically naive. In other cases, the interaction was somewhat modified. Merton would lay out a substantive sociological analysis which he had himself carried out and then Lazarsfeld would pose these same or similar questions. And in at least one case, having finally felt that he understood what the theorist meant, he attempted to express this understanding in a formalization. This was in the joint paper with Merton on homophily (Lazarsfeld & Merton, 1954).

I do not attempt here to describe the relative roles of Merton and Lazarsfeld at Columbia generally; this is a complex task I could not hope to carry out, but there was a complementarity in their roles, and they had different styles of work. (For example, Merton's magnetism acted largely *through* his brilliant, and sometimes almost hypnotic, lectures in which he threw out ideas, and depended on the force of the ideas themselves to mobilize those who heard them to pursue the ideas. Lazarsfeld's power occurred wholly apart from his lectures and depended much more on active pursuit of those in whom he was interested.) Because of these complementarities, a description of the role of one of them at Columbia leaves large gaps and holes, and gives an unbalanced picture of what was happening. In the examination of any interdependent system, a quantitative methodologist would tell us that specifying only one equation where there are two simultaneous equations gives biased estimates. And it is no less so in this case. But because I cannot carry out the full analysis, I can only warn that the bias exists.

Paul never hesitated to defer to those with whom he wanted to interact. He never pretended to know more than he did, though he often pretended to know less. He deferred to mathematical statisticians and mathematicians, just so they would work on his problems. He deferred to Robert Merton and other sociological theorists, as I've described above. He deferred to Ernest Nagel, in the process inducing Nagel not only to carry on with him the seminar in mathematical sociology, but also to write, for the Bureau's research program, a paper uncovering the logic of functional analysis. The latter episode is instructive: Lazarsfeld had some ideas about functional analysis, but his desire to see the logic analyzed and the problem solved was greater than his desire to see a particular set of ideas dominate. He felt Nagel was more likely to successfully analyze functional analysis than he. So he posed to Nagel the *problem*, rather than arguing for a particular *solution*. Yet he would not simply accept what Nagel first did, but continued to push, asking nagging questions, until he was satisfied (see Nagel, 1956).

It is past time to finish, so I must stop. Before I do, however, I must apologize to those of you who knew Paul Lazarsfeld better and longer than I did, and who could have described the rich fabric of his life with incidents that would have evoked powerful images in all who knew him and given a flavor of his presence to those who did not.[16] My view of Lazarsfeld and his work is confined by the limits of my experience. I knew him only in the last twenty-five years of his life and was in his immediate orbit for only four years. Thus my perception of Paul is a very selective and partial one.

But if I have fixed your attention for a longer time than you anticipated on a particular direction in sociology, as I hope I have done, this is in the Lazarsfeld spirit. He would be happy to know that a large number of people had been pressed into service, thinking about problems that occupied him.

---

[16]An evocation of some of those images, and something of the flavor of Lazarsfeld's presence, can be found in some of the papers in the volume published in honor of Lazarsfeld. See Merton, Coleman and Rossi, eds., (1979).

REFERENCES

Barton, A.H. Paul Lazarsfeld and the Invention of the University Applied Social Research Institute. Unpublished ms. scheduled for publication in Burkart Holzner and Jiri Nehnevajsa, eds., *Organizing for Social Research.*

Berelson, B., Lazarsfeld, P.F., & McPhee, W. *Voting.* Chicago: University of Chicago Press, 1954.

Campbell, D. & Clayton, K. N. "Avoiding Regression Effects in Panel Studies of Communication Impact." *Studies in Publication Communication,* 1961, *3,* 99-118.

Coleman, J. S. *The adolescent society.* New York: Free Press, 1961.

Coleman, J. S. *Introduction to mathematical sociology.* New York: Free Press, 1964.

Coleman, J. S., Katz, E., Menzel, H. *Medical innovation.* Indianapolis: Bobbs-Merrill, 1966.

Coleman, J. S. "The Mathematical Study of Change." In H.M. Blalock & A.D. Blalock, (eds.), *Methodology in social research.* New York: McGraw-Hill, 1968.

Coleman, J. S. "Properties of Collectivities." In Coleman, J.S., Etzioni, A., & Porter, J. (eds.), *Macrosociology: Research and theory.* Boston: Allyn & Bacon, 1970.

Coleman, J. S. "The University and Society's New Demands upon It." In Kaysen, C. (ed.), *Content and context: Essays on college education.* New York: McGraw Hill, 1973.

Coleman, J. S. "Sociological Analysis and Social Policy." In Bottomore, T., & Nisbet, R. (eds.), *A history of sociological analysis.* New York: Basic Books, 1979.

Glock, C.Y., "Organizational Innovation for Social Science Research and Training," In R.K. Merton, J.S. Coleman, & P.H. Rossi (eds.), *Qualitative and quantitative social research: Papers in honor of Paul F. Lazarsfeld.* New York: Free Press, 1979. Chapter 5.

Goodman, Leo A.. "The Analysis of Qualitative Variables Using Parsimonious Quasi-Independence Models, Scaling Models, and Latent Structures." In R. K. Merton, J. S. Coleman and P. H. Rossi (eds.), *Qualitative and quantitative social research—Papers in honor of Paul F. Lazarsfeld.* New York: Free Press, 1979, 119-137.

Jahoda, M., Lazarsfeld, P. F., & Zeisel, H. *Marienthal: The sociography of an unemployed community* (translated from the German by the authors with J. Reginall and T. Elsaesser). Chicago, Aldine, 1971.

Katz, E., & Lazarsfeld, P. F. *Personal influence.* New York: Free Press, 1955.

Kendall, P., & Lazarsfeld, P. F. "Problems of Survey Analysis." In Merton, R. K. & Lazarsfeld, P. F. (eds.), *Continuities in social research: Studies in the scope and method of 'The American Soldier'.* New York: Free Press, 1950.

Lazarsfeld, P. F., Berelson, B., & Gaudet, H. *The people's choice.* New York: Columbia University Press, 1948.

Lazarsfeld, P. F., & Merton, R. K. "Friendship as a Social Process." In Berger, M., T. Abel and C.H. Page (eds.), *Freedom and control in modern society: In honor of Robert Morrison MacIver.* Newark: Van Nostrand, 1954.

Lazarsfeld, P. F. (ed.), *Mathematical thinking in the social sciences.* New York: Free Press, 1954.

Lazarsfeld, P. F. & Thielens, W. *The academic mind.* New York: Free Press, 1958.

Lazarsfeld, P. F. & Menzel, H. "On the Relation Between Individual and Collective Properties." In Etzioni, A. (ed.), *Complex organizations: A sociological reader.* New York: Holt, Rinehart, & Winston, 1961.

Lazarsfeld, P. F., Klein, L. R., & Tyler, R. W. *The behavioral sciences: Problems and prospects.* Boulder, Colorado, 1964.

Lazarsfeld, P. F. *Qualitative analysis.* Boston: Allyn & Bacon, 1972.

Lipset, S., Trow, M., & Coleman, J. S. *Union democracy.* New York: Free Press, 1956.

Merton, R. K., Coleman, J. S., & Rossi, P. H. (eds.), *Qualitative and quantitative social research: Papers in honor of Paul F. Lazarsfeld.* New York: Free Press, 1979.

Nagel, E. "A Formalization of Functionalism." In Nagel, *Logic without metaphysics*. New York: Free Press, 1956.

Pelz, D. C. & Andrews, F. M. "Detecting Causal Priorities in Panel Study Data." *American Sociological Review,* 1964, *29,* 836-848.

Sills, D. "Paul F. Lazarsfeld." In *International Encyclopedia of the Social Sciences,* v. 18. New York: MacMillan-Free Press, 1980.

Simon, H. A. "The Meaning of Causal Ordering." In Merton, *et al.* (eds.), *Qualitative and quantitative social research: Papers in honor of Paul F. Lazarsfeld*. New York: Free Press, 1979.

Weber, M. *On the methodology of the social sciences*. New York: Free Press, 1949.

About the Contributors

Robert Bierstedt is Professor of Sociology at the University of Virginia. He is a former Vice-President of the American Sociological Association, a former President of the Eastern Sociological Society, and is currently a member of the Board of Directors of the American Council of Learned Societies. He has written *The Social Order* (4th ed., 1974) and a number of his essays on sociological theory have been published under the title *Power and Progress* (1974).

James S. Coleman is Professor of Sociology at the University of Chicago and Senior Study Director at the National Opinion Research Center, University of Chicago's counterpart to Columbia's Bureau of Applied Social Research. He is a member of the National Academy of Sciences, the American Philosophical Society, the American Academy of Arts and Sciences, and the National Academy of Education. Among his books are *The Adolescent Society* (1961), *Introduction to Mathematical Sociology* (1964), and *Power and the Structure of Society* (1973).

Leonard S. Cottrell, Jr. is Emeritus Professor of Sociology and Social Psychology at the University of North Carolina. He has served, among other posts, as Professor of Sociology and Anthropology and Dean of the College of Arts and Sciences at Cornell University, as Director of Survey Research in the War Department during World War II, and as Social Psychologist and Secretary of the Russell Sage Foundation. His many professional honors include the 1965 Merit Award by the Eastern Sociological Society. His publications reflect his deep interest in Mead and include *Developments* *in Social Psychology, 1930–1940* (1941); "The Self as an Emergent Social Interaction" (1965); and "George Herbert Mead and Harry Stack Sullivan: An Unfinished Synthesis" (1978).

G. Franklin Edwards is Professor of Sociology at Howard University. He is a member of the American Sociological Association, the Eastern Sociological Society, and the District of Columbia Sociological Society. He is the author of *The Negro Professional Class* (1959); "E. Franklin Frazier," in *Black Sociologists: Historical and Contemporary Perspectives* (1974), a volume edited by James E. Blackwell and Morris Janowitz; and "Occupational Mobility of Negro Professional Workers" in E. W. Burgess and D. J. Bogue, eds., *Contributions to Urban Sociology* (1964). He is the editor of *E. Franklin Frazier on Race Relations* (1966).

Helen MacGill Hughes is currently President of the Eastern Sociological Society and Vice-President of the American Sociological Association (ASA). She was, for seventeen years, in the editorial office of the *American Journal of Sociology* ending as managing editor. She served as editor and compiler of the ASA project, *Sociological Resources for Social Studies in Sociology* and as editor of the ASA series, *Issues and Trends in Sociology*. She is the author of *News and the Human Interest Story* (1947) and editor of *The Fantastic Dodge: The Autobiography of a Girl Drug Addict* (1961).

Robert K. Merton is University Professor Emeritus and Special Service Professor at Columbia University. A member of the National Academy of Sciences, the American Philosophical Society, the National Academy of Education and Foreign Member of the Royal Swedish Academy of Sciences, he has been awarded the Talcott Parsons Prize for the Social Sciences by the American Academy of Arts and Sciences. His books include *Social Theory and Social Structure* (1949, 1968), *The Sociology of Science* (1973), and *Sociological Ambivalence* (1976).

Talcott Parsons is generally recognized as the master sociological theorist of the middle half of our century. He took an active part in the life of the sociological community, having served as President of the Eastern Sociological Society and the American Sociological Association. He was a member of the American Philosophical Society and, for five years, President of the American Academy of Arts and Sciences, which named its prize in the social sciences in his honor. His many books include the masterworks *The Structure of Social Action* (1937) and *The Social System* (1951) and, most recently, *Action Theory and the Human Condition* (1978).

Matilda White Riley is Associate Director for Social and Behavioral Research, National Institute on Aging. She is currently on leave from Bowdoin College where she is Fayerweather Professor of Political Economy and Sociology. Senior member of the Institute of Medicine of the National Academy of Sciences, and a former Fellow at the Center for Advanced Study in the Behavioral Sciences, she is the recipient of the Lindback Award for Social Research from Rutgers University, and the Andrus Award in the Social Sciences from the University of Southern California. Her books include *Sociological Research* (2 vols., 1963), *Aging and Society* (3 vols., 1968–1972), and *Aging from Birth to Death* (1979).

Jackson Toby is Professor of Sociology and Director of the Institute for Criminological Research at Rutgers University. He was a consultant to the Youth Development Program of The Ford Foundation from 1959 to 1963 and sociologist-designer of the episode, *Delinquency,* created for Sociological Resources for Secondary Schools, a project of the American Sociological Association funded by the National Science Foundation. Recent publications include "The New Criminology Is the Old Sentimentality," *Criminology* (February 1979); "Societal Evolution and Criminality: A Parsonian View," *Social Problems* (April 1979); and "Delinquency in Cross-Cultural Perspective" in LaMar T. Empey, ed., *Juvenile Justice* (1979).

Robin M. Williams, Jr. is the Henry Scarborough Professor of Social Science at Cornell University. He has served as President of the Eastern Sociological Society, the American Sociological Society, and the Sociological Research Association, and is a member of the American Philosophical Society and the American Academy of Arts and Sciences. His writings include *American Society: A Sociological Interpretation* (3rd ed., 1970); "Relative Deprivation" in L.A. Coser, ed., *The Idea of Social Structure* (1975), and *Mutual Accommodation: Ethnic Conflict and Cooperation* (1977).

Index of Names

Numbers in *italics* indicate where complete references are listed.